"Richard Swinburne is famous for arguing from the conceivability of my disembodiment to my having an immaterial part. Weir's argument is not open to the criticisms levelled against Swinburne's, and the engine driving the argument is entirely different and entirely original. I was very impressed."

Dean Zimmerman, *Rutgers University*

"If you thought substance dualism was confined to history, then think again. Ralph Weir has developed one of the most compelling arguments for mental substance in contemporary philosophy. Essential reading for anybody working on the problem of consciousness."

Philip Goff, *Durham University*

"Weir shows that recent philosophy of mind is hampered by an unreflective abhorrence for the idea of the soul – an attitude which is at odds with serious reflection on the mind-body problem. A vastly important book for anyone serious about understanding human nature."

Benedikt Paul Göcke, *Ruhr University Bochum*

The Mind-Body Problem and Metaphysics

This book evaluates the widespread preference in philosophy of mind for varieties of property dualism over other alternatives to physicalism. It takes the standard motivations for property dualism as a starting point and argues that these lead directly to nonphysical substances resembling the soul of traditional metaphysics.

In the first half of the book, the author clarifies what is at issue in the choice between theories that posit nonphysical properties only and those that posit nonphysical substances. The crucial question, he argues, is whether one posits nonphysical things that satisfy an Aristotelian-Cartesian independence definition of substance: nonphysical things that could exist in the absence of anything else. In the second half, the author argues that standard and Russellian monist forms of property dualism are far less plausible than we usually suppose. Most significantly, the presuppositions of one of the leading arguments for property dualism, the conceivability argument, lead by parity of reasoning to the view that conscious subjects are nonphysical substances. He concludes that if you posit nonphysical properties in response to the mind-body problem, then you should be prepared to posit nonphysical substances as well. Mainstream philosophy of mind must take nonphysical substances far more seriously than it has done for the best part of a century.

The Mind-Body Problem and Metaphysics will be of interest to scholars and advanced students working in philosophy of mind, metaphysics, and the history of philosophy.

Ralph Stefan Weir is Lecturer in Philosophy at the University of Lincoln and Associate Member of the Faculty of Theology and Religion at the University of Oxford. His recent publications include "Bring Back Substances!" (*Review of Metaphysics*, 2021), "Can a Post-Galilean Science of Consciousness Avoid Substance Dualism?" (*Journal of Consciousness Studies*, 2021), and "Does Idealism Solve the Problem of Consciousness?" (*Routledge Handbook of Idealism and Immaterialism*, 2021).

Routledge Studies in Contemporary Philosophy

The Ethics of Interpretation
From Charity as a Principle to Love as a Hermeneutic Imperative
Pol Vandevelde

The Nature and Practice of Trust
Marc A. Cohen

A Plea for Plausibility
Toward a Comparative Decision Theory
John R. Welch

Living with the Dead
On Death, the Dead, and Immortality
J. Jeremy Wisnewski

Free Will's Value
Criminal Justice, Pride, and Love
John Lemos

Emotional Self-Knowledge
Edited by Alba Montes Sánchez and Alessandro Salice

Global Justice and Recognition Theory
Dignifying the World's Poor
Monica Mookherjee

The Mind-Body Problem and Metaphysics
An Argument from Consciousness to Mental Substance
Ralph Stefan Weir

For more information about this series, please visit: www.routledge.com/Routledge-Studies-in-Contemporary-Philosophy/book-series/SE0720

The Mind-Body Problem and Metaphysics
An Argument from Consciousness to Mental Substance

Ralph Stefan Weir

NEW YORK AND LONDON

First published 2024
by Routledge
605 Third Avenue, New York, NY 10158

and by Routledge
4 Park Square, Milton Park, Abingdon, Oxon, OX14 4RN

Routledge is an imprint of the Taylor & Francis Group,
an informa business

© 2024 Ralph Stefan Weir

The right of Ralph Stefan Weir to be identified as author of this
work has been asserted in accordance with sections 77 and 78 of
the Copyright, Designs and Patents Act 1988.

All rights reserved. No part of this book may be reprinted or
reproduced or utilised in any form or by any electronic, mechanical,
or other means, now known or hereafter invented, including
photocopying and recording, or in any information storage or
retrieval system, without permission in writing from the publishers.

Trademark notice: Product or corporate names may be trademarks
or registered trademarks, and are used only for identification and
explanation without intent to infringe.

ISBN: 978-1-032-45768-0 (hbk)
ISBN: 978-1-032-45769-7 (pbk)
ISBN: 978-1-003-37860-0 (ebk)

DOI: 10.4324/9781003378600

Typeset in Sabon
by SPi Technologies India Pvt Ltd (Straive)

To my Sage and Illustrious parents, Sue and Dave.

Contents

Acknowledgements	*x*
Abbreviations	*xi*
Introduction	1
1 Why Does Everyone Hate the Soul?	6
2 The Decline of Substance Dualism and the Substance-Property Distinction	31
3 A Defence of the Independence Definition of Substance	58
4 Four Theories of Mind and the Place of Russellian Monism	77
5 The Strangeness of Property Dualism	95
6 Parity of Reasoning Demands Nonphysical Substances	109
7 The Consequences of the Parity Argument for Nonphysical Substances	134
Conclusion	154
Appendix	*158*
Bibliography	*159*
Index	*172*

Acknowledgements

Thanks are due to Arif Ahmed, Sue Capener, Harry Cleeveley, Tim Crane, Christina Faraday, Joshua Farris, Richard Holton, Samuel Hughes, Maxime Lepoutre, Alex Moran, Donnchadh O'Conaill, Olley Pearson, Stephen Priest, Brandon Rickabaugh, Mikołaj Sławkowski-Rode, David Weir, and Dean Zimmerman for providing comments on some or all of the manuscript, as well as to participants in the Postgraduate Session of the 2017 Joint Session of the Mind Association and the Aristotelian Society, the Serious Metaphysics Group at the University of Cambridge, Martine Nida Rümelin's seminar series on the subject of experience at the University of Fribourg, a workshop of the New Generation Research Exchange at the University of Warsaw, a meeting of the Lincoln Philosophy Salon and a visiting lecture organised by Johnathan Price at Pusey House, Oxford, where parts of the argument were presented. I am grateful to my colleagues at the University of Lincoln, in particular Daniel Came, Gary Francione, Mark Hocknull, Olley Pearson, Brian Pitts, and Nick Zangwill for making it an extremely congenial place to work. I am indebted to John Cottingham, Benedikt Göcke, Philip Goff, Paul Lodge, Colin McGinn, Hugh Mellor, Alex Norman, Anthony O'Hear, Andrew Pinsent, Howard Robinson, Marija Selak, Richard Swinburne, Raymond Tallis, Nick Waghorn, and His Holiness the Dalai Lama for valuable conversations as well as various adventures and opportunities during the book's composition, and to the Arts and Humanities Research Council, Jesus College, Cambridge, Blackfriars Hall and the Ian Ramsey Centre for Science and Religion, Oxford, the Humanities Research Institute of the University of Buckingham, the Philosophy Department of the Central European University and the John Templeton Foundation for support at different stages during the project. Finally, I am especially grateful to Stephen Priest and Roger Scruton for initiating my interest in the topic of this book and for many years of friendship and support.

Abbreviations

AG Leibniz, Gottfried Wilhelm. (1989). *Philosophical Essays*. Trans. Roger Ariew and Dan Garber. Indianapolis: Hackett.

AT Rene Descartes. (1964–76). *Oeuvres de Descartes*. Ed. Charles Adam and Paul Tannery. Revised edition. Paris: Vrin/C.N.R.S.

CSMK Rene Descartes. (1984–91). *The Philosophical Writings of Descartes*. Ed. John Cottingham, Robert Stoothoff, Dugald Murdoch, and Anthony Kenny. Cambridge University Press.

NIV The Holy Bible. New International Version. Colorado Springs, CO: Biblica Inc.

ST Thomas Aquinas. (1948). *Summa Theologiae*. Trans. Fathers of the English Dominican Province. New York: Benziger Brothers.

Introduction

The mind-body problem has been central to Western philosophy since classical antiquity. The most influential philosophers of the ancient and medieval periods, Plato, Aristotle, Augustine, and Aquinas all devoted individual works to it. And the importance accorded to the mind-body problem has only increased with time. Since the seventeenth century, it has been widely regarded as pivotal to philosophy in general.

In the preface to the second edition of his *German Metaphysics* (1751) Christian Wolff distinguishes three responses to the mind-body problem. Materialism says that everything is ultimately material. Idealism says that everything is ultimately mental. Substance dualism says that there are both material and mental things and that these are different substances. Through Baumgarten and Kant, Wolff's trichotomy shaped the way later theorists approach the mind-body problem, and the Wolffian positions retain a kind of classical status (cf. Double 1985, 386; Spackman 2012, 742; Schwitzgebel 2014, 674).

When Wolff was writing, Descartes' substance dualism and Leibniz's idealism were the leading positions, so much so that Wolff was not able to identify a clear example of a materialist. He had to make do with Spinoza. Wolff might have named Hobbes, but Hobbes' theory of mind commanded no school in the eighteenth century. In Wolff's day, the fundamentality of minds was a point of widespread consensus.

This situation has changed remarkably. The present-day incarnation of materialism, physicalism, overtook substance dualism and idealism in the middle of the twentieth century to become the leading response to the mind-body problem and a cornerstone of the naturalistic worldview that dominates present-day philosophy. (Physicalism is close to traditional materialism both in spirit and in content as I explain in § 4.1 in this volume.)

At the same time, substance dualism and idealism have become decidedly unpopular. For example, Searle (2004, 48) says that 'Idealism ... has been dead as a doornail among nearly all of the philosophers whose

DOI: 10.4324/9781003378600-1

2   Introduction

opinions I respect, for many decades.' Similarly, Kim (2005, 151) says that 'substance dualism has not been taken as a serious option in mainstream philosophy of mind since the early twentieth century.' Both assessments are issued approvingly, and this reflects a widespread attitude in present-day philosophy.

The unpopularity of substance dualism and idealism is not entirely accounted for by the rise of physicalism, however. It is also partly due to a second development: the emergence of property dualism. The rise of physicalism has shifted the balance of credence that we invest in responses to the mind-body problem. The rise of property dualism has transformed our conception of the options available.

Property dualism says that there are nonphysical *properties* but that there is no need to posit nonphysical substances such as Cartesian souls or Leibnizian monads. It comes in a standard and a Russellian monist form. (§ 4.4 explains why it makes sense to class the leading Russellian monist positions as property dualist.) Property dualism gained prominence in the final decades of the twentieth century, in works such as Jackson (1982) and Chalmers (1996) and quickly became the leading alternative to physicalism. This position does not feature in Wolff's trichotomy, and its recent ascent has reshaped research in the philosophy of mind.

From the perspective of detached theorising the rise of property dualism is puzzling. For the term 'substance' has a number of historical uses and no standard use in present-day metaphysics. For this reason, it has never been clear exactly what property dualists take themselves to be denying when they eschew nonphysical substances. Property dualists do not tend to clarify this, as I explain in § 2.2.

Neither is it clear what the advantage of positing nonphysical properties whilst resisting nonphysical substances is supposed to be. Property dualists sometimes gesture at the problem of mind-body interaction as a reason to prefer property dualism (e.g. Chalmers 1996, 124–5; Kim 2005, 70–92). This makes little sense however. For property dualism faces the same problems about interaction as substance dualism, as the same property dualists tend to acknowledge (e.g. Chalmers 1996, 150; Kim 2005, 156).

From the perspective of intellectual fashion the rise of property dualism makes greater sense. For ever since Ryle's (1949) assault on the 'dogma of the ghost in the machine' nonphysical substances have been treated with mistrust. Many theorists share Dennett's (1991, 37) suspicion that anyone who posits 'mind stuff' must be driven by a reactionary desire 'to keep science at bay'. Nonphysical substances tend to be grouped alongside healing crystals and astrology as things beyond the pale of scientific thinking.

Rejecting nonphysical substances is one way that property dualists can signal their commitment to the scientific spirit. They often amplify this gesture by calling their version of dualism 'naturalistic' and by comparing

Introduction 3

the addition of mental properties to our ontology to Maxwell's introduction of electromagnetism to physics. For example, after classing his position as property dualism, Chalmers (1996, 127) tells us that 'this view is entirely compatible with a contemporary scientific worldview and is entirely naturalistic.'

This diplomacy appears to have been effective. From Double (1985) onwards, there has grown a consensus in the philosophy of mind according to which nonphysical substances can be dismissed out of hand whereas nonphysical properties must be taken seriously. (See § 2.1 for several examples of this view.) Today, property dualism is widely seen as one of the leading responses to the mind-body problem.

The received view in the philosophy of mind has, then, changed strikingly since Wolff's day. Physicalism has soared to eminence. Property dualism has established itself as the leading alternative. And substance dualism and idealism have been pushed into the background. For at least 70 years, nonphysical substances have been out of vogue, whether in the form of Cartesian minds or Leibnizian monads or Aristotelian intellects.

The new status quo has intellectual fashion behind it. But it is not obviously well-founded. In particular, the idea that property dualism is preferable to substance dualism, and idealism seems to have arisen out of nowhere. This should make us uneasy. For the historical philosophers who posit nonphysical properties regularly attribute these to nonphysical substances. It is possible that they had a good reason for doing so.

A pivotal question for present-day philosophy, then, is whether it is really feasible to respond to the mind-body problem by positing nonphysical properties without nonphysical substances. Understandably, this question has not been given much attention. The task of debating physicalism has left little room for other issues. But physicalism has been losing ground for some time (cf. Koons and Bealer 2010). And so there is growing need for serious reflection on the alternatives.

The present enquiry addresses this need. The outcome is dramatic. Once the surrounding issues have been clarified, the room for both standard and Russellian monist forms of property dualism turns out to be far narrower than we usually suppose. Most significantly, the presuppositions of one of the leading arguments for property dualism, the conceivability argument, appear to lead by parity of reasoning to the existence of nonphysical substances. (I defend this claim at length in Chapter 6.)

What little room is left for property dualism involves making controversial claims. There are two main options. The first posits a 'transcendental ego,' of the sort described by Husserl (1913) and Sartre (1936–7), to hook mental properties to the physical world. The second posits brute metaphysical necessities to rule out nonphysical substances. Property dualists are likely to find both options unattractive (see §§ 7.4–7.5).

4 Introduction

I conclude that if you are going to posit nonphysical properties in response to the mind-body problem, then you should be prepared to posit nonphysical substances as well. More precisely, you should be prepared to posit nonphysical minds that satisfy the Aristotelian-Cartesian independence definition of substance defended in Chapter 3: minds that could exist in the absence of anything else, including any physical body, and that therefore resemble the immaterial souls posited by traditional cultures the world over.

Although this conclusion is dramatic, it should not be surprising. For property dualism has never been subjected to proper scrutiny, despite contradicting historical wisdom. Historical consensuses can be overturned, of course. But this requires new insights. In the present case, these have been lacking. Theorists have taken it for granted that we can posit nonphysical properties without nonphysical substances, and because resistance has come mainly from physicalism, the special problems facing property dualism have been overlooked.

If it is true that the viable anti-physicalist positions require nonphysical substances, the effect on the philosophy of mind ought to be considerable. This would mean a return to the view that something resembling Wolff's trichotomy exhausts the main responses to the mind-body problem, and hence to the philosophical status quo of the early eighteenth century. Furthermore, if anti-physicalist positions continue to grow in popularity, it means that we must once again take mental substances seriously, however extravagant this may seem.

Summary

This book is mainly an intervention in recent analytical philosophy of mind. In Chapter 1, I explain why this intervention has a significance that extends far beyond the subdiscipline in which it occurs. For recent philosophy of mind exemplifies a much wider trend in our intellectual culture, which may be summed up as an abhorrence for anything resembling an immaterial soul. This attitude exists throughout the natural sciences, social science, and humanities, and it is one of the peculiar features of our age. Chapter 1 describes this trend, and explains why the subsequent, narrower, and more technical discussion is needed.

Chapters 2–4 are preparative. Chapter 2 raises a puzzle about the opposition to nonphysical substances that has characterised mainstream philosophy since Ryle (1949) and sets out on the task of clarifying the issue. Chapter 3 defends the definition of substance adopted in Chapter 1 against an influential objection that has held back discussion. Chapter 4 defines the boundaries between physicalism, idealism, substance dualism, and property dualism and explains why Russellian monism should be seen not as a distinct theory to the four listed but as a variation that can be made on each, and whose main exemplars in the recent literature are versions of property dualism.

Chapters 5–7 are executive. Chapter 5 explains why property dualism is an intuitively strange position and introduces three arguments for thinking that present-day opponents of physicalism must posit nonphysical substances. Chapter 6 takes up the most powerful of these arguments, the 'parity argument,' and presents it in detail. Chapter 7 draws out the consequences of the parity argument and addresses some objections. Readers impatient to get to the main issue can jump from Chapter 1 to Chapter 5, referring back to earlier chapters as necessary. Readers who would like to see the main argument in summary immediately should read §§ 5.5.2–5.5.3.

As far as I am aware, there has been no previous attempt to reinstate Wolff's trichotomy in the context of present-day philosophy. Double (1985) comes the closest. Nonetheless, there are signs of a resurgence of interest in substance dualism and idealism, including several volumes dedicated to re-examining these positions which have appeared whilst this one was being written (e.g. Robinson 2016; Goldschmidt and Pearce, 2017; Loose et al. 2018; Swinburne 2019; Farris and Göcke, 2021; Farris 2023; Rickabaugh and Moreland, 2023). These works do not anticipate the arguments of the present enquiry, but they make its arguments timely.

1 Why Does Everyone Hate the Soul?

The mind-body problem is the problem of explaining why it is that, in addition to ordinary physical properties, humans have mental or spiritual properties. An ancient response to the mind-body problem says that the reason why we have these mental or spiritual properties is that, in addition to our physical bodies, humans have immaterial minds or souls. Recent intellectual culture exhibits intense animosity towards the idea that humans have immaterial minds or souls. This chapter describes the strangely hostile treatment that the idea of the soul receives in contemporary thought and explains why this attitude needs rethinking.

1.1 The Mind-Body Problem and the Soul

You have many properties of the sort that belong to ordinary physical objects such as a rock. Shape and weight, for example. You also have properties that involve moving parts, like those of a more complex physical object such as a clock. Respiration and cardiac circulation, for instance. On the other hand, you have a range of properties that do not, we usually suppose, belong to ordinary physical objects. You have beliefs, intentions, desires, the ability to choose, and to take responsibility for your actions. Most vividly of all, there is something it is like to be you, from the inside as it were. We do not usually suppose that there is something it is like to be a rock or a clock – or even a computer or a plant.

The mind-body problem is the problem of explaining why you have these radically different kinds of properties. There exists one very ancient and very widespread response to the mind-body problem. This response says that the reason why, unlike an ordinary physical object, you also have the kind of mental or spiritual features that you have is that, unlike an ordinary physical object, you have an immaterial mind or soul.

Your body, on the view in question, is the principal bearer of physical properties, such as shape, weight, and respiration. Your mind or soul is the principal bearer of mental or spiritual properties, such as belief,

DOI: 10.4324/9781003378600-2

Why Does Everyone Hate the Soul? 7

agency, and conscious experience. Your body and soul are very intimately related. So long as they are united, we might go so far as to say that you are *an incarnate soul* or an *animate body*. Nonetheless, body and soul are distinct.

The view that humans have immaterial souls in addition to material bodies – soul-body dualism as it is sometimes called – has been unpopular of late. Philosophical movements as diverse as Quinean naturalism, Wittgensteinianism, Deconstruction, neo-Aristotelianism, and countless others find common ground in their firm rejection of soul-body dualism (though rather than acknowledging this common ground, they often accuse one another of covert dualism). Opposition to dualism in recent philosophy is, moreover, characterised by a surprising degree of animosity. For many, dualism is not just mistaken, it is odious.

Recent hostility towards the idea of the soul is by no means confined to philosophy. The same attitude exists throughout the natural sciences, social sciences, and humanities. It is not going too far to say that we live in a psychephobic age, and to a corresponding degree, a somaphilic age. Present-day intellectuals never tire of reminding us that we have bodies. But you risk causing considerable consternation if you suggest that they might also have a soul.

I think that the mind-body problem has become a nexus of bad scholarship, feeble argument, and general wrong-headedness, mainly because of the strange horror present-day theorists have of anything resembling an immaterial soul. This book argues that the idea of an immaterial mind or soul should be treated far more seriously than it has been in recent analytical philosophy of mind. The discussion is technical and restricted to just one of many reasons for reviving the idea of the soul. Nonetheless, it goes some way towards challenging the psychephobia that has characterised recent philosophy of mind. In the remainder of this chapter, I put the comparatively narrow project of this book in its wider context.

The hostility to the soul that characterises recent intellectual culture can be seen in three widespread misconceptions. Firstly, soul-body dualism is an idiosyncratic, Western view, largely due to Plato or Descartes. Secondly, soul-body dualism is responsible for all that is wrong with the Western world. Thirdly, soul-body dualism has little or nothing going for it theoretically. I describe these misconceptions in turn and explain why I regard them as completely unfounded. Doing so will bring out the very strange place the idea of the soul has in contemporary intellectual culture.

Three clarificatory remarks before we set out. Firstly, the idea that humans have immaterial minds or souls is compatible with *both* soul-body dualism *and* idealism. Although this chapter focuses on soul-body dualism, the conclusion of this book is that we should take more seriously the idea that *either* soul-body dualism *or* idealism obtains. Secondly, I use

8 *Why Does Everyone Hate the Soul?*

'soul-body dualism' as a less technical term for what later chapters call 'substance dualism.' The relationship between these terms will become clear in due course. Thirdly, although I focus on the case of humans, much of what I say will apply equally to animal minds. The Cartesian idea that we should adopt entirely different accounts of human and animal minds is not plausible. In many respects, Descartes has been wrongly maligned, but here his opponents are right.

1.2 Misconception 1: Soul-Body Dualism Is a Platonic or Cartesian Idiosyncrasy

One reason why the mind-body problem is interesting is that it is an area where detached philosophical reflection carries us into the territory of religion – or religion as traditionally conceived. And while my interest in the mind-body problem did not arise from any religious commitment, it has always seemed to me that the utter failure of materialism to account for the mental or spiritual half of our existence is one reason for taking religion seriously. It came as a surprise, therefore, when I discovered that many contemporary Christian thinkers are no less fierce opponents of the soul than postmodern sociologists or new atheists.

The materialism of present-day Christian thinkers is surprising, in part, because the conception of human nature shared by more or less all historical Christian thinkers from the Church Fathers to the twentieth century is unambiguously dualist. Christian materialists do not try to deny this fact. Instead, they represent it as an extremely long-standing blunder. For soul-body dualism is not, they contend, the view of the *first* Christians, as represented by the New Testament. Rather, Christian dualism reflects the early corruption of Christianity by Greek philosophy.

An early proponent of Christian materialism was Thomas Hobbes, who claimed that 'the enemy has sown spiritual errors by mingling with scriptur the vain and erroneous philosophy of the Greeks, especially of Aristotle.' According to Hobbes, 'the soul in Scripture signifieth always either the life or the living creature; and the body and soul jointly, the body alive' (Leviathan Ch. xliv). But Hobbes's position is difficult to maintain. For countless biblical passages seem to contradict it. Take Matthew 10:28, for example, where Jesus tells his disciples not to fear 'those who kill the body but cannot kill the soul' but to 'be afraid of the One who can destroy both soul and body' (NIV, Matthew 10:28). Or consider 2 Corinthians 5:6–10 where Paul says,

> We are always confident and know that as long as we are at home in the body we are away from the Lord. … We are confident, I say, and would prefer to be away from the body and at home with the Lord. … For we

must all appear before the judgment seat of Christ, so that each of us may receive what is due us for the things done while in the body.

(NIV, Corinthians 5:6–10)

If it were true that the soul in scripture signifieth always the life of the living creature or the body alive, then 'those who kill the body, but cannot kill the soul' would of course be meaningless. And a writer who agreed with Hobbes's materialism would not speak of a person being 'away from the body' or contrast the things done 'in the body' with those done later.

The difficulty of maintaining Hobbes's position has not gone unnoticed amongst biblical scholars. Indeed, it is now widely recognised that the New Testament contains many passages that suggest that persons are capable of surviving bodily death. The surprising thing is that, having acknowledged this, many biblical scholars *continue* to deny that the New Testament embraces a kind of soul-body dualism.

The theologian N. T. Wright has done as much as any scholar to show that according to the New Testament, persons survive bodily death in an intermediate state before bodily resurrection. And yet Wright is adamant that the New Testament does not affirm dualism. Wright (2016) argues that the New Testament view is instead a form of 'holism' on which a human is an 'ontologically differentiated unity.'

I have no objection to the use of the term 'holism' in this context. No doubt, some views of human nature are more holistic, others more atomistic. But we should not suppose that 'holism' is an antonym of 'dualism'. The antonym of 'dualism' is 'monism'. And so we can ask: is the conception of human nature suggested by the New Testament a holistic *monism* according to which humans are wholly material, or a holistic *dualism* according to which we also have immaterial souls? On Wright's reading, the New Testament view is clearly holistic *dualism*, notwithstanding his protests to the contrary.

Wright's position leads him to make some odd statements. For example, he says that 'it simply won't do to demonstrate that the NT shows awareness of aspects of human life which appear to be non-material and to conclude from that that some kind of "dualism" therefore envisaged.' Likewise, respecting Paul's statement at 2 Corinthians 12 that he does not know whether an experience took place 'in the body or apart from the body' Wright says,

The fact that he can consider the possibility that the experience might not have been 'in the body' does indeed indicate that he can contemplate non-bodily experiences, but … I don't think one can straightforwardly argue from this to what is now meant, in philosophical circles, by 'dualism.'

(Wright 2016)

10   *Why Does Everyone Hate the Soul?*

This will sound very strange to anyone trained in philosophy. *Of course,* this is what we mean by 'dualism.' If I suggest in a philosophy of mind seminar that we can go on having experiences without our bodies, I will be swiftly labelled a dualist – I know because I have often done so.

Wright also places great emphasis on the fact that the Bible does not usually use the word 'soul' (*psyche*) when describing the disembodied existence of persons. Having observed that Paul is clear about the continued existence of persons between bodily death and resurrection Wright adds,

> But he never names the *psyche* as the carrier of that intermediate existence. ... Had the earliest Christians wanted to teach that the 'soul' is the part of us which survives death and carries our real selves until the day of resurrection, they could have said so. But, with [a] solitary exception in Revelation [6.9], they never do.
>
> (Wright 2016)

This *is* very strange. Even if the New Testament *never* used '*psyche*' in this way, '*psyche*' would remain a completely appropriate term for the part or aspect of a person that survives bodily death, according to a common Ancient Greek usage, as the New Testament authors *would, of course, have been well aware*. Besides which, any view that posits an immaterial something in virtue of whose persistence persons can survive without their bodies is a kind of dualism irrespective of whether it calls that thing the 'soul': the terminology makes no difference to the metaphysics. Moreover, as Wright himself observes, the New Testament *does* use 'psyche' in this way (and not only in Revelation 6.9, as the earlier example from Matthew 10:28 shows).

It seems to me, therefore, that we should call a spade a spade and recognise that, insofar as we are using the categories of present-day philosophy of mind, the New Testament embraces a form of mind-body or soul-body dualism. Indeed, it embraces a *much more thoroughgoing* form of dualism than much that goes by the name in recent philosophical discussions, as we shall see.

Wright is by no means the only biblical scholar who goes to great lengths to deny that New Testament embraces dualism despite the evidence to the contrary. Those who are interested can consult the excellent work on the issue by John Cooper (2000, 2001, 2007, 2009a, 2009b, 2015, 2018), Joshua Farris (2015, 2020), J. P. Moreland (2014, 40–73), and Brandon Rickabaugh (2018a, 2018b, 2019), as well as Weir (2022, forthcoming). Here, it is enough to observe that there exists a thriving tradition in biblical scholarship of arguing that the New Testament opposes dualism on the basis of arguments that are bound to leave the uninitiated nonplussed.

Why Does Everyone Hate the Soul?   11

Something that Christian materialists do not always realise is that their attempts to expunge soul-body dualism from the New Testament are just one instance of a very widespread scholarly phenomenon. Indeed, the repetition of essentially the same pattern across numerous scholarly fields suggests that it reflects a powerful and deep-seated force in the current intellectual climate.

There exists, for example, a parallel state of affairs respecting Judaism, concerning the Tanakh, the Talmud, and later Jewish authorities. Consider Maimonides, the 'Rambam,' the most influential Jewish thinker of the Middle Ages. In his article 'The Soul and the Body in the Philosophy of the Rambam' Avshalom Mizrahi (2011) states that for Maimonides 'the body is the home of the soul, and the soul guides the body. That means the body and the soul are one unit ... body and soul are one.' Likewise, in an introduction to medieval Jewish views of the soul, Daniel Davies cautions us that

[w]hen they spoke about souls they were not speaking of things that continue to exist as ghosts of material things that have passed away. What people like Maimonides and Halevi meant, when they said that something has a soul, is that the thing is alive.

(Davies 2022)

From what these sources say, and from what they do not say, one might come away with the impression that Maimonides endorsed some kind of monism, broadly continuous with contemporary materialism. Indeed, Davies's statements respecting Maimonides sound just like Hobbes's on the Bible.

When we turn to Maimonides himself, however, the picture is completely different. In his magnum opus, *Mishneh, Torah, Repentance*, Maimonides asserts that 'in the world to come, there is no body or physical form, only the souls of the righteous alone, without a body, like the ministering angels' (Maimonides c.1176–c.1178, Ch. 8). Likewise, respecting certain bodily goods, Maimonides says,

They are only considered of great benefit to us in this world because we possess a body and a physical form. In a situation, where there is no body, all of these matters will be nullified. There is no way in this world to grasp and comprehend the ultimate good which the soul will experience in the world to come. ... In truth, there is no way to compare the good of the soul in the world to come to the bodily goods of this world.

(Maimonides c.1176–c.1178, Ch. 8)

Maimonides, it turns out, is completely unambiguous in his affirmation of soul-body dualism.

12 *Why Does Everyone Hate the Soul?*

If we turn to the Ancient Egyptians, we find a similar story. Famously, Herodotus reports that the Egyptians were there first to posit an immortal soul that survives bodily death to be successively reborn. As Thomas Mcevilly observes in his book, *The Shape of Ancient Thought* (which merits quoting at length) Herodotus's testimony was once widely accepted. However,

> [f]or the last couple of generations, despite the facts that Herodotus seems genuinely to have travelled in Egypt and that he was a leading authority on that culture among the Greeks of that time, his claim that the doctrine came from there has been widely discredited by scholars. They have been, in fact, somewhat curt and authoritarian on this point, almost disapproving, as if the question should never have been raised in the first place. One says, 'The Egyptians had no such theory,' without arguing the point. Another says, also without argumentation, 'The Egyptians never had such a doctrine,' and 'This is regarded as a closed question.' And another '[W]e now know that Herodotus was totally wrong. Metempsychosis is foreign to the Egyptians' way of thinking.'
>
> (Mcevilley 2002, 127)

It is worth noting Mcevilley's puzzlement at the censorious tone of the sources he cites, a tone that characterises many scholarly discussions of soul-body dualism.

The article that 'led to almost universal rejection of Herodotus II.123 by Western classicists' (McEvielley 2002, 128) is Louis Žabkar (1963). Žabkar's central contention is that the Egyptians could not have entertained the idea of metempsychosis because it requires a Greek notion of soul-body dualism alien to Egyptian thought:

> The Egyptian concept of man … is not a composite of the body and soul, and death does not mean a separation of the soul from the body. … To translate the *ba* or any of the words here discussed as "soul"… would be a matter of grave inaccuracy.
>
> (Žabkar, 1963, 60–2)

The problem with Žabkar's reasoning is that so long as the Egyptian sources describe *some* part or aspect of human persons that survives bodily death, their view will be sufficiently dualistic to make sense of metempsychosis however unlike Greek soul-body dualism it is in other respects. And Egyptian sources describing the separation of *ba* and body at death clearly *are*, to the requisite extent, dualist:

> The curious point is that the serious replies that cry out to be made to this simplistic argument have not been made. … That there is a dualism

between the *ba* and the body, and that the *ba* in certain circumstances separates from the body and ascends to the sky on the death of the body is undeniably true; the dualism is there. ... The Egyptian's way of conceptualizing the parts of the person was different from the Greeks', but it does indeed involve a dualism and a separation of parts, one invisible part (call it spiritual if you will) ascending to the sky, the other visible part (call it physical if you will) remaining on or in the earth.

(Mcevilley 2002, 128–9)

The differences between the (many and varied) Greek conceptions of *psyche* and the (perhaps equally many and varied) Egyptian conceptions of the *ba* should not blind us to the fact that insofar as the categories of contemporary philosophy are concerned, the Egyptian sources entail a kind of dualism.

I hope that the reader is alive to just how bizarre is the circumstance exemplified by these scholarly expositions of Christian, Jewish, and Egyptian views on human nature. The sources cited exhibit a tenacious resolve to deny that the tradition under discussion embraced dualism, in the teeth of what appears to be unmistakable evidence to the contrary.

The story does not end there. Edward Slingerland (2013, 7) observes that 'an almost universally accepted truism among scholars of Chinese religion is that, while "Western" thought is dualistic in nature, early Chinese thought can be contrasted as profoundly "holistic."' We see here the same contrast between dualism and 'holism' that we saw in the biblical scholarship. And again, we must ask: is the Chinese view described here a holistic *monism* on which there is only the body, or is it holistic *dualism* on which there is also something resembling an immaterial soul?

The answer, as Slingerland goes on to show, is emphatically the latter. There exists strong evidence of belief in persons surviving bodily death as early as the Shang dynasty (c. 1600 BCE–1045 BCE). By the time of the Han (202 BCE–220 CE), the textual evidence of soul-body dualism is overwhelming. As Slingerland says,

[Ancient Chinese] afterlife beliefs – as well as the belief in other supernatural beings such as ancestral spirits, nature deities, or high gods – were not only widespread, but also fundamentally parasitic on some sort of mind-body dualism.

(Slingerland 2013, 12–13)

A conception of human nature that permits ancestral spirits to survive bodily death might, no doubt, be considered 'holist' in some important sense. But it is certainly profoundly dualist.

14 *Why Does Everyone Hate the Soul?*

Variations on the same theme abound in discussions of African traditions beyond that of Ancient Egypt. Nelson Ukwamedua (2022, 1), for example, contrasts the 'holistic' Igbo conception of human persons with the dualism of Plato and Aquinas, stating that 'in Igbo ontology, there is no distinction between body and soul' because 'the attention is on man as a complete being.' Ukwamedua adds that for the Igbo, 'death is not the separation of body and soul as what happens at death is not explicit. ... Corporeal death is not the end of existence but that death is rather a gateway to another realm of existence.' And yet, as with the other 'holistic' views discussed, it is clear that the Igbo position is a holistic *dualism* involving an immaterial something in virtue of whose persistence persons may survive bodily death. Azenabor (1999) admits of a similar response.

A distinctive strategy for resisting the idea that African conceptions of human nature involve a form of soul-body dualism may be found in the claim that some African traditions, in particular the Akan, favour 'quasi-physicalism' (Wiredu 1983; Quame 2004). This suggestion merits more detailed discussion elsewhere. But for the present, it is sufficient to observe that the 'quasi-physicalism' that Kwasi Wiredu and Safro Quame attribute to the Akan tradition posits a soul-like component of humans that does not satisfy current philosophical definitions of the physical and that survives bodily death. Hence Kwame Gyekye (1995, 85–103) and Hassekei Mohammed Majeed (2013) are right to argue that the Akan view is more perspicaciously described as 'dualist' than as 'quasi-physicalist.'

An especially audacious example of the scholarly determination to interpret traditional cultures as anti-dualist, whatever the evidence, may be found in Glen Mazis's (2011) discussion of the North American Anasazi. Mazis' central contention is that the religious preoccupation with the sky reflected in the Anasazi built environment can teach us to 'overcome our mind-body dualism.' He explains,

> [The] rupture of earth and sky is fundamental to the metaphysics, religious creeds, overvalued rationalism, reductive science, and technological imperialism that have plagued the Greek to modern European tradition. From its inception in Platonic thought, this dualistic philosophical vision has relied on the injunction to separate mind from body. The built environment of the Anasazi ... [seems] to address a unity of earth and sky. ... If we are to overcome our mind-body dualism, we will have to look to the sky again, not for escape this time, but because as many Native American peoples knew, its home is in the earth.
>
> (Mazis 2011, 19)

Mazis's article is worth reading for its beautiful phenomenology. But insofar as it is supposed to convince us that the Anasazi were anti-dualists in

Why Does Everyone Hate the Soul? 15

their conception of human persons, the argument is simply missing. There is no reason why a society with the built environment of the Anasazi should not turn out to be dualists – Platonists, even. After all, Plato's dualism was preceded, and influenced by that of Indo-Iranian cultures that were no less spiritually preoccupied with the sky than the Anasazi.

It is also worth noticing Mazis's talk about '*our* mind-body dualism' (my emphasis). This too is odd. Insofar as Mazis is addressing today's Western and Western-influenced intellectual culture, he is in fact addressing an ardently *anti-dualist* culture, perhaps the only unambiguously anti-dualist culture that has *ever* attained ascendance over its dualist rivals. Mazis's assumption that his readers belong to a Western intellectual culture that is distinguished by a preference for dualism is *the reverse of the truth*.

The Anasazi left no written records, so it is hard to determine whether they were really the anti-dualists Mazis seems to suppose them to be. But more all less all North American indigenous cultures that we do know about do in fact exhibit the belief that persons survive bodily death and continue to play a part in the religious practices of the community. To that extent, they clearly qualify as dualist in the sense in which the term is used in contemporary philosophy. There is little reason to suppose that the Anasazi were an exception.

This last point is important. Religious practices involving the spirits of the deceased are in fact as close to universal as anything in human culture. In a well-known study, Lyle Steadman, Craig Palmer, and Christopher Tiller (1996) revisit the 16 cases identified in Guy Swanson's classic 1963 investigation of 50 indigenous cultures as not involving such practices. The authors find evidence of belief in the continued existence of deceased persons in *every single case*. While we could do with more evidence here and there, the big picture is plain: something resembling soul-body dualism is ubiquitous in traditional cultures the world over.

Neither are formal philosophical elaborations of soul-body dualism a peculiarly Platonic or Cartesian affair. Pythagoras and Anaxagoras appear to have embraced dualism well before Plato. The Aristotelian tradition followed suit, at least as it was widely understood in the ancient world and revived in the Middle Ages. And the classics of Confucian, Daoist, Hindu, Jain, and Islamic philosophy are frequently as unambiguously dualist as Plato's *Phaedo* or Descartes's *Meditations*. See, for example, Kong Yingda's *Wujing Zhengyi*, the anonymously authored *Taiping jing*, Isvara Krishna's *Samkhyakarika*, Kanada's *Vaisheshikasutra*, Umaswati's *Tattvarthasutra*, or Avicenna's *Maqala fi'l-nafs*. All are classics in their respective traditions, and all affirm the existence of something resembling an immaterial soul that can exist separately from the body.

This is not to say that there have been no historical exceptions to soul-body dualism. There exist special cases such as Buddhism and Stoicism

16 *Why Does Everyone Hate the Soul?*

that must be considered separately. There also exist unambiguous historical examples of materialist monism such as Carvaka and Epicureanism.
These have typically been in the minority, however, while dualism has been
predominant.

Why is it that scholars treat the pervasive dualism of our forebears as a
shameful secret to be swept under the rug? There are plenty of local factors
one could mention. Christian theologians are often eager to emphasise the
theological importance of the body and regard dualism as a distraction.
Anthropologists frequently exaggerate the exotic character of other cultures. And many social scientists and humanists are influenced by the deconstructionist idea that we should oppose binary oppositions wherever
they lurk, as well as the deconstructionist idea that there is nothing wrong
with tendentious interpretation.

It would be a surprising coincidence, however, if local factors independently gained sufficient traction to account for the dualism-minimising practices exhibited throughout recent scholarship. It is more probable
that there exists some deeper source of dualism minimising which has
encouraged local developments that accord with it. I do not know what
this deep-seated explanation is. Indeed, I find the whole situation quite
mysterious. But it is probably connected to the two other misconceptions I have mentioned: the belief that dualism is to blame for manifold
Western societal ills and the belief that dualism has nothing going for it
theoretically.

1.3 Misconception 2: Soul-Body Dualism Is Responsible for Everything Wrong With the West

The claim that soul-body dualism is a distinctively Western view due to
Plato or Descartes is often accompanied by the assertion that dualism is
responsible for just about everything that is wrong with the Western world.
We have already seen Mazis assert that Plato's dualism is answerable for
the European tradition's 'overvalued rationalism, reductive science, and
technological imperialism.' Dualism is also regularly implicated in such
evils as environmental destruction, medical malpractice, and social injustice of every kind (see e.g. Plumwood 1993, Pfeifer 2009; Ventriglio and
Bhugra 2015).

The claim that soul-body dualism is a Platonic or Cartesian idiosyncrasy
has a superficial plausibility to it, at least before one looks at the relevant
sources or reflects on how natural soul-body dualism is. By contrast, the
claim that dualism is responsible for large-scale societal evils is, at face
value, farfetched. This might explain why the practice of blaming dualism
for such evils is comparatively rare in analytical philosophy, the relatively
sober discipline to which this book belongs.

Elsewhere, however, the practice of holding dualism responsible for large-scale societal evils is a commonplace and time-honoured custom. Mario Di Gregorio describes an early example of the kind of attitude that prevails in the famous anti-dualist scientist Ernst Haeckel (1834–1919) in the following terms:

> His hostility to dualism was such that over time he would come to label anything he disliked as dualist. In perfect Orwellian fashion, he held the motto 'monist good – dualist bad' as his main guiding mantra.
>
> (Di Gregorio 2016)

So influential was Haeckel's hostility to dualism that it led to the foundation, in 1906, of an organisation dedicated to the cause: the German Monist League (Hübinger 2023).

It is easy to demonstrate that soul-body dualism is not that Platonic or Cartesian idiosyncrasy that many scholars represent it as being. It would be much harder to prove that dualism is not responsible for the extraordinary range of societal ills laid at its doorstep. Part of what makes the charge farfetched is that there exists no credible methodology for determining whether superficially unrelated social phenomena result from people's views about the philosophy of mind. This also makes the claim hard to refute.

It is possible, however, to evaluate the kind of support that is put forward in support of the claim that dualism is responsible for the West's ills and iniquities. The evidence is far from overwhelming.

Frequently, as in Mazis's paper, no support at all is given. For many scholars, the thesis that dualism is responsible is not a hypothesis but an axiom. Others have presented the case for regarding dualism as a malignant force in detail, however. One of the most influential and most thorough examples is Val Plumwood's (1993) classic exposition of ecofeminism, *Feminism and the Mastery of Nature*. I will treat Plumwood's book as representative of the kind of arguments that are put forward.

Plumwood's argument has three parts. Firstly, historical soul-body dualists regard the soul as superior to the body. Secondly, historical dualists associate the superiority of soul to body with objectionable judgements, such as the superiority of master to slave, coloniser to colonised, or male to female, thereby creating a web of dualisms that structure Western thought. Thirdly, because some of the dualisms in the web are objectionable, the whole web must be repudiated, the soul-body distinction along with it.

The strategy of treating soul-body dualism as an important part of a web of evil dualisms is very common and goes back at least as far as Haeckel. It is a powerful device that permits one to trace anything from the Belgian

18 Why Does Everyone Hate the Soul?

Congo (Sartwell 2019) to the War on Terror (Porter 2006; Wilson 2009) back to Plato's philosophy of mind. There are, however, several problems with this kind of reasoning.

The first part of Plumwood's argument – the claim that historical dualists regard the soul as superior to the body – is largely correct. Plato, in particular, represents embodiment as a misfortune and escape from the cycle of death and rebirth as our highest goal. Plato's views on this question accord with the Jain philosophical ideas that appear to have influenced him via Orphism (Mcevilley 2002, 197–204). Other historical dualists, especially Christians, have been much more positive about embodiment. But even Christian dualists tend to represent the soul as more important than the body.

The first part of Plumwood's argument may, then, be accepted. For two reasons, the second part – Plumwood's claim that historical dualists situate the superiority of soul to body in a web of evil dualisms, along with the superiority of master to slave, coloniser to colonised, and so on – is much less convincing.

Firstly, Plumwood's evidence for the web of evil dualisms tends to be highly indirect and conjectural. Plato's cave associates the inferiority of the material world with that of women because the cave is like a womb (Plumwood 1993, 93). Descartes's theory of mind leads to a 'solipsism' that 'treats the other as alien to the self, excluding the possibility of mutual recognition or exchange' (Plumwood 1993, 117). Logicians favour classical logic because the classical understanding of negation encodes a 'radical exclusion of the alien other' (Plumwood 1993, 57). These claims are, at best, far from obvious.

In some cases, the evidence is simply absent. For example, Plumwood (1993, 105) claims without argument that Plato has no conception of 'a common human nature in contrast to non-human nature; slaves, for example, are little different from animals.' And yet, Plato's *Phaedrus* (249b) explicitly identifies humans as the unique bearers of the rational faculties explained by his theory of recollection, and his *Meno* (80a–86d) famously has Socrates support that theory by demonstrating the presence of those rational faculties in Meno's slave.

If you look for a pattern everywhere, you are likely to find it whatever the evidence. All the more so if you treat the pattern as a 'deep structure,' 'buried' beneath the surface (Plumwood 1993, 190). The doubtful character of Plumwood's evidence leaves open the possibility that the web of evil dualisms that she finds at the foundations of Western intellectual frameworks is the product of illusory pattern perception.

Secondly, there is a systematic selective bias Plumwood's reconstruction the web of dualisms that structures Western thought. For example, Plumwood throws Plato's soul-body dualism together with his putative

Why Does Everyone Hate the Soul? 19

affirmation of the superiority of master to slave, of male to female, and other such objectionable evaluations. But Plumwood leaves out Plato's affirmation of the superiority of justice over injustice, honesty over dishonesty, of the life of a philosopher over that of a tyrant – matters about which Plato is much more explicit and emphatic. No explanation is given for this inconsistency.

Even if we accept that soul-body dualism is part of a web of dualisms that structures Western thought, the impression that the dualisms in this web are in general morally objectionable appears, therefore, to be unfounded. If there is such a web, then many of the dualisms it contains will be ones we ought to keep.

The third part of Plumwood's argument – the claim that because the web contains objectionable dualisms, soul-body dualism must be repudiated – is also unpersuasive. Suppose we *did* have good evidence that soul-body dualism has had a place in a web of dualisms every other component of which is objectionable. This *still* would not show that there is anything wrong with either the distinction between soul and body or even with the evaluation of soul as superior to body. Soul-body dualism is not to be convicted by association.

We must reject the superiority of master to slave, coloniser to colonised, and so on. But before we reject the distinction between soul and body, we must consider the arguments in its favour – arguments of the sort discussed later in this book. Something odd about Plumwood's methodology is that, although she concludes that we must reject even the nonevaluative distinction between soul and body, she does not engage with those arguments. Her enquiry ignores the real profundity of the mind-body problem.

Insofar as it is represented by Plumwood's book, the argument that soul-body dualism is responsible for manifold Western societal ills is, then, unconvincing. It should be added that, if soul-body dualism *has* sometimes been invoked for objectionable purposes, this is hardly evidence that dualism is to blame. Soul-body dualism has been part of the belief system of most humans across the globe and throughout history. In excusing or rationalising their behaviour, humans will appeal to whatever lays to hand. So it will be no surprise if soul-body dualism has sometimes been mixed up in rationalisations of widely evidenced historical evils, even if it was entirely innocent of bringing about those evils.

In order to decide whether soul-body dualism is in fact the harmful view it is made out to be, we should have to consider whether dualism has served as a cause and not merely as a rationalisation for the iniquities attributed to it. And we should have to consider, not only those occasions on which the soul-body distinction has been invoked in defence of, or in the vicinity of, some objectionable practice, but also converse cases.

20 *Why Does Everyone Hate the Soul?*

Gregory of Nyssa's soul-body dualism did not prevent him from making a moral stand against slavery that has no parallel in the ancient world. On the contrary, Gregory appeals to the soul-body distinction in making his case. 'How many obols did you reckon the equivalent of the likeness of God? ... He who knew the nature of mankind rightly said that the whole world was not worth giving in exchange for a human soul' (Gregory of Nyssa 1993, 72–4). Mary Astell's soul-body dualism did not prevent her from making a stand against female subordination that has earned her the title of the first female English feminist. Astell invoked Cartesian dualism as part of her argument (Bryson 1998).

At the same time, Haeckel's monism did not prevent him from championing scientific racism and eugenics (Hawkins 1997, 32–45). There is, in fact, a well-known case for thinking that the work of the German Monist League assisted in the rise of Nazism (Gasman 1975). Neither did Stalin's (1938) materialism prevent the atrocities of the Gulag and the Holodomor, nor Chairman Mao's (cf. Knight 1990, 10) the horrors of the Great Leap Forward and the Cultural Revolution.

Countless cases of beneficent dualism and malignant materialism might be given before we had to resort to the strategy of alleging the existence of examples 'buried' beneath the surface. Works such as Plumwood's simply ignore this. The anti-dualist narrative is nourished by a diet of one-sided examples.

I do not mean to imply that the anti-dualism of the German Monist League, Stalinist Russia, or Maoist China was *responsible for* the evils that followed. I only say that the claim that materialism is to blame for Nazism or the Gulag is no more absurd than the claim that dualism is to blame for the slave trade or climate change. And yet it is only the latter claims that are widely asserted by contemporary thinkers.

An impartial assessment of the impact of opinions about the philosophy of mind on large-scale societal evils would be a massive and quixotic undertaking. No such undertaking has been attempted. Until it has, the claim that dualism is responsible for this or that large-scale societal evil should be treated not as a hypothesis demanding serious evaluation but as an interesting symptom of modern psychephobia.

Though baseless, the perception that dualism is deeply malignant might help to explain why scholars downplay the dualistic leanings of traditions they wish to present in a good light – whether for the purpose of screening their religious faith from scientific criticism, or of doing down evil Western culture, or simply of treating their subject of study charitably. This second strand of psychephobia – dualism blaming – might, therefore, help explain the first – dualism minimising. The converse is also true: the idea that dualism is responsible for what is wrong with the West assumes that dualism is distinctively Western. Both misconceptions are closely

Why Does Everyone Hate the Soul? 21

connected to the third and most important: the idea that soul-body dualism has nothing going for it theoretically.

1.4 Misconception 3: Soul-Body Dualism Has Nothing Going for It Theoretically

An early purveyor of the myth that soul-body dualism 'hails chiefly from Descartes' was Gilbert Ryle (1949, 1), in his influential book *The Concept of Mind*. Ryle devoted most of that work to arguing that soul-body dualism is fundamentally and disastrously wrong. And while Ryle's arguments are no longer widely accepted, his contention that there exist no good grounds for believing in an immaterial soul still reflects the received view both in the analytical philosophical tradition to which he belonged and more widely.

Before considering whether that received opinion is right, three clarifications are in order. Firstly, I have claimed that the scholars discussed above make obviously false or baseless claims about dualism. I do not mean to imply that the works cited are therefore, generally, of low quality. On the contrary, the subordination of the need for good evidence or argument to the cause of anti-dualism in otherwise high-quality sources – many that are justly considered classics – is part of what makes this pattern so worthy of note.

Secondly, the discussion in § 1.2 had much to do with afterlife beliefs. This is because belief in disembodied survival is powerful evidence of soul-body dualism. It is less susceptible to nit-picking objections than other kinds of evidence. Afterlife beliefs will come up again, from time to time, in what follows. But I am interested in afterlife beliefs, here, solely as an indication of the underlying dualist conception of human nature. Soul-body dualism might be true and important irrespective of what one thinks about death and the afterlife. And the pervasiveness of dualism across cultures might be due to its truth and importance, whether or not there is anything in the afterlife beliefs that presuppose it.

Thirdly, it is not my principal object in what follows, either in this chapter or the rest of the book, to refute materialism. Rather, my purpose is to explain why, in view of the challenges facing materialism, the idea of the soul ought to be treated seriously. I explain in outline in this section why I think those who reject materialism are right. And in Chapters 5 and 6, I present a novel argument against materialism which, for reasons explained in § 6.3, I regard as especially powerful. Nonetheless, my focus will be on showing that those who already regard materialism as untenable must return to the idea of an immaterial mind or soul. This is worthwhile because, while there has been a recent backlash against materialist theories of mind, the leading opponents of materialism have followed the herd in going out of their way to avoid positing anything resembling an immaterial soul.

22   *Why Does Everyone Hate the Soul?*

At least two kinds of reason have been given for believing in immaterial souls: those based on empirical investigation and those based on philosophical argument. I consider these in turn. (I set aside, here, reasons based on divine revelation, mystical insight, or altered states of consciousness as not having a claim on readers who have not undergone the requisite conversion, mystical episode, or narcotic spree.)

In 1882, the Society for Psychical Research was founded with the principal aim of seeking empirical evidence for the existence of the soul. Its founding members included many distinguished thinkers and even one future British prime minister. They sought both direct evidence by means of séances and hauntings, and indirect evidence in phenomena such as extra-sensory perception and near-death experiences.

The literature produced by the Society for Psychical Research and the wider paranormal research programme it inspired makes for fascinating reading. It has impressed thinkers as rigorous and ingenuous as William James and Alan Turing. And it contains some striking stories, such as that of Henry Sidgwick's unsettling post-mortem communication to his friends: 'We no more solve the riddle of death by dying than we solve the problem of life by being born.' I introduce the topic of paranormal research here, however, only to give my opinion that it has not produced a convincing case for the soul.

In his 1939 presidential address to the Society for Psychical Research, Oxford's Wykeham Professor of Logic, H. H. Price said,

> If our study is to become an experimental science in the full sense of that phrase, we must be able to *produce* the phenomena whenever we like; or if you prefer, we must be able to *ensure* that they will happen. It is not enough to be able to detect and measure them when they do happen.
>
> (Price 1939, 18)

So far as I can tell, this never happened: there is no paranormal phenomenon that obviously demands a nonphysical explanation and that we can produce at will for scientific study.

This is not to say that paranormal research merits no serious attention or that its practitioners must be excessively credulous or dishonest. So far as I can tell (which may not be very far) researchers such as Rupert Sheldrake are no less committed to the scientific spirit than their more conventional colleagues. Their indifference to the consternation of some parts of the scientific community is entertaining and probably admirable. And if some paranormal research *has* been deceitful, this does not distinguish it from regular science. A certain amount of scientific fraud is ubiquitous and perhaps inevitable (cf. Bright 2021). It should not be taken to discredit an unfashionable field any more than a mainstream one.

Why Does Everyone Hate the Soul? 23

Nonetheless, I would not put any weight on paranormal research in making the case for the soul. When we turn to philosophy, the situation is completely different. It is true that 60 years ago, philosophy of mind seemed to be approaching a materialist consensus. But the consensus never arrived. Instead, philosophy of mind has been marked by a series of influential challenges to materialism, leading to a resurgence of anti-materialist theories. And while philosophers have attempted to minimise the implications of these developments for the traditional idea of the soul, it is impossible to overlook their significance.

It is now widely recognised that materialism struggles to accommodate the mental or spiritual half of human nature, even by those who hope that it will ultimately succeed. This is largely due to work on the problem of consciousness, the issue on which this book focuses. But complementary and, in my judgement, equally decisive arguments can be made respecting other mental or spiritual matters including but not limited to intentionality, reason, personal identity, subjecthood, unity, agency, moral worth, and moral responsibility. I hope to discuss some of these in a future book.

The problem of consciousness concerns what is sometimes called *phenomenal consciousness*: the fact that there is something it is like to be you, from the inside – the fact that you have a first-person perspective replete with colours, sounds, sensations, ideas, and the like. Phenomenal consciousness is distinguished from functional consciousness, roughly: the ability to perform certain behaviours in response to one's environment. 'Functional *consciousness*' so understood, is a misnomer. For it need not involve anything mental or experiential any more than the behaviour of an automatic door. For this reason, I will use 'conscious' only in the sense of 'phenomenally conscious' in what follows.

The fact that you are conscious seems certain. Even if you cannot be sure that you are not dreaming or hallucinating, you can be sure that you are having the experiences you are having. At the same time, the fact that you are conscious radically separates you from ordinary material objects. At least as we usually conceive of them, rocks and clocks and plants are, as it were, *all physical exteriority*. They have third-person properties that can be observed from the outside, but no first-person conscious interiorities of their own.

I describe the most influential arguments against materialism about consciousness in § 5.1. At their heart is the observation that no characterisation of a purely physical system such as the human body or brain a priori entails the existence of conscious experience. That is to say, there is no logical or conceptual connection between the physical characteristics of a system, however complex or sophisticated, and consciousness. The arguments infer, by one path or another, that consciousness must be

24 *Why Does Everyone Hate the Soul?*

something additional, over and above any physical system with which it is associated.

In my judgement, when properly supported, existing arguments against materialism about consciousness are entirely sound. The difficulty of maintaining materialism can also be brought out by considering the materialist options available. It is worth pointing out here that there exist two kinds of materialist: casual materialists who have not thought deeply about the issue, and informed materialists who have.

Casual materialists include academic philosophers who have not worked on the area, specialists in other disciplines, and members of the wider public. For this group, the problem getting consciousness from matter can seem comparable to a geometric puzzle that appears impossible but might turn out to have a satisfactory solution. Consider Sam Loyd's (1858) 'Famous Trick Donkeys' (Figures 1.1 and 1.2):

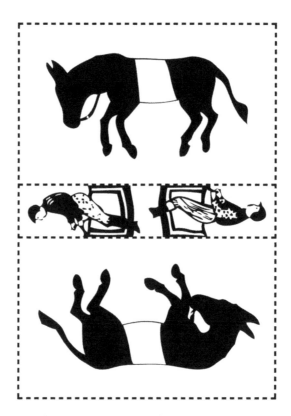

Figure 1.1 Sam Loyd's (1958) Famous Trick Donkeys (creative commons).
Source: https://en.wikipedia.org/wiki/File:Sam_Loyd%27s_Trick_Donkeys.svg.

The player must rearrange three images to represent two riders on two donkeys. Typical players try countless unsuccessful arrangements before finding the solution. Many give up before getting there. The puzzle can seem impossible. But when players are faced with the solution there is an 'ah-ha!' moment in which all becomes clear, and any doubts concerning the solubility of the puzzle disappear:

Figure 1.2 Sam Loyd's (1958) Famous Trick Donkeys solved (creative commons).

Casual materialists often assume that there exists this kind of satisfactory 'ah-ha!' solution to the problem of getting consciousness from matter. They often suppose that the solution is already known to experts in philosophy or brain science, and they are sometimes encouraged in this supposition by the misleading statements of such experts. Casual materialists are, as a result, sanguine about their own inability to explain why some physical systems have first-person perspectives ablaze with technicolour phenomenology while others do not.

Informed materialists have thought deeply about the problem of consciousness and are familiar with the literature. As a result, they tend to recognise that getting consciousness from matter is not like solving a geometric puzzle. The difference is that materialist theories never provide, and are not generally expected to provide, the kind of illuminating 'aha!' explanation that we have for Loyd's Trick Donkeys. Instead, the leading materialist theories focus on *reconciling us to the lack of such an explanation*.

The result is that materialist theories of consciousness end up adopting one of two strategies. Some claim that consciousness does not really exist. The idea that we are conscious is, on this view, some kind of mass delusion

26 *Why Does Everyone Hate the Soul?*

or persistent theoretical error. Others assert that consciousness does exist, and is the same thing as some physical phenomenon, even though we are incapable of seeing how. (In a way, there is a third strategy which quietly stipulates that by 'consciousness' will be meant some physical or physically realisable thing, such as a function of the nervous system, and then explains how *that* is physical. But this approach only counterfeits a materialist explanation of consciousness by covertly changing the subject.)

This is why, despite the colossal ingenuity and resourcefulness of contemporary materialist philosophers, specific materialist theories always seem disappointing and never gain general acceptance. Materialist theories are, in this respect, quite unlike the solution to Lloyd's Trick Donkeys, which satisfies everyone and ends all controversy. If it were more widely known that the strategies described are all that informed materialists have to offer, there would probably be fewer casual materialists. It is plausible, therefore, that the position of materialism in our intellectual culture is fragile, and might quickly collapse once word gets out that the experts do not really have the answers.

Open-minded readers might ask, could there not nonetheless be some undiscovered 'aha!' solution to the problem of getting consciousness from matter that *will* satisfy everyone and end all controversy once we have it? After all, it took 365 years before Andrew Wiles proved Fermat's last theorem. And so far as we know, it took more than two millennia before August Amthor solved Archimedes' cattle problem. Perhaps the mind-body problem is a comparably fiendish, yet ultimately soluble puzzle.

The comparison is misleading. For the problem of giving, for the mind-body problem, the kind of satisfactory 'aha!' explanation that we have for Fermat's last theorem, Archimedes' cattle problem, or Lloyd's Trick Donkeys, is not merely unsolved. It has been demonstrated to be unsolvable. For such a solution would require an a priori entailment from a physical system to consciousness. And even most materialists grant that anti-materialist thought experiments of the sort described in § 5.1 show that no such entailment exists. That is why materialists focus on reconciling us to the lack of such an explanation, rather than on providing it.

It would be more illuminating, therefore, to compare the problem of getting mind from matter to the problem of squaring the circle, which Lindemann and Weierstrass proved to be impossible in 1882. It is a historical irony that Hobbes purported to have overcome both in the seventeenth century.

If we were not living in an age of widespread abhorrence for the idea of the soul, then the renewed dissatisfaction with materialism that has characterised recent philosophy of mind might be expected to bring with it a corresponding renewal of interest in soul-body dualism. We find here,

Why Does Everyone Hate the Soul? 27

however, a parallel to the anti-soul biases described earlier. For although many theorists now regard materialism as untenable, they have gone out of their way to avoid recognising the positive implications of this view for the old idea of the soul.

As I explain in Chapter 2, the received opinion in recent philosophy is that, although there exist powerful arguments that consciousness involves nonphysical *properties*, these properties, if such exist, should be regarded as belonging to the brain or body. As a result, there is no need to posit an immaterial mind or soul that is a separate property-bearer in its own right. In the terminology that has become standard, the case against materialism has led to widespread interest in 'property dualism,' but not in 'substance dualism.' ('Substance' has a technical sense here to be discussed in the following chapters.)

The received opinion is reflected neatly in a couple of lines from Yuval Noah Harari's widely read book, *Homo Deus*. On page 52, Harari asserts that there is 'zero scientific evidence' that humans have souls. And yet three pages later he says, 'How is it, then, that when billions of electric signals move around in my brain, a mind emerges that feels [...]? As of 2016, we have absolutely no idea' (Harari 2016, 52–5). It is characteristic of contemporary intellectual culture that Harari can make these assertions without putting two and two together and concluding that there may be something in the idea of the soul after all.

This book argues that the received view, according to which recent arguments against materialism should lead us to posit nonphysical properties only and not nonphysical substances, is unwarranted. The result is that anyone who accepts the case for nonphysical properties will be under great pressure to accept the existence of nonphysical substances resembling immaterial souls. Since many contemporary thinkers do recognise that there is a strong case for positing nonphysical properties, the idea of an immaterial soul should be treated much more seriously than it has been in recent philosophy.

I will not anticipate the arguments to come here. Instead, I will conclude this chapter by commenting on two worries the reader might have. First, the reader might be thinking 'but don't we *know* that there is a fundamental problem for soul-body dualism concerning how the two interact?' There are a few things to say in response.

The idea that there exists some disastrous interaction problem for soul-body dualism is, to some extent, a myth. People often speak as though Pierre Gassendi and Elizabeth of Bohemia showed that Descartes's dualism could not accommodate mind-body interaction back in the seventeenth century and that this objection has been fatal. But in fact, the kind of objection raised by Gassendi and Elizabeth plays no role in the contemporary discussion. The argument suggested by their comments, if it goes beyond the mere demand for an explanation, appears to presuppose that interaction requires physical impact. There is no reason to accept that presupposition.

There *does* exist a very different interaction problem, known as the causal-closure argument, that many present-day theorists do regard as posing a serious challenge to dualism. The causal-closure argument is based on the principle that every physical effect is brought about by a chain of sufficient physical causes. It seems to follow that physics leaves no work for a non-physical mind or soul to do in determining how the body behaves. I discuss the causal-closure argument in detail in Weir (2021c).

For two reasons, the causal-closure argument does not pose a serious challenge to the claim that opponents of materialism should return to the idea of an immaterial soul. Firstly, although property dualists sometimes gesture at the causal-closure argument as a reason for preferring property dualism to substance dualism, in fact, the argument poses exactly the same problem for both kinds of dualism (see § 2.2). The practice of treating the interaction problem as a decisive objection to substance dualism but as indecisive with respect to property dualism is, it seems, just another example of contemporary psychephobia.

Secondly, the principle on which the causal-closure argument is based – the claim that all physical effects are brought about by chains of sufficient physical causes – is itself little more than an article of faith. The causal-closure principle is accepted, not because it has been confirmed by some exacting empirical test, but because it is useful in arguing against dualism.

Two kinds of support for the causal-closure principle get offered (see e.g. Papineau 2001). Firstly, it is sometimes said that in inanimate matter, under the kind of conditions in which we have studied it, all physical effects are brought about by sufficient physical causes. It is then inferred that the same will be true of animate organisms including humans. But of course, this inference is deeply question-begging. For the truth of interactionist dualism – the kind on which the soul makes a difference to what the body does – would make no difference to the behaviour of inanimate matter.

Secondly, it is sometimes said that empirical work on the human body itself shows that in this system, physical effects are always brought about by sufficient physical causes. Now, this really would pose a problem for interactionist dualism if the evidence were there – if, for example, we could model the dynamics of someone's nervous system in sufficient detail to predict what will happen next, given the physical causes present, and show that our predictions are accurate. But the actual evidence that gets put forward falls so far short of this as to be laughable. It usually comes down to the observation that it has not been shown that this is *not* what would happen if we were able (which we are not) to carry out such a test (e.g. Papineau 2001, 27).

It is worth adding that even if the causal-closure principle were well supported, the game would hardly end there. For there exist non-standard interactionist and non-interactionist forms of soul-body dualism that are immune to the causal-closure argument, even if they might be vulnerable to arguments of other kinds. I discuss some of these in Weir (2021c) and also take seriously the strategy proposed by Goff (forthcoming).

For these reasons, I do not regard the interaction problem as a threat to soul-body dualism. For science-engaged discussions of the causal-closure argument that are sympathetic to interactionist dualism, the reader should consult the recent work of Alin Cucu and Brian Pitts (2019; Pitts 2020; Cucu 2022).

The second worry I will mention is less specific. It consists in a sense of unease about how strange the idea that humans have immaterial souls appears against the backdrop of our wider, largely naturalistic worldview. The soul, one feels, is something too vast to introduce without making a wider difference. This is disconcerting. Accepting that humans have immaterial souls is like detecting extra-terrestrial life or discovering a parallel universe. (In a sense it *is* detecting extra-terrestrial life *and* discovering a parallel universe.)

I suspect that most of the real uneasiness about soul-body dualism arises, not from the interaction problem, but from the sense that positing an immaterial soul must have massive and unpredictable knock-on effects on our conception of the world and our place in it. And I think that dualists sometimes exacerbate the problem by making out that their position requires only a minor adjustment to our ordinary view of things. John Henry Newman (1849) is more perspicacious when he says that a person with a soul 'has a depth within him unfathomable, an infinite abyss of existence; and the scene in which he bears part for the moment is but like a gleam of sunshine upon its surface.'

To some extent, I share this unease. The idea that we have to posit something resembling an immaterial soul is embarrassing. It does not fit well into our ordinary, naturalistic picture of the world. I doubt that it will fit into any picture that feels so elegant and complete. (An appearance of elegance and completeness can be had cheaply by leaving out whatever is difficult to explain.) If the problem of consciousness can only be solved by a return to nonphysical substances, then the world is much more mysterious than we ordinarily suppose.

To address this concern properly, it would be necessary to embark on a metaphysical investigation that would take us far beyond the scope of this book. For now, in partial mitigation, I would urge that the alternatives – the materialist strategies outlined in this chapter – are at any rate *no less embarrassing*. One denies the most obvious of all truths: that you are conscious (cf. Strawson 2018). The other affirms what looks very much like a

30   *Why Does Everyone Hate the Soul?*

contradiction: that one's conscious experience is inexplicably the same thing as some fundamentally unconscious physical thing. (For all the ink that has been spilled over the question, I think this *simply is* a contradiction.)

The idea that we possess immaterial souls might be mysterious, but at least it is not obviously false. If it entails that our ordinary naturalistic worldview is less true or less complete than we usually suppose, so much the worse for our ordinary naturalistic worldview.

With that said, I will turn to the main project of this book, that of showing that those theorists who go so far as to grant that consciousness requires nonphysical properties must take the further step and posit nonphysical substances resembling the soul of traditional cultures the world over. In doing so, I leave in the background the issue of *whether* we must take the initial step of rejecting materialism. Hence, what follows is a project with which materialists might sympathise. After all, there could hardly be better news for materialism than the discovery that the only alternative is to embrace an idea so popularly detested as that of the soul.

2 The Decline of Substance Dualism and the Substance-Property Distinction

Dualism is the view that in addition to physical things, there exist non-physical mental things. Property dualism says that the nonphysical mental things are limited to properties; substance dualism says that they also include substances. The received view in present-day philosophy is that the only serious kind of dualism is property dualism. This chapter argues that the received view should be reconsidered. For it seems to be based neither on any influential argument nor even on a clear understanding of how the two positions differ. To this end, we must first clarify what 'substance' and 'property' mean here. The second half of the chapter does so.

2.1 The Fall of Substance Dualism and the Rise of Property Dualism

The term 'substance dualism' is new, but the position it names is very old. Substance dualism is standardly attributed to Plato, Augustine, and Descartes, and more controversially to Aristotle and Aquinas. I explain in § 4.3 why these attributions are plausible. Substance dualism was still considered one of the leading responses to the mind-body problem at the start of the twentieth century. Broad (1925) treats it as such, and Ryle (1949, 1) goes so far as to call Descartes's 'dogma of the ghost in the machine' the 'official doctrine' to which 'most philosophers, psychologists and religious teachers subscribe, with minor reservations.'

Not long after this, however, Double (1985, 383) reports that 'few philosophers believe in Cartesian ghosts anymore.' More recently, Kim (2005, 151) claims that 'substance dualism has not been taken as a serious option in mainstream philosophy of mind since the early twentieth century.' As the quotations listed on the next page demonstrate, many present-day philosophers concur.

Both Ryle and Kim are exaggerating. There were many opponents of the 'official doctrine' in Ryle's day. Both Broad (1925) and Russell (1927)

DOI: 10.4324/9781003378600-3

32 The Decline of Substance Dualism

depart significantly from Descartes. And Carnap (1932) is naturally read either as an early physicalist or as an early logical behaviourist along with Hempel (1935). There were also several mainstream defences of substance dualism between the early twentieth century and Kim's 2005 book. Plantinga (1970) and Swinburne (1986) are clear examples.

It is true, nonetheless, that substance dualism lost much of its long-standing popularity in the middle of the twentieth century. This reversal appears to have been initiated, in analytical philosophy at least, by the behaviourist arguments of Ryle (1949) and Wittgenstein (1953). It was subsequently reinforced by arguments for physicalism, in particular the causal-closure argument which is advanced in an early form by Lewis (1966). (As I explain in § 4.1, 'physicalism' is the modern, science-inspired version of materialism.)

The decline of substance dualism was followed, after a time, by widespread interest in property dualism. This was due, to a considerable degree, to a series of influential works that challenged the capacity of physicalism to accommodate conscious experience. These include Nagel (1974), Jackson (1982), Levine (1983), McGinn (1989), and Chalmers (1996). Some, like Nagel (1974) Levine (1983), and McGinn (1989), raise concerns about physicalism without endorsing dualism. But others, including Jackson (1982) and Chalmers (1996), defend a return to dualism. They are joined by later works such as Kim (2005).

These recent works defend property dualism only, not substance dualism. They agree that phenomenal properties are 'fundamentally new features of the world,' as Chalmers (1996, 125) puts it. But they hold off from positing nonphysical substances as the bearers of these properties. I follow Schneider (2012a, 61, fn. 1) in treating Jackson (1982), Chalmers (1996), and Kim (2005) as the most important defences of property dualism, so described. Zimmerman (2010, 120, fn. 3) provides a longer list. But of those Zimmerman adds, only Strawson (1994) has had comparable influence. I return to Strawson in Chapter 4.

It is also in the late twentieth century that the labels 'substance dualism' and 'property dualism' become common. Michel's et al. (2011) data show that these terms were hardly used before the 1970s. Marked increases occur after 1974 and 1982. (It is tempting to credit this to Nagel (1974) and Jackson (1982). This does not explain why the initial increase is confined to the UK corpus however.) It appears to have been the need to differentiate the ascendant dualism of Jackson (1982) and others from the unpopular dualism of Plato, Augustine, and Descartes that gave the terms 'substance dualism' and 'property dualism' general circulation.

Shortly after property dualism entered mainstream philosophy, theorists began to report a broad consensus about the relative merits of property dualism and substance dualism. According to this consensus, substance dualism is highly implausible, whereas property dualism is an important position, which must be taken seriously. Here are some recent samples:

> The fact is that substance dualism has played a very small role in contemporary discussions of philosophy of mind. ... Dualism is no longer a dualism of two sorts of substances; it is now a dualism of two sorts of properties.
>
> (Kim 2006, 51)

> Unlike substance dualism, property dualism remains a respectable position within philosophy of mind, defended by Chalmers (1996) and others.
>
> (Zimmerman 2006, 114)

> The official doctrine is dead in only one of its ontological aspects: substance dualism may well have been repudiated but property dualism still claims a number of contemporary defenders.
>
> (Tanney 2009, x)

> It is widely thought that mind–body substance dualism is implausible at best, though mere "property" dualism is defensible and even flourishing.
>
> (Lycan 2013, 533)

Similar reports can be found in Double (1985), Ruhnau (1995), Francescotti (2001), Searle (2004, 41–4), Zimmerman (2010), Schneider (2012a), Heil (2012), Yang (2015), and Loose et al. (2018).

These citations provide evidence of a *perceived* consensus and only indirect evidence of a consensus. Still, as Bourget and Chalmers (2014, 466) suggest, the received wisdom of a community is plausibly defined not by what most people believe, but by what most people believe most people believe. The received wisdom in the philosophy of mind, so described, is that the only serious kind of dualism is property dualism.

2.2 The Preference for Property Dualism Lacks Support

The received wisdom in the philosophy of mind, then, is that opponents of physicalism should favour property dualism, not substance dualism. This section argues that, for two reasons, the received view deserves to be reassessed. Firstly, the preference for property dualism does not seem to have been driven by any influential argument. Secondly, this preference does not appear to be based on a clear understanding of what a nonphysical 'substance' would be.

34 *The Decline of Substance Dualism*

2.2.1 No Influential Argument for Preferring Property Dualism

Substance dualism loses its long-standing popularity in the middle of the twentieth century. In the late twentieth and early twenty-first century, theorists start taking property dualism seriously as a solution to the problems physicalism faces accommodating consciousness. Finally, there emerges a widespread view that although substance dualism need not be taken seriously, property dualism is a respectable position.

This story contains a lacuna. It does not explain why recent theorists see property dualism as preferable to substance dualism. And it is remarkably difficult to find a satisfactory explanation for this. For the main advantages and the main disadvantages attributed to property dualism seem to be features it shares with substance dualism. Insofar as these features are concerned, substance dualism seems just as attractive as property dualism. (I will argue later, of course, that substance dualism is in fact *more* attractive.)

The main advantage of property dualism over *physicalism* is that it rejects the thesis that consciousness is physical. As a result, property dualism is compatible with the leading arguments against physicalism such as the knowledge argument and the conceivability argument which I introduce in § 5.1. But this is clearly not an advantage over substance dualism. For substance dualists also reject the thesis that consciousness is physical.

It is natural to assume, therefore, that property dualism earns its important position in present-day philosophy by rejecting the thesis that consciousness is physical *whilst* avoiding one or more of the objections that brought about the decline of substance dualism. But this does not seem to be the case either.

As I have said, the decline of substance dualism appears to have been initiated by the behaviourist arguments of Ryle (1949) and Wittgenstein (1953). But these are usually seen as arguments against dualism *of any kind*, not just substance dualism (cf. Tanney 2009, x; 2015). And in any case, present-day opponents of physicalism tend not to treat these arguments seriously to begin with. (For my response to Wittgenstein on this issue, see Weir (2021d).) So even if property dualism were less vulnerable to behaviourist arguments than substance dualism, this would not explain its preferential treatment.

The decline of substance dualism was perpetuated by later physicalist arguments. The most important of these is a problem about mind-body interaction known as the causal-closure argument, which is advanced in an early form by Lewis (1966) and more recently by Papineau (2001, 2002, 2009). But this too is standardly presented as a case against dualism generally, and property dualists have offered no explanation of why their position should be less vulnerable to it than substance dualism. Quite the opposite as the passage from Kim (2005, 156) quoted in a moment shows.

The Decline of Substance Dualism   35

I have mentioned that I distinguish between a standard version and a Russellian monist version of property dualism. It should be acknowledged that Russellian monism *is* widely thought to carry an advantage over traditional dualism when it comes to the causal-closure argument (cf. Chalmers 2016a). However, as I explain in § 4.4, the definitive elements of Russellian monism are compatible with physicalism, substance dualism, and idealism, as well as property dualism. So, Russellian monism gives property dualism no special advantage.

The situation, then, is perplexing. It is widely supposed that property dualism is preferable to substance dualism. And yet there is no widely attested advantage of property dualism over substance dualism. The preferential treatment given to property dualism appears to be unfounded.

It might be hoped that the classic defences of property dualism will cast some light on this puzzle. But these works are unilluminating here. For example, Jackson (1982) does not mention the choice between substance dualism and property dualism at all. He just assumes that the nonphysical things he argues for are properties, not substances. In a follow-up, Jackson (1986) specifies that he is only proposing 'attribute dualism,' in response to Churchland's (1985) suggestion that Jackson is committed to 'ectoplasm.' But Jackson (1986) does not give any reason for favouring 'attribute dualism,' and serious substance dualist positions do not get discussed.

Chalmers (1996) also assumes without explanation that the nonphysical things he posits are properties. At one point Chalmers (1996, 124–5) emphasises that he is proposing a kind of property dualism only, not substance dualism. But he does not argue that property dualism is preferable to substance dualism. And more recently Chalmers (2010, 139) has clarified that he understands 'property dualism' in a broad way that entails that there are nonphysical properties whilst remaining neutral on nonphysical substances.

Initially, Kim (2005) looks more promising. For Kim (2005, 70–92) argues at length that substance dualism must be rejected. But Kim only rejects nonphysical substances on the basis that they could not act causally on physical things. (Chalmers (1996, 124–5) can also be read as rejecting substance dualism on this basis.) This is not helpful. For as I have said, the same charge is often pressed against property dualism and, all the more puzzlingly, Kim (2005) himself is one of the chief prosecutors:

What has become increasingly evident over the past thirty years is that mental causation poses insuperable difficulties for all forms of mind-body dualism – for property dualism no less than substance dualism.

(Kim 2005, 156)

36 *The Decline of Substance Dualism*

Kim's solution is to endorse a noninteractionist form of property dualism. (I use 'noninteractionist' here for views on which mental causes do not have physical effects.) As a result, it is not clear what is supposed to motivate Kim's preference for property dualism over substance dualism after all. For substance dualism also comes in both interactionist forms like Descartes's and non-interactionist forms like Malebranche's and Leibniz's. (I mean the theory Leibniz recommends as a corrective to Descartes's interactionist dualism at *Monadology* (AG 223); Leibniz himself is an idealist.)

Of the three defences of property dualism discussed here, only Kim (2005) makes a case for the superiority of property dualism to substance dualism, and that case seems implausible by its own lights. Less influential defences of property dualism such as those listed by Zimmerman (2010, 120, fn. 3) tend to be no more enlightening. The received view that property dualism is preferable to substance dualism is widely evinced. But it seems to be supported by no influential argument.

2.2.2 Unclarity About 'Substance'

As I have explained, there is no widely attested advantage of property dualism over substance dualism. This is one reason to suspect that the received view about the merits of these two positions is not well-founded. A second reason is that there is little clarity in the literature on the mind-body problem about what the difference between substance dualism and property dualism consists in.

The distinctive feature of substance dualism is that it posits nonphysical substances, not just nonphysical properties. But 'substance' is not part of the standard vocabulary of present-day philosophy. And as I explain in the next section, there exist multiple historical uses of 'substance.' So to understand the difference between substance dualism and property dualism, we need some indication of what 'substance' means here.

Theorists who invoke the distinction between substance dualism and property dualism tend not to explain what 'substance' means. For example, shortly after stating that his arguments lead only to property dualism and not substance dualism, Chalmers (1996, 125) adds that 'the issue of what it would take to constitute a dualism of substances seems quite unclear to me' (1996, 125). More recently, Chalmers says on the same theme,

> I take the key question to be whether there is a dualism of objects as well as of properties, and in particular whether there are fundamental objects over and above the objects in physics or whether there are merely further fundamental properties that attach to existing fundamental or nonfundamental objects.

> (2010, 139, fn. 36)

The idea that 'substance' means the same as 'object' in this context provides some guidance. But without a definition of 'object,' this is limited. For example, it would be surprising if substance dualism were defined as a view that posits nonphysical objects in the sense of 'object' that contrasts with 'subject.'

Kim is no clearer. He (2005, 150) glosses 'Cartesian mental substances' as 'minds conceived as concrete immaterial things outside physical space in causal interaction with material things located within physical space.' Kim's description is suggestive. But it is insufficiently precise for serious theorising. For he does not explain which of the characteristics mentioned is supposed to be sufficient for substancehood.

Kim might just be assuming that a mind is a substance. Or he might be using 'thing' as a synonym for 'substance.' If so, his gloss is uninformative. Alternatively, Kim might be implying that concreteness, and with it the capacity to act causally, is sufficient for substancehood. (See § 2.4.1 for the idea of 'concreteness.') Arguably, there is precedent for this in Leibniz's definition of substances as things that are 'capable of action' (AG 207). But it is hard to see how concreteness could be sufficient for substancehood if substance dualism is to contrast with property dualism. For as I explain in § 2.4, many philosophers view properties as concrete.

It is not only defences of property dualism that leave the distinction between substance dualism and property dualism imprecise. Some of the works I have cited question the presumption that property dualism is preferable to substance dualism. These too tend to be imprecise about the difference between the two positions. For example, Zimmerman (2010) characterises substance dualism as the view that

> [f]or every person who thinks or has experiences, there is a thing – a soul or spiritual substance – that lacks many or most of the physical properties characteristic of non-thinking material objects like rocks and trees; and that this soul is essential to the person, and in one way or another responsible for the person's mental life.
>
> (Zimmerman 2010, 119–20)

Like Chalmers's and Kim's descriptions, Zimmerman's gives us an approximate sense of what substance dualism involves. But once again, it is not clear which if any of the characteristics mentioned is supposed to be sufficient for substancehood (except the term 'substance' itself).

Although they are imprecise, the examples given here are comparatively useful characterisations of 'substance' in the context of the mind-body problem. It is also common for theorists to discuss substance dualism only indirectly through allusions to 'spirits' (Lewis 1983, 361) 'ectoplasm'

38 *The Decline of Substance Dualism*

(Churchland 1985, 25) or 'mind stuff' (Dennett, 1991, 37). These terms provide very little information about the kind of entities they refer to.

Without clarity on the meaning of 'substance,' it is hard to see how we could be confident that nonphysical substances should be taken less seriously than nonphysical properties. Rather, the received view that property dualism is preferable to substance dualism seems to have arisen out of nowhere, without any influential argument in its favour, or any precise understanding of what this view involves.

2.3 What Is a 'Substance'?

The present-day preference for property dualism stands in need of reappraisal. In order to carry out this task, we need to get clear on what we mean by 'substance' and 'property.' In the remainder of this chapter, I argue that, in the context of present-day philosophy of mind, we should draw this distinction in terms of an Aristotelian-Cartesian independence definition of substance. In the following chapter, I address an influential objection to that definition. I explain how the definition of substance that I defend relates to the main responses to the mind-body problem in Chapter 4.

2.3.1 Three Characterisations of Substance: Aristotle, Descartes, Locke

The substance-property distinction enters the Western canon at the start of the Aristotelian corpus in *Categories* (1a). Aristotle's definition of substance in the *Categories* is adopted very widely indeed until the Early Modern period when definitions of substance proliferate. The most influential Early Modern definitions of substance are Descartes's independence definition and the substratum definition associated with Locke. This section introduces these three approaches to substances. The next section explains why it is Descartes's independence definition that is relevant to the difference between substance dualism and property dualism. More detail on historical and contemporary conceptions of substance may be found in Weir (2021a, 2023) and (O'Conaill 2022).

At *Categories* (1a), Aristotle introduces what seem to be two kinds of properties: those that are 'said of' something in the way that 'two-legged' can be said of a human being, and those which are 'in' something in the way that the colour white is 'in' an individual body. He distinguishes things that are 'said of' and/or 'in' things from 'primary substances,' such as an individual human or an individual horse. Primary substances, Aristotle says, are not 'said of' nor 'in' other things. Rather everything else is 'said of' or 'in' primary substances (2a11–36).

The *Categories* definition is negative. It says that a substance is not something that is 'said of' or 'in' other things. And so, assuming that the 'said of' and 'in' relations are the relations by which a property belongs to its bearer, a substance is not a property. The nature of the 'said of' and 'in' relations is contentious. But Aristotle suggests that they are such that properties cannot exist without the substances they are said of or in (*Categories* 1a24–5, 2b5–6). Properties cannot exist on their own.

Aristotle (4a10) adds that primary substances are distinctive in that they are the only things that can 'receive contraries' by undergoing change. It is not obvious that this follows from his definition, however. On an alternative view, properties themselves have second-order properties and can undergo change with respect to these. For example, the colour of a rose might become more saturated as it blooms.

In the Second Replies (AT VII, 161) Descartes introduces a definition of substance that closely resembles that of the *Categories*. Descartes says that a substance is that 'in which whatever we perceive immediately resides.' (Translations of Descartes are from the CSMK.) By 'whatever we perceive' he means 'any property, quality or attribute of which we have a real idea.' Descartes does not say here that substances do not reside in other things in this way, but this is probably implied. If so, the Second Replies definition appears to be equivalent to the *Categories* definition minus the 'said of' relation.

This is no surprise. Aristotle's *Organon*, of which the *Categories* is the first part, had served as the standard introduction to philosophy generally and to logic in particular for at least 1,200 years in the West when Descartes was writing (see Pini 2008, 148–9). This same tradition was the basis of the Jesuit curriculum that introduced Descartes and Mersenne to philosophy at La Flèche (Societas Jesu, 1599, 398).

Descartes also has a second definition of substance, however. In the *Meditations* (AT VII 44), Fourth Replies (AT VII 226), and *Principles of Philosophy* (AT VIII A 24), Descartes says that a substance is something 'capable of existing independently,' 'that can exist by itself,' or 'which exists in such a way as to depend on no other thing for its existence.' He contrasts substances, so defined, with properties ('modes,' 'qualities,' and 'attributes') which he says, in agreement with Aristotle, cannot exist without other things.

On the interpretation I favour, to say that x could exist 'by itself,' etc., just means that x could exist unaccompanied, or equivalently, that the existence of x does not necessitate the existence of anything other than x. On this view, Descartes's innovation is to explicitly affirm that substances can do what Aristotle says that properties cannot. So Descartes's definition can be seen as either a clarification or a moderate augmentation of Aristotle's. I defend this interpretation in Chapter 3 and in Weir (2021a).

The *Categories* definition and the independence definition, on this understanding, are close relatives. It seems that anything that satisfies the

40 *The Decline of Substance Dualism*

independence definition must satisfy the *Categories* definition. For the independence definition says a substance is something that can exist without anything else. A substance, so defined, cannot be 'said of' or 'in,' or otherwise belong to something else in a way that entails that it is incapable of existing unaccompanied.

It is less clear whether anything that satisfies the *Categories* definition must satisfy the independence definition. The *Categories* definition leaves it open that a substance might depend on something else for its existence in some third way, which does not involve being 'said of' or 'in' it in the way that properties are 'said of' or 'in' their bearers. If this can happen, then something might satisfy the *Categories* definition but not the independence definition. On the other hand, it might be that there *is* no other way for one thing to depend on another for its existence. In that case, the two definitions are equivalent.

In the *Principles*, Descartes says that only God satisfies the independence definition in an unqualified way. This is because Descartes thinks other things can only exist with the concurrence of God. But Descartes also uses the independence definition to distinguish between *created* substances and properties:

> In the case of created things, some are of such a nature that they cannot exist without other things, while some need only the ordinary concurrence of God in order to exist. We make this distinction by calling the latter 'substances' and the former 'qualities' or 'attributes' of those substances.
>
> (AT XI B 24–5)

On a natural interpretation, Descartes defines created substances as things that satisfy the independence definition when we restrict our attention to the domain of nondivine things.

It is hardly an exaggeration to say that whereas before 1662 the *Categories* definition expressed the received understanding of substance throughout the Western world, after 1662, the independence definition took its place. For in 1662, Antoine Arnauld and Pierre Nicole's *L'Art de Penser*, known in English as the Port Royal Logic, usurped the preeminent role of Aristotle's *Organon* in philosophical education. *L'Art de Penser* is an emphatically Cartesian work, and it helped to transmit Descartes's understanding of substance far and wide.

It is important to distinguish these two closely related approaches to substance from a third approach associated with Locke's *Essay Concerning Human Understanding*. Locke describes a substance as 'the supposed, but unknown support of those qualities, we find existing, which we imagine cannot subsist, *sine re substante*, without something to support

The Decline of Substance Dualism   41

them.' (*Essay* II xxiii 2) He seems to imply that a substance is an additional ingredient that must be combined with properties for something to exist. Insofar as this is Locke's intention, his conception of substance resembles the Aristotelian notion of prime matter or Bergman's (1967) notion of 'bare particulars' more than it does Aristotle's or Descartes's conception of substance.

To avoid confusion, recent discussions adopt Locke's alternative term 'substratum' for the extra entity that underlies something's properties, whilst reserving the term 'substance' for the substratum plus the properties. Proponents of 'bare particulars' tend to posit one substratum, in this sense, per particular. Locke can also be read as positing just one substratum underlying all particulars.

Commentators debate whether Locke is really in favour of positing substrata or whether he introduces the idea merely to criticise it. Later British empiricists such as Hume (*Treatise*, § 1.4) and Russell (1948) echo Locke's discussion but are more explicit in their opposition to substrata. If Locke *is* introducing the substratum view of substance to criticise it, then we might say that there are three important ideas of substance in the history of Western philosophy: the idea defended by Aristotle, the idea defended by Descartes, and the idea attacked by British empiricists.

Comments such as Locke's have encouraged the assumption that earlier accounts of substance are also meant to pick out an extra ingredient that must be combined with something's properties for it to exist (cf. Broackes 2006). This assumption cannot be easily sustained. Aristotle's examples of substances are plants and animals, not substrata that must be combined with properties to yield plants and animals. Descartes's examples of substances are minds and bodies, not substrata that must be combined with properties to yield minds or bodies.

In the next subsection, I explain why, of the three definitions introduced here, the *Categories* definition and the independence definition are the only serious candidates for the definition of 'substance' in the sense that is relevant to substance dualism. I also explain why, if the *Categories* definition and the independence definition are not in fact equivalent, then the independence definition is the best candidate.

2.3.2 Substance Dualism and the Independence Definition

The main reason for thinking that the independence definition has the best claim to be considered canonical when we are characterising substance dualism is that the independence definition is the one that Descartes favours when he is putting forward his theory of the mind, and he is the paradigm substance dualist. A secondary reason is that the independence

42 *The Decline of Substance Dualism*

definition captures the commonplace association between substance dualism and the possibility of disembodiment. I explain these in turn.

The claim that Descartes is the paradigm substance dualist is unlikely to receive much resistance. In fact, it is widely taken for granted (cf. Levin 1979, 49; Double 1985; Chalmers 1996, 124–5; Kim 2005, 151; Rodriguez-Pereyra 2008; Lycan 2009). Qualified dissent can be found in Cottingham (1985) and Clark (2003), however, and I briefly comment on this.

Cottingham (1985) argues that aspects of Descartes's thought on the special status of the 'union' of mind and body might make it more reasonable to think of his position as a kind of 'trialism' rather than a kind of 'dualism.' However, Cottingham grants that of the 'trialist' views he finds in Descartes, those that intuitively conflict with substance dualism are also those that conflict with Descartes's official position. So it still makes sense to treat Descartes as the paradigm substance dualist so long as we focus on his official position.

Clark (2003, 258) doubts that Descartes counts as a substance dualist because, although he posits material and immaterial substances, the immaterial substances do not play a certain kind of explanatory role that is important to Clark's reading of Descartes. Although Clarke's comments deserve more attention elsewhere, they do not seem to threaten Descartes's status as a substance dualist. For 'substance dualism' does not usually carry any connotation about the explanatory role played by the nonphysical substances, so long as they exist.

Even Cottingham and Clark agree that there is at least an important sense in which Descartes is a substance dualist. It is this sense that should guide us when we are trying to define the position more clearly. I now argue on this basis that we should prefer the independence definition to the substratum definition and, insofar as they differ, the *Categories* definition when we are defining substance dualism. I begin with the substratum definition.

I have already mentioned that Descartes's use of 'substance' does not pick out Lockean substrata. For this would be incompatible with his standard examples of substances. Furthermore, the substratum view is incompatible with (i) Descartes's claim to Burman that taken together, 'the attributes are the same as the substance' (AT V 154–5; cf. Markie 1994, 76), and (ii) Descartes' suggestion in the *Fifth Objections and Replies* that to know a substance is to know its attributes (cf. Broackes 2006, 160–2).

Rather, Descartes seems to be a proponent of the 'bundle view,' insofar as this means that a substance is nothing over and above its properties. This coheres with his doctrine that the 'principal attributes,' thought and extension, are not really distinct from the substances, mind and body (AT VIII, A 28–30). Importantly, in the sense that is relevant here, the bundle view says that there is nothing more to a substance than its properties.

The Decline of Substance Dualism 43

This does not mean that the properties are separable from or more fundamental than the substance.

There is reason, then, to believe that Descartes rejects the existence of substrata. If so, the paradigm example of substance dualism involves no substrata. This gives us good grounds to reject the substratum definition as a candidate for the definition of substance that characterises substance dualism.

The choice, then, is between the *Categories* definition and the independence definition. This choice is complicated (or simplified, depending on how you look at it) by the fact that these definitions could turn out to be equivalent. I have already said that anything that satisfies the independence definition must satisfy the *Categories* definition. For the *Categories* definition certainly implies that *only* a substance could exist by itself. The question is whether the *Categories* definition implies that *all* substances can exist by themselves.

Descartes himself is probably assuming that the *Categories* definition and the independence definition are equivalent. For he seems to imply that the only way something could be incapable of existing by itself is if it is a property of something else (cf. AT XI B 24–5 quoted earlier). And the *Categories* definition certainly implies that the properties of things do not count as substances. This would explain why Descartes gives no indication that the two definitions concern different senses of 'substance.'

However, the question of the actual relationship between the two definitions raises complicated interpretive and theoretical questions. These can be harmlessly evaded by saying that *if* the *Categories* definition does not turn out to be equivalent to the independence definition, *then* we should prefer the independence definition when defining substance dualism. Two reasons support this judgement.

The first reason is that, again, Descartes is the paradigm substance dualist, and the independence definition is his preferred definition of substance. By adopting the independence definition, we ensure that our definition of substance dualism reflects the paradigm example of the position.

The second reason is that substance dualism is closely associated with the idea of disembodiment (Ryle 1949; Crane 2001, 37–8; Searle 2004, 41; Nida-Rümelin 2010, 191; Zimmerman 2010, 119; Montero 2013, 108). It is this that encourages talk of 'spirits' and 'ghosts.' This association is reasonable. For the classic substance dualist theories of Plato, Augustine, and Descartes, as well as the more recent theories of Plantinga (1970) and Swinburne (1986), consistently affirm the possibility of disembodiment.

On the reading of the independence definition that I have given, it entails that a nonphysical substance could exist without anything else, and therefore without a body. So, the independence definition makes sense of the association between substance dualism and the possibility of disembodiment.

44 *The Decline of Substance Dualism*

By contrast, if the *Categories* definition is not equivalent to Descartes's, this is because it is compatible with the thesis that a nonphysical substance cannot exist on its own. In that case, the mind might be a nonphysical substance, in the sense captured by the *Categories* definition, even though it cannot exist without a body, so long as it is not 'said of' or 'in' that body in the way that properties are. This would undermine the widely accepted view that substance dualism entails the possibility of disembodiment.

For two reasons, then, insofar as the two differ, the independence definition has a better claim than the *Categories* definition to capture the sense of 'substance' that is relevant to substance dualism. I, therefore, adopt the independence definition in what follows.

This makes especially good sense when we are defining 'substance' in preparation for arguing that property dualists must posit nonphysical substances, as I do in Chapters 4–7. For a definition that did not require that nonphysical substances have independent existence would make this conclusion weaker and hence less interesting. Moreover, property dualists explicitly distance themselves from Descartes (e.g. Chalmers 1996, 124–5; Kim 2005, 151). So the claim that property dualists must posit nonphysical substances of the kind that Descartes posits is straightforwardly interesting.

Having said this, it is harmless to describe a position as substance dualist in a weaker sense than that characterised by the independence definition so long as we are clear about what we mean. Incidentally, when Martine Nida-Rümelin (2006) describes her position as 'substance dualist,' it appears to be in some such weaker sense. (The same might be true when Chalmers (2016b) expresses sympathy for 'substance dualism.') But Nida-Rümelin (2010) later drops the label 'substance dualism' precisely because she is not committed to the view that minds have independence existence in a sense that would permit them to exist disembodied.

2.4 What Is a 'Property'?

Insofar as the mind-body problem is concerned, we should count as substances all and only those things that satisfy Descartes's independence definition. If property dualism is a genuine alternative to substance dualism, this must be because properties do not satisfy the independence definition: they cannot exist by themselves. Defences of property dualism such as Jackson (1982), Chalmers (1996), and Kim (2005) do not attempt to show this. In this section, I describe the main theories of properties and explain why it is plausible that properties do indeed differ from substances in their inability to exist by themselves. Following this, I explain how we should understand property dualism, addressing some complications that arise out of the intricacy of contemporary theories about properties.

The Decline of Substance Dualism   45

2.4.1 Two Approaches to Properties

Exactly how we express the difference between substance dualism and property dualism will depend on the theory of properties that we assume to be true. An important fault line exists between those theories that posit concrete properties and those that do not. In this subsection, I set out this difference. The following subsections explain why property dualism seems to constitute a genuine alternative to substance dualism on theories that posit concrete properties and those that do not. Readers easily exhausted by technical minutiae are encouraged to skip ahead to § 2.4.5.

The meanings of 'concrete' and 'abstract' vary. Lewis (1986, 81–6) distinguishes four versions of this distinction. The most common account, however, and the one that is relevant here, says that concrete things are both spatiotemporal and capable of standing in causal relations, whereas abstract things are neither. Something is spatiotemporal if it is either spatial or temporal or both. Everyday objects are standardly regarded as concrete. Numbers, sets, and universals are often regarded as abstract.

A second distinction that differentiates theories of properties is the distinction between particulars and universals. A particular is a *unique*, *unrepeatable* entity, something that can feature in the world only once. A universal is a *common*, *repeatable* entity, something that can feature in the world multiple times. Everyday objects, as we usually understand them, are standardly regarded as particulars. Properties are often regarded as universals.

The difference between theories that posit concrete properties and those that do not can be illustrated by example. Suppose that you encounter a red pillar box. Proponents of concrete properties will say that the colour red is a component of the pillar box located at its surface, which causes you to have the kind of experience you are having when you behold it. Opponents of concrete properties will say that the only thing in front of you is the pillar box, which causes you to have the kind of experience you do *by being red*.

Usually, the distinction between theories that posit concrete properties (which I regard as elegant and plausible) and theories that do not (which I regard as awkward and implausible) is all that is important. But it will sometimes be useful to refer to specific theories of either genus, of which there are five.

Three of the five posit concrete properties. First, there is a liberal form of platonism that posits *both* abstract universals *and* concrete particular property-instances. For liberal platonists, the pillar box is red *partly* because it instantiates the abstract universal *redness*, but it instantiates that universal by comprising a concrete *redness* instance. Following Williams (1953a and b), particular property-instances are widely known as 'tropes,'

46   The Decline of Substance Dualism

though historically they were often called 'qualities' or 'modes.' If we see his Forms as abstract universals, then Plato himself appears to be a liberal platonist (Demos 1948; Mertz 1996, 83–118).

The second theory that posits concrete properties is the moderate kind of nominalism that rejects the existence of universals but affirms the existence of tropes. A moderate nominalist will say that the pillar box is red *solely* because it comprises the particular colour trope it does. Moderate nominalism is liberal platonism without the universals. Ockham appears to be a moderate nominalist in this sense (cf. Spade and Panaccio, 2019, Section 5). So are the great trope nominalists, Williams (1953a and b) and Campbell (1990).

The third theory that posits concrete properties is the theory of concrete universals. Concrete universals are an ontological crossbreed intended to do the work of abstract universals and tropes at the same time. A proponent of concrete universals will say that the pillar box is red because it comprises a concrete *redness* component that is at one and the same time *also a component* of other red things. Concrete universals are sometimes attributed to Aristotle (cf. Ackrill 1963, 73; Owen 1965). However, Armstrong (1978) is a much clearer example, and a very influential one, so I call the theory of concrete universals 'Armstrongianism.'

As I have said, I find theories that posit concrete properties elegant and plausible (at least those that posit concrete *particular* properties anyway). History shows that this is the usual view. However, there has arisen in the twentieth century (so far as I can tell) a pair of extremist ontologies which reject the existence of concrete properties. The first is an austere form of platonism. This position posits abstract universals but rejects concrete property-instances. The second is an extreme version of nominalism. This position rejects abstract universals, concrete universals, *and* tropes, replacing all properties talk with nominalist circumlocutions.

An austere platonist will say that the pillar box is red *solely* because it instantiates the abstract universal redness. Extreme nominalists will introduce some theoretical machinery so that when speaking strictly, they can avoid reference to properties of all kinds. For example, they might say that for the pillar box to be red is solely a matter of its belonging to the set of red things (cf. Lewis 1986).

I cannot name any historical examples of austere platonism or extreme nominalism. Important recent examples can be found in van Inwagen (2014) and Lewis (1986), respectively, though Lewis does not wholeheartedly endorse the position he develops. Both positions can be traced to Quine.

A diagram of the five theories outlined here can be found in the appendix. Thankfully, the specific differences between theories of properties can usually be ignored. However, the generic difference between theories that

The Decline of Substance Dualism   47

do or do not recognise the existence of concrete properties is often important. For ideas that we naturally express by referring to concrete properties frequently require careful reformulation to satisfy the ontological thrift of austere platonists and extreme nominalists. An important example arises concerning the distinction between property dualism and a position known as 'nonreductive physicalism'.

2.4.2 The Difference Between Property Dualism and Nonreductive Physicalism

Now that we have distinguished the main theories of properties, it will be possible to consider what exactly the difference between property dualism and substance dualism consists in. But before doing so, it will be useful to pre-empt a commonplace confusion about the relationship between property dualism and the position properly called 'nonreductive physicalism.' For whilst the positions that ordinarily go by these names are very different, nonreductive physicalism is sometimes referred to as 'property dualism.' To explain this, it is necessary to say something about the history of physicalism.

Physicalism is the thesis that everything is physical, where 'physical' refers to the things described by physics (for more detail see § 4.2). Physicalism is not a totally universal thesis, however. For, many well-known physicalists such as Quine (1995) and van Inwagen (2014) posit abstract things. And it is usually agreed that abstracta are not amongst the things that physics says exist.

This might be taken to show that the literature is confused, and that we should not count Quine or van Inwagen as physicalists after all. This would cohere with the occasional use of 'physicalism' in the literature on abstract objects for the thesis that there are no such things.

It makes more sense, however, to see this as a case of context restricting the domain of discourse (cf. Boole 1854, 42; Lewis 1986, 3). When we talk about physicalism, we implicitly restrict our attention to the domain of concrete things. This is sensible because the debate about whether there are abstract things turns on different issues to the debate about whether there are nonphysical concrete things. If 'physicalism' were used for the view that answers both questions negatively, it would not be a useful term (cf. Double 1985, 389–90). Physicalism, then, is really the claim that in the domain of *concrete* things, everything is physical.

The question arises: what of those things that are not explicitly described by physics – organisms, artifacts, and conscious experiences, for example? The standard reply is that those things that are not explicitly described by physics stand in some special relation to those that are. The relation in question must be sufficiently intimate that the not-obviously-physical

48   *The Decline of Substance Dualism*

things can correctly be regarded as no real addition to the trivially physical things – as 'nothing over and above' them, as it is usefully, albeit cumbersomely, put.

The philosophers who established the importance of physicalism in twentieth-century philosophy, U. T. Place (1956) and J. J. C. Smart (1959) argue that mental things (such as sensations) are *identical* to physical things (such as brain processes). For this reason, they are known as 'identity physicalists.' By contrast, more recent physicalists tend to replace the identity relation with something less demanding, such as supervenience or grounding. A supervenience physicalist says that mental things are necessitated by physical things, a grounding physicalist says that the mental things exist in virtue of physical things.

Since the 1970s, it has been common to regard Place (1956) and Smart (1959) as proponents of an especially extreme version of identity physicalism, known as the 'type-identity' theory. This contrasts with the 'token-identity' theory which originates with Nagel (1965) and Davidson (1970).

The distinction between types and tokens is, essentially, the distinction between universals and their concrete instances. The only difference, if there is a difference, is that 'type' can be used to refer both to universals proper – the kind posited by platonists and Armstrongians – and to nominalist substitutes for universals or the sort described by Lewis (1986). The mental type *pain*, therefore, may be thought of as the universal *pain*. A token pain is some concrete instance of that universal, such as the pain Caesar felt when Brutus stabbed him.

The type-identity theory says that every mental type is identical to some physical type. If the type-identity theory is true then the mental type *pain* must be identical to some physical type that is instantiated on all and only those occasions when pain is instantiated. The traditional candidate for the physical type that is identical to pain is c-fibres firing. (Strictly, talk of c-fibres belongs to biology, not physics. But theorists tend to take it for granted that the biological is ultimately physical.)

If the type-identity theory is true then it should in principle be possible to deduce a theory of psychology from physics by using the identities of mental types with physical types as 'bridge laws' that connect mental and physical descriptions. The resulting psychological theory will be 'reducible' to physics in the sense of intertheoretical reduction defined by Ernest Nagel (1961). The type-identity theory is, in this sense, a form of 'reductive physicalism.'

Hilary Putnam (1967) famously argues that psychology is not reducible to physics in the sense defined by Nagel. For according to Putnam, many mental types are 'multiply realizable' in the sense that they can be instantiated by very different kinds of physical token. For example, Putnam

The Decline of Substance Dualism 49

suggests that the nervous systems of octopuses, because they are very different from those of humans, might instantiate the mental types pain and hunger without instantiating the physical types that, in humans, realise pain and hunger.

If Putnam is right, then the type-identity theory is false. But it does not follow that physicalism is false. For the fact that there exist mental types that are not identical to physical types might only mean that there exist multiple useful ways of carving up one wholly physical concrete reality.

Still, a physicalist who rejects the reducibility of the mental to the physical must adopt a different formulation of physicalism. The solution that departs the least from the type-identity formulation is the token-identity formulation. The token-identity formulation says that all tokens – that is all concrete instances of types – are identical to physical tokens. Perhaps the pain Caesar felt when Brutus stabbed him was c-fibres firing, whereas the pain that Cleopatra felt when the cobra bit her was a-fibres firing, but both were physical. Supervenience and grounding formulations are also available.

Token-identity physicalism, supervenience physicalism, and grounding physicalism are all forms of 'nonreductive physicalism' in that they are not sufficient for the reducibility of psychology to physics in the sense defined by Nagel (1961). (More strictly: they are not sufficient for the reducibility of psychology to physics *unless* our bridge laws are permitted to be so complex as to make the reduction relation uninteresting.) Most contemporary physicalists are, in this sense, nonreductive physicalists.

Nonreductive physicalism sometimes gets referred to as 'property dualism.' This is because the thesis that mental types are not identical to physical types can be understood as the thesis that there are two kinds of property: physical and nonphysical. It should be emphasised, however, that nonreductive physicalism entails that properties of the second kind are 'nonphysical' *only* in the sense that they do not share their extensions (or perhaps intensions) with physical terms. For example, for a nonreductive physicalist, the property *pain* is a nonphysical property only in the sense that there is no specific physical property had by all and only those beings that are undergoing pain, *not* because being in pain involves anything over and above physical things such as brain processes. This is compatible with the physicalist claim that there only exist physical things.

Either the 'nonphysical' properties are abstracta (abstract universal, sets of possibilia, etc.) in which case they are not in the domain that physicalism concerns or they are concreta (concrete universals, word or thought tokens) in which case nonreductive physicalism entails that they *are* physical things no less than atoms, rocks, or planets, even though they do not share their extensions (the set of things they refer or belong to) with physical terms. This is perfectly coherent. After all, atoms, rocks, and planets do not have extensions at all, let alone extensions they share with physical terms.

50   The Decline of Substance Dualism

Where 'dualism' is being used in the sense that contrasts with physicalism, therefore, nonreductive physicalism is no closer to dualism – even to property dualism – than reductive physicalism. As Chalmers (1996, 125) says, even biological fitness is plausibly a nonphysical property in the sense that is relevant to nonreductive physicalism. And yet biological fitness does not threaten physicalism as it is usually understood.

'Property dualism,' as the term is ordinarily used, refers to a much stronger position than nonreductive physicalism. Property dualism says that there are properties that do not stand to trivially physical things in the relation that defines physicalism: properties that are 'fundamentally new features of the world' as Chalmers (1996, 125) puts it. Only property dualism in this second sense is a kind of dualism in the sense of 'dualism' that contrasts with physicalism.

A final comment on the token-identity theory before moving on. I have said that of the theories of properties described in the previous subsection, I prefer those that posit concrete properties. One advantage of such theories is that they allow us to speak simply of physicalism as a claim about what exists in the domain of concrete things. Strictly, opponents of concrete properties must treat talk about properties 'existing' in the concrete domain as shorthand for talk about properties being *concretely instantiated*.

This creates obstacles for the task of defining physicalism. For concrete properties, if they exist, are clearly candidates for the relata of relations such as identity or grounding. But it is not obvious that we can talk about the concrete 'instantiation' of a property being identical to or grounded in something. The difficulty is evident in discussions of the token-identity theory.

The token-identity theory says that every concrete particular is identical to some physical concrete particular. If we have concrete particular properties of the sort posited by liberal platonists and moderate nominalists in our domain of discourse, then the token-identity theory will be sufficient for physicalism and incompatible with dualism. But if we prohibit reference to concrete properties, in the manner of austere platonists and extreme nominalists, the token-identity theory will be insufficient for physicalism. For it will place no constraint on what properties things may possess. Hence, the token-identity theory *without* concrete properties is compatible with *real* property dualism – the kind that contrasts with physicalism. (As for what happens if, like Armstrong, we posit concrete *universals* but not concrete particular properties, the issue is a complicated one and had better be passed over here.)

Naturally, this causes confusion, especially given that some theorists (e.g. Melnyk 2003) take it for granted that the tokens involved in token-identity physicalism include concrete properties, whilst others (e.g. Papineau 2009) take it for granted that they do not. Theorists end up using the same terms to describe very different views.

In fact, there exist classic expositions of the token-identity theory of both varieties. Nagel (1965) treats token-identity as a relation between concrete properties such as 'this water's (now) being frozen.' Davidson (1970) treats token-identity as a relation between concrete property-bearers only. On its own, Davidson's identity claim is therefore insufficient for physicalism. This is why he proposes to combine the identity claim with a supervenience claim (Davidson 1970, 88).

It is not clear if it is possible to make the token-identity theory, by itself, sufficient for physicalism without assuming the existence of concrete properties. Perhaps this could be done by positing identities between concrete 'states,' 'events,' or 'property-instancings' understood in a suitably fine-grained way (cf. Schneider 2012b, 720, fn. 3.). It might be worried, however, that these are really just concrete properties by another name. And ontological misers are likely to object to other fine-grained concreta on the same grounds as concrete properties.

As we will shortly see, there exists an obstacle to formulating property dualism without referring to concrete properties that parallels the obstacle to formulating token-identity physicalism without referring to concrete properties. And this too has caused confusion. In the next subsection, I explain how we should understand property dualism on the presumption that there exist concrete properties. In the following subsection, I explain how we might revise that account for the benefit of opponents to concrete properties.

2.4.3 Property Dualism With Concrete Properties

Like physicalism, dualism is usually regarded as a claim about the concrete world. If somebody holds that the mental property *pain* is nonphysical in the sense that it is an abstract universal, whilst maintaining that all concrete instances of pain are wholly physical, this will make that person a platonist, but not a mind-body dualist. For this reason, it is natural to understand property dualism as the claim that in addition to physical things, there exist nonphysical concrete properties, but no nonphysical substances.

If property dualism, so defined, qualifies as a genuine alternative to substance dualism, this must be because concrete properties do not satisfy the independence definition of substance. The good news for property dualism is that there exists some precedent for this thesis in the literature on concrete properties.

Whilst recent philosophy tends to avoid talking about substances, there does exist a discussion of how properties (e.g. the shape of a desk) differ from un-property-like parts (e.g. the leg of a desk) on the supposition that

52   The Decline of Substance Dualism

both are concrete components of their bearers. The classic answer is that concrete properties are 'abstract' not in the usual sense which applies to nonspatiotemporal, acausal things, but in a second sense which applies to things that are brought to mind by means of *abstraction*, 'a process of selection, of systematic setting aside' as Campbell (1990, 3) puts it (cf. Wood, 1944, 2; Williams 1953a and b; Lewis 1986, 85–6).

The suggestion that properties are brought to mind by abstraction is intuitively plausible. For example, it is plausible that one brings the shape of a desk before one's mind by starting with the whole desk, then setting aside its colour, size, and so on, until only the shape remains. The shape one arrives at might be considered as spatiotemporal and causally vigorous as the desk to which it belongs. If so, the shape is concrete in the first sense of the concrete-abstract distinction introduced in this chapter. But the shape is property-like in virtue of being abstract in the second sense – in that it is brought to mind by abstraction.

This is not yet a satisfactory explanation of the difference between concrete properties and other concreta, however. For the process of abstraction has not been specified in sufficient detail to explain why the leg of the desk, for example, does not also count as abstract. After all, one can bring the leg of a desk before one's mind by starting with the whole desk and then setting aside the top and the other legs. And yet, a leg is naturally regarded as a part, in a sense of 'part' that contrasts with 'property.'

Williams (1953a and b, 7) gestures at a more satisfactory explanation when he proposes that tropes (i.e. particular concrete properties) have a 'special form of incompleteness' such that 'a cat and the cat's tail are not tropes, but a cat's smile is a trope.' The implication is that a cat's tail can exist separately from the rest of the cat, whereas its smile *pace* Lewis Carrol cannot. If so, then Williams's 'special form of incompleteness' describes precisely those concreta that do not satisfy the independence definition of substance.

Williams's proposal is plausible. For intuitively, concrete properties, whether they are understood as tropes or as universals, cannot exist without other properties of the things to which they belong. For example, it is plausible that the shape of a desk could not exist without a size. And it is plausible that the pitch of a note could not exist without a volume or timbre. And yet, shape seems to be genuinely distinct from size, and pitch from volume and timbre – after all these properties vary independently of one another.

If it is true that concrete properties cannot exist by themselves, then we might say that the process of abstraction that defines the second sense of 'abstract' occurs only when you begin with a concrete thing and then subtract elements *without which the remainder could not exist*. This would explain why the leg of a desk does not strike us as property-like in the way that its shape, colour, or surface does.

The Decline of Substance Dualism   53

The upshot is that concrete properties do not seem to satisfy the independence definition of substance. This is good news for property dualism since it suggests that property dualism is a genuine alternative to substance dualism.

To avoid confusion about the two senses of 'abstract,' it is useful to use Williams's other term and say that, insofar as they cannot exist by themselves, concrete properties are 'incomplete.' And to avoid confusion with other senses of 'incomplete,' we might say that they are 'metaphysically incomplete.' (By contrast, we might call a cat that is missing its tail 'naturally incomplete' and a vase that is missing its handle 'artificially incomplete'). This terminology echoes Descartes (AT VII 221–2) who also uses 'complete' and 'incomplete' for things that do and do not satisfy the independence definition.

It is also useful to call the things without which a metaphysically incomplete entity could not exist its 'metaphysical complements.' For example, it is plausible that the shape of a desk and the rest of the desk minus its shape are metaphysical complements; likewise the timbre of a sound and the rest of the sound minus the timbre.

Property dualism seems like a genuine alternative to substance dualism because it is plausible that properties cannot exist by themselves: they appear to be metaphysically incomplete. It may be added that property dualism evades substance dualism only if every nonphysical property *has a physical metaphysical complement*. For otherwise the nonphysical property and its complement would, together, make up a nonphysical substance.

As it happens, after suggesting that concrete properties cannot exist by themselves, Williams (1953a and b, 79–80) goes on to disown this proposal on the basis that it would make possible the inference from the existence of a concrete property to the existence of its bearer. Williams regards such inferences as suspect because they are not analytic. He regards these inferences as nonanalytic because they deduce a composite from reflection on a component rather than deducing a component from the analysis of a composite.

If Williams is right that concrete properties can exist by themselves, this would be bad news for property dualists. For it would entail that *everything* is in fact a substance in the sense that is relevant to substance dualism, including the nonphysical properties that make up a person's conscious life.

Few property dualists will share Williams's concern, however. For as I explain in Chapter 5, property dualists tend to be committed to a degree of modal rationalism in view of which the inferences that trouble Williams will seem innocuous. Moreover, the idea that a property such as a timbre could exist by itself seems much less plausible than the thesis that we can infer from the existence of a timbre to the existence of a pitch, a volume, and whatever other properties timbres go with. (If Williams is right that it

54 The Decline of Substance Dualism

is not analytic, then the inference from the existence of a timbre to that of a pitch is a plausible example of synthetic a priori justification.)

It is possible to formulate arguments for the metaphysical incompleteness of properties on the basis of such intuitions. The argument might go as follows. Suppose a property, such as a timbre, exists on its own. We can ask: is this thing a sound – something audible – or not? If it is a sound, then it must have a pitch, because all sounds have pitches. If it is not a sound, it cannot have a timbre, because only sounds have timbres. It follows that a timbre is not the kind of thing that can exist on its own. Similar arguments might be adopted for other cases.

For the purposes of this book, however, I need not insist that properties are metaphysically incomplete. I need only claim that *if property dualism constitutes a genuine alternative to substance dualism, then* properties must be metaphysically incomplete, and that the consequent of this conditional is plausible enough to make the task of arguing that property dualists must posit nonphysical substances on other grounds a serious one. So I will not defend the metaphysical incompleteness of properties in greater detail here.

2.4.4 Property Dualism Without Concrete Properties

Dualism is a claim about the concrete world. For this reason, a formulation of property dualism as a view on which there exist nonphysical properties will puzzle austere platonists and extreme nominalists – theorists who reject the existence of concrete properties. Witness van Inwagen:

> Nonphysical properties cannot be understood as properties that are not physical ... for on that reading of 'nonphysical property,' all properties are nonphysical properties ... I have been unable to find in print a definition of 'nonphysical property' that seems to me both to be intelligible and likely actually to capture what property dualists mean.
>
> (Van Inwagen 2014, 246)

Van Inwagen takes the view that all properties are nonphysical because he is an austere platonist – the only properties he posits are abstract universals – and abstract things are usually regarded as nonphysical. For van Inwagen, the sentence 'there are nonphysical properties' expresses a truism that has nothing to do with the mind-body problem or the position that property dualists mean to express.

In my judgement, the fault lies with austere platonism and extreme nominalism. Nonetheless, it is desirable to have a way of formulating property dualism that does not require concrete properties. A good strategy for producing a formulation of property dualism that does not require concrete properties draws on the literature on grounding.

The Decline of Substance Dualism 55

These days, many theorists formulate physicalism as the view that those things that are not trivially physical are 'grounded in' physical things. Grounding is ordinarily understood as a noncausal explanatory relation commonly expressed when we say that one thing exists or obtains 'in virtue of' another. It is hoped that grounding will be strong enough to guarantee that the things that are not trivially physical are nothing over and above those that are without being unnecessarily demanding – unlike supervenience and identity formulations respectively, according to influential criticisms of those formulations (e.g. Haugeland 1982; Horgan 1993).

We saw in § 2.4.2 that austere platonism and extreme nominalism create a problem for formulating token-identity physicalism. A parallel problem arises for grounding physicalism. For it is not clear why a grounding formulation of physicalism should place any constraints on the properties that concrete things have, if there are no concrete properties to serve as the relata of the grounding relation.

A quick fix would be to introduce fine-grained concrete events, states, or property-instancings and to let these serve as the relata of grounding. But as I mentioned earlier, opponents of concrete properties are unlikely to be content to posit other fine-grained concreta at what appears to be the same cost in parsimony.

A more ecumenical solution takes advantage of the fact that, although it is usually treated as a relation, grounding can also be treated as an *operation*, represented by a sentential operator such as 'because' (see Fine 2001, 16; 2012 43). This allows us to express physicalism in a way that is neutral about the existence of concrete properties. For example, we can say that physicalism requires that concrete things have the properties they have *because* of the physical properties that they have or *because* of the physical facts about the world more generally, in the sense of 'because' associated with grounding.

Property dualism can also be expressed without implying the existence of concrete properties by using a grounding operator. For the claim that some things have nonphysical properties can be clarified as meaning that some things have properties other than those that they possess *because* of their physical properties, or *because* of the physical facts about the world generally, in the grounding sense of 'because.' Having properties may then be understood in wholly austere platonist or extreme nominalist terms.

With our special sense of 'because' in hand, the difference between substance dualism and property dualism can now be expressed as it was in § 2.4.2 without causing confusion to ontological extremists such as van Inwagen. That is, substance dualism remains the view that there exist nonphysical substances as characterised by the independence definition. And property dualism remains the view that whilst some things have nonphysical properties, there are no nonphysical substances.

56 The Decline of Substance Dualism

The status of property dualism as a genuine alternative to substance dualism will still rest on the assumption that properties are metaphysically incomplete. However, this must be understood not as the claim that a trope or concrete universal is not the kind of thing that can exist on its own, but as the claim that an abstract universal or a nominalist substitute thereof is not the kind of thing that can be concretely instantiated on its own. This claim will remain plausible for the reasons already given: it is hard to make sense of shape being instantiated without size or timbre without pitch or volume.

As it happens, I am not convinced that we should use 'grounding' to define physicalism. This is because grounding definitions require the things that are not identical to trivially physical systems of particles, fields, and forces should be *less fundamental* than them. This requirement seems unreasonable. Suppose someone claims that a plant, for example, is neither identical to nor less fundamental than a physical system of particles, fields, and forces, but is nonetheless nothing over and above that system. That ought to be sufficient for physicalism about the plant.

For this reason, I prefer to define physicalism with the phrase 'nothing over and above' rather than with grounding. This preference creates no new problem for formulating physicalism and property dualism without presupposing that there exist concrete properties, however. For we can define a sense of 'because' that stands to 'nothing over and above' as the grounding sense stands to grounding. The definition of physicalism and property dualism will then remain the same.

Readers who have persevered with this section see why I regard austere platonism and extreme nominalism as awkward. But once the sentential operators have been defined it is easy to translate between descriptions that require the existence of concrete properties and descriptions that do not. Descriptions of the former kind are less complicated and more vivid, and so I favour the language of concrete properties in what follows.

2.4.5 The Role of Properties

It is often observed that theorists associate a range of theoretical roles with the term 'property,' not all of which can be served by the same kind of things (e.g. Lewis 1986, 67; Oliver 1996 11–12). The take-home point of this section is that, when we are distinguishing substance dualism and property dualism, the role of properties is that of contrasting with substances and hence that of being metaphysically incomplete. This remains the case whatever roles we associate with the term 'property' in other contexts.

For this reason, there is no need to defend the characterisation of properties suggested here against the view that some of the things we intuitively think of as properties are in fact capable of existing by themselves and are therefore metaphysically complete as Williams (1953a and b) and Campbell

(1983, 1990) suggest. Such metaphysically complete 'properties' are 'in Hume's sense substances' as Campbell (1983, 186) puts it. Hume's sense is Descartes's sense, and it is the sense that is relevant in this enquiry.

Likewise, there is no need to defend the characterisation of properties given here against the view that some of the things we intuitively think of as parts are in fact inseparable from their owners and therefore metaphysically incomplete as Moran (2018) has recently argued. In the sense that is relevant to the contrast between substance dualism and property dualism, such nondetachable parts may count as properties.

2.5 An Obstacle for the Independence Definition of Substance

One reason why the widespread preference for property dualism over substance dualism needs to be reassessed is that it does not seem to be based on a clear understanding of the difference between the two positions. I have argued that, in this context, 'substance' should be taken to refer to things that do, and 'property' to things that do not, satisfy Descartes's independence definition of substance.

It would be desirable to advance directly at this stage to the principal task of this enquiry: that of explaining why opponents of physicalism must posit nonphysical substances. However, this would leave an important task undone. For Descartes's independence definition, as I have interpreted it, faces an influential objection, which has prevented recent philosophers from making use of it. I introduce and address this objection in Chapter 3.

3 A Defence of the Independence Definition of Substance

As characterised in the previous chapter, the independence definition of substances says something very simple: a substance is something that could exist by itself. This formulation of the independence definition is widely rejected both as a reading of Descartes and as a tool for present-day philosophy. Opponents of the formulation of the definition favoured here object that *nothing* could be a substance in the sense specified because nothing could exist without any properties. This concern may be referred to as the 'property-dependence objection.' This chapter responds to the property-dependence objection and addresses some surrounding issues.

3.1 The Metaphysical Reading and the Causal Reading

This section and the next explain why, the property-dependence objection aside, the formulation of the independence definition of substance that I favour is the most natural reading of Descartes. Descartes says that a substance is something that is 'capable of existing independently,' 'that can exist by itself,' or 'which exists in such a way as to depend on no other thing for its existence' (AT VII 44, 226; VIII 24). There exist two readings of these claims. The metaphysical reading and the causal reading say, respectively, that x is a substance if and only if

(i) the existence of x does not necessitate the existence of anything else ('metaphysical independence'); or
(ii) the existence of x need not have been caused by anything else ('causal independence').

Lowe (1998, 137) and Rodriguez-Pereyra (2008) adopt the metaphysical reading. Loeb (1981), Bennett (2001, 134–5), and Stuart (2003) adopt the causal reading. Hoffman and Rosenkrantz (1997, 20–2) discuss both, and Markie (1994) combines the two. As I have already indicated, I prefer the metaphysical reading.

DOI: 10.4324/9781003378600-4

A Defence of the Independence Definition of Substance   59

There are four reasons to favour the metaphysical reading over the causal reading. By contrast, aside from the property-dependence objection, only one reason is given in favour of the causal reading, and this reason, as I shortly explain, is obviously defective. This makes the metaphysical reading clearly preferable.

The first reason to favour the metaphysical reading is that Descartes's language persistently suggests unaccompanied, rather than merely uncaused existence. This is especially clear when Descartes says that created substances can exist 'without other things' (*sans quelques autres*) excluding God, or 'without any other creature' (*absque omni alia creata*) at (AT IX B 47) and (AT III 429), respectively. (The first quotation is an addition to the French text of the *Principles*, but these additions were added or approved by Descartes. 'Created thing' would be a better translation of '*creata*' in the second quotation since 'creature' in English suggests an animal.)

If Descartes meant that substances can exist uncaused, he could easily have increased the perspicacity and informativeness of his characterisation of substances by making this explicit. But Descartes never indicates that it is causal independence that he has in mind. It follows from Gricean considerations that Descartes means that a substance is something that can exist without anything else at all, not just without a cause.

A second advantage of the metaphysical reading is that it explains why Descartes classes the mind as a substance, whilst the causal reading leaves this a mystery. Descartes claims that we can clearly and distinctly imagine the mind existing in the absence of other things and that what we can clearly and distinctly imagine is possible. It follows that the mind can exist in the absence of other things (e.g. AT VII 78). If so, minds satisfy the independence definition of substance on the metaphysical reading.

By contrast, Descartes does not discuss whether we can imagine the mind existing without having been caused to do so by other things. And so, it is not clear why he should think that minds are substances on the causal reading. The causal reading makes Descartes's application of the term 'substance' to minds mysterious. (Rodriguez-Pereyra (2008) argues for the metaphysical reading on similar grounds.)

The third reason to prefer the metaphysical reading is that it makes sense of Descartes's claim that whenever we perceive a property, we can infer that it must belong to a substance (AT VIII A 25). As Markie (1994) points out, on the causal reading, it is unclear why Descartes would say this. For there is no obvious inference from the existence of a property to the existence of something causally independent to which it belongs.

Markie claims that a causal reading is still justified because Descartes's comment at (AT VIII A 25) is a problem for any reading of the independence definition. But this is incorrect. On the metaphysical reading, Descartes's claim at (AT VIII A 25) is intuitively plausible. If a property is

60 *A Defence of the Independence Definition of Substance*

something that cannot exist unaccompanied, then to exist it must be accompanied by some further thing; if the pair could not exist unaccompanied either, they must be accompanied by something further still. If we repeat this process, it seems that we are bound to get to something – a substance – that can exist unaccompanied.

The fourth reason to favour the metaphysical reading is that it makes sense of the difference between substances and properties, whereas the causal reading does not. Descartes makes it clear that the independence definition is supposed to define substances to the exclusion of properties ('attributes,' 'qualities,' or 'modes' in his terminology). On the metaphysical reading, this means properties cannot exist without other things.

This makes sense. For as I mentioned in § 2.3, the claim that properties cannot exist without other things was proposed long before Descartes by Aristotle, and as I explained in § 2.4, this claim is intuitively plausible. So, we can see why Descartes might see the distinction between substances and properties as the distinction between things that can and cannot exist unaccompanied. Descartes would just be clarifying Aristotle's definition of substance by making it explicit that substances can do what Aristotle says properties cannot.

By contrast, it is not at all clear why Descartes would think that substances, but not properties, can exist uncaused. For there does not seem to be any precedent for this idea in earlier philosophy. And far from being independently intuitive, it seems incoherent. For a substance must have some properties (cf. AT VIII A 25). And so, if a substance exists uncaused, so too it seems must its properties (apart from those it acquires later).

For example, Descartes seems to think that God exists uncaused and has certain necessary properties (AT VIII A 26). What causes those properties to exist? Not God, since that would make the effect logically prior to the cause. But not something other than God either since that would make God dependent on something else's existence. (It is for this reason that Markie (1994, 68–9) rejects a purely causal reading. His reason for retaining a causal component is the property-dependence objection, which I address in this chapter.)

There is more to say about this final point, especially as Descartes's understanding of causation is in some respects closer to that of his scholastic contemporaries than it is to the views that dominate today (cf. Schmaltz 2007). Even so, it is hard to imagine how the distinction between properties and substances could be understood as the distinction between things that do and do not need causes.

For four reasons, then, the metaphysical reading seems much more natural than the causal reading. Apart from the property-dependence objection, by contrast, scholars seem to have put forward only one reason to favour the causal reading. And as Rodriguez-Pereyra (2008) argues, this reason is obviously defective.

A Defence of the Independence Definition of Substance   61

The reason sometimes given for adopting the causal reading is as follows. In the *Principles*, Descartes claims that created things cannot be substances in an unqualified sense, because they depend on God. Some commentators suggest that this shows that Descartes has causal independence in mind. For the dependence of created things on God is causal dependence (e.g. Loeb 1981, 94–5; Stuart 2003, 87–8; Broackes 2006, 137–8; Chappell 2008, 261).

The problem is that this argument supports the causal reading over the metaphysical reading only if Descartes holds that created things depend causally *but not metaphysically* on God. For otherwise, Descartes's reason for saying that created things are not substances in an unqualified sense could equally be that they depend metaphysically on God. If Descartes holds that created substances depend metaphysically on God, then the only argument for the causal reading of his independence definition fails.

As Rodriguez-Pereyra, (2008, 84–5) points out, it is clear that Descartes does hold that created things depend metaphysically as well as causally on God. That is, Descartes does not only think that created things are caused by God, but also that created things could not possibly exist unaccompanied by God. The qualification about created substances, therefore, does nothing to support the causal reading of the independence definition, and all other considerations count in favour of the metaphysical reading.

3.2 Strong and Weak Metaphysical Readings

The metaphysical reading of the independence definition is, then, clearly preferable to the causal reading. There is a further question about how to formulate the metaphysical reading. Rodriguez-Pereyra (2008, 80) expresses the metaphysical reading as the claim that x is a substance if and only if x 'can exist without any other entity.' Rodriguez-Pereyra's formulation is ambiguous between the claim that x is a substance if and only if

(i) x does not necessitate that there exists some y such that y is something other than x ('strong metaphysical independence'); and

(ii) there is no y such that y is something other than x, and x necessitates that y exists ('weak metaphysical independence').

The claim that x is strongly metaphysically independent is the claim that x can exist in total isolation. By contrast, the claim that x is weakly metaphysically independent is consistent with the thesis that for some set of entities, $\{a, b, c...\}$ x cannot exist without *either a* or b or c, etc. so long as there is no particular member of the set that x needs in order to exist.

For reasons that I explain in the next section, it is clear that Rodriguez-Pereyra is committed to the weak formulation. So is Lowe (1998, 1510).

62 *A Defence of the Independence Definition of Substance*

This seems to be a mistake, however. For Descartes's statements of the independence definition, read idiomatically, permit the strong formulation only.

For example, Descartes says that a substance is something that can exist 'without' (*sans, absque*) 'other things' or (for created substances) 'any other created thing' (AT IX B 47; III 429). The weak formulation is only compatible with these expressions if Descartes is speaking in an unusual way, so that for x to be able to exist 'without other things,' it is sufficient that there is no other thing *in particular* that x needs in order to exist.

This would be highly unidiomatic. We would not say that Ada Cornaro can tango 'without any other dancer' just because any partner will do. Nor would we say that neat vodka can serve as a cocktail 'without other ingredients' just because no other ingredient in particular is essential. Likewise, when Descartes says that a substance can exist without any other thing, it is natural to suppose that he is saying that a substance can exist, not just without any other thing in particular, but without any other thing at all.

Descartes also says that a substance is capable of existing '*per se.*' English translations, including the CSMK, typically render '*per se*' in this context 'by itself' or 'on its own.' This too is only compatible with the strong metaphysical reading.

There is good reason to think that the CSMK is correct. For example, when Descartes says that substances can exist 'on their own' (*per se solae*) at (AT VII, 222), he is backing up the argument at (AT VII, 219) that the mind could exist with thought 'and it alone' (*cum hoc solo*). In the earlier location, Descartes is certainly talking about the mind existing without anything else at all. It is therefore natural to suppose that in the later location, he is expressing the same idea.

It is also worth considering Descartes's use of 'complete thing' (*res completa*) and 'incomplete thing' for substances and nonsubstances, respectively (AT VII, 222). It is clear why a proponent of the strong metaphysical independence definition might use this terminology. For something that satisfies the strong metaphysical definition is complete in that it is *not missing anything* – there are no gaps that need filling. By contrast, it would be very confusing for a proponent of the weak metaphysical definition to call substances 'complete.' For something that only satisfies the weak but not the strong definition *is* incomplete in that *it is missing something* – there is a gap that needs filling by some metaphysical complement.

The strong formulation of the metaphysical reading seems clearly preferable to the weak formulation, just as the metaphysical reading seems clearly preferable to the causal reading. I do not think it is going too far to say that, given ordinary linguistic conventions, the weak formulation is simply incompatible with Descartes's statements. Proponents of the weak metaphysical reading can of course dismiss Descartes's

A Defence of the Independence Definition of Substance   63

language as misleading. But they need some reason to do so. Lowe (1998) (whose focus is not Descartes scholarship) and Rodriguez-Pereyra (2008) provide no reason.

3.3 The Property-Dependence Objection

On the strong metaphysical reading, the independence definition says that x is a substance if and only if x does not necessitate that there exists some y such that y is something other than x. I have argued that this is the natural reading of Descartes's characterisation of substance. Recent discussions of substance often start out with the strong metaphysical formulation of the independence definition in mind. But the strong metaphysical formulation is usually rejected on the basis that nothing could satisfy it because nothing could exist without any properties. This section introduces this objection more fully and explains why it rests on a misunderstanding.

3.3.1 The Property-Dependence Objection in Recent Philosophy

Two of the most important works on substance in recent philosophy are Hoffman and Rosenkrantz (1997) and Lowe (1998). Both take the independence definition as their starting point, and both favour a metaphysical reading. However, Hoffman, Rosenkrantz, and Lowe raise an objection which leads them to reject the independence definition as Descartes formulates it.

Hoffman and Rosenkrantz (1997, 22, 44) and Lowe (1998, 142–3) argue that nothing could satisfy Descartes's independence definition because no candidate substance will be able to exist without having properties with which it is nonidentical. For example, even a Cartesian mind must have some properties, some 'attributes,' 'qualities,' and 'modes.' And it seems clear that none of these properties is identical to the mind to which it belongs. (In fact, Descartes does seem to regard the 'principal attribute' of thought as identical to the mind to which it belongs. But the problem remains, respecting its other attributes, qualities, and modes.)

This is the property-dependence objection. Put another way, the property-dependence objection says that nothing can satisfy the strong metaphysical independence definition because any candidate substance depends metaphysically on its own properties. Hoffman and Rosenkrantz (1997, 44) and Toner (2011) raise a parallel issue with respect to the parts of composite substance, which we may call the 'part-dependence objection.'

It is plausible that all things have properties, whereas only some things have parts. For this reason, the property-dependence objection seems more powerful than the part-dependence objection. On the other hand, as I explain shortly, it is plausible that the property-dependence objection only

64 A Defence of the Independence Definition of Substance

arises if there exist concrete properties. So, opponents of concrete properties might view the part-dependence objection as more important. In any case, it is possible to treat both objections together.

Hoffman, Rosenkrantz, and Lowe treat the property-dependence objection to the independence definition as decisive. (I address some less important objections advanced by Hoffman and Rosenkrantz in § 3.4.) In response, they advance radical revisions to the independence definition of substance. Lowe (1998, 144–5) proposes that we replace independence of existence with independence of identity. This leads him to formulate the following definition:

(T7) x is a substance if and only if x is a particular and there is no particular y such that y is not identical with x and the identity of x depends on the identity of y.

(Lowe 1998, 151)

Hoffman and Rosenkrantz (1997, 48) introduce a hierarchy of categories with 'entity' at 'level A,' 'abstract' and 'concrete' at 'level B,' and so on. After a protracted discussion, they formulate the following definition:

(D3) x is a substance = df. x instantiates a level C category, $C1$, such that: (i) $C1$ could have a single instance throughout an interval of time, and (ii) $C1$'s instantiation does not entail the instantiation of another level C category which could have a single instance throughout an interval of time, and (iii) it is impossible for $C1$ to have an instance which has as a part an entity which instantiates another level C category, other than Concrete Proper Part, and other than Abstract Proper Part.

(Hoffman and Rosenkrantz 1997, 65)

The resulting definitions are interesting in their own right. But they give up on any attempt to capture the intuitive idea of a substance as something that can exist by itself. As a result, they depart significantly from Descartes, and they do not entail that a nonphysical substance could exist disembodied. For these reasons, they have little claim to be considered relevant when we are characterising substance dualism.

3.3.2 The Property-Dependence Objection in Descartes Scholarship

It is also the property-dependence objection that leads many Descartes scholars to adopt the causal reading or the weak metaphysical reading of the independence definition rather than the strong metaphysical reading. For example, when Markie (1994) first introduces the independence

A Defence of the Independence Definition of Substance   65

definition, he seems to have in mind a metaphysical reading. However, he then asks, respecting some of Descartes's examples of substances,

> Does not the rock also 'need' and 'depend on' its material parts? ... Do not God, a rock, Descartes's mind, and Descartes's body all 'depend' on their essential attributes since they could not exist without them, and on qualities in general since they could not exist without some?
> (Markie 1994, 66)

This is a statement of the property-dependence objection, as well as the neighbouring part-dependence objection. Markie proposes on this basis that 'to let us move forward' we should 'assume that Descartes is concerned, at least partially, with a form of causal independence.'

Markie is joined by Bennett (2001) and Stuart (2003) in giving the property-dependence objection as the main reason to adopt a causal reading of the independence definition. The motivation appears to be that the property-dependence objection is so devastating to the independence definition as Descartes *seems* to intend it that we are justified in assuming out of charity that he means something else.

Likewise, it is in addressing the property-dependence objection as it applies to modes that Rodriguez-Pereyra implicitly adopts the weak metaphysical reading over the strong metaphysical reading. Rodriguez-Pereyra (2008, 80) dismisses the property-dependence objection on the basis that 'although mind and body need modes to exist, they do not need any particular modes to exist.' He concludes that mind and body do not depend on modes in a way that disqualifies them from being substances.

Clearly, this response will at most be successful on the weak metaphysical reading only. For the weak reading only requires that there is no other thing *in particular* without which a substance could not exist. The strong metaphysical reading, by contrast, requires that a substance could exist without anything else at all. If so, it is no defence of the status of mind and body as substances that 'they do not need any particular modes to exist.'

In fact, it is not clear that Rodriguez-Pereyra's response to the property-dependence objection even works for the weak metaphysical formulation. For although is true that a substance will not need any particular mode to exist, supposing that modes are nonnecessary properties, the same will not be true of necessary properties or parts, and so the property-dependence and part-dependence objections will still apply to these.

Rodriguez-Pereyra (2008, 81–2) acknowledges that it is a consequence of the independence definition as he interprets it that a substance cannot have any necessary properties distinct from itself. He suggests that this is acceptable to Descartes because Descartes says that every substance has

66 A Defence of the Independence Definition of Substance

exactly one principal attribute (which is a necessary property) and that the principal attribute is only conceptually distinct from the substance.

This response is initially promising as a defence of the weak metaphysical definition on behalf of Descartes. But it is successful only if principal attributes are the *only* necessary properties or parts that Descartes attributes to substances. And on the contrary, Descartes seems to say, for example, that duration, as well as the principal attribute of extension, are necessary properties of bodies (AT VIII A 26). Moreover, it seems that duration and extension must be distinct properties from one another since minds have duration but not extension.

Furthermore, as Markie (1994, 65) points out, after stating the independence definition in the *Fourth Replies*, Descartes says that it is satisfied by various composite substances. It is hard to see why Descartes should think that these composite substances have none of their parts necessarily.

Rodriguez-Pereyra does not discuss necessary parts. And he deliberately ignores necessary properties such as duration (2008, 76, fn. 13). This leaves his reading of the independence definition vulnerable to both the property-dependence objection and the part-dependence objection as they apply to necessary properties and parts. So the weak metaphysical reading does not even appear to offer a good response to the property-dependence objection in return for its unidiomatic reading of Descartes's statements.

3.3.3 Responding to the Property-Dependence Objection

The property-dependence objection has been very influential. It appears to be the main reason for the disfavour accorded to the strong metaphysical formulation of the independence definition, both as a reading of Descartes and as a tool for present-day philosophy. The same objection has also prevented recent defences of substance dualism such as Swinburne (2018, 136) from clearly defining 'substance.'

I now explain why the property-dependence objection should not be regarded as a threat to the strong metaphysical formulation of the independence definition after all. If this is right then, for the reasons already given, that formulation should be considered the best reading of Descartes and therefore the most appropriate characterisation of 'substance' in the sense that defines substance dualism.

To narrow down the problem, it will be useful to begin by considering the domain over which the independence definition quantifies. For Descartes, the domain of the independence definition clearly includes minds, bodies, and their modes, qualities, and attributes, which he treats as concrete properties. And insofar as we are concerned with created substances, it clearly excludes God.

A Defence of the Independence Definition of Substance 67

Descartes does not specify the domain in greater detail. But as Boole (1854, 42) and Lewis (1986, 3) point out, we often operate with implicit restrictions on the domain over which we are quantifying, leaving these to be determined by context. In fact, there is good reason to treat the independence definition as quantifying over the domain of contingent concrete things only. If this restriction is not implicit in Descartes's use of 'substance,' it is compatible with it, and it makes sense given our ordinary understanding of substance dualism.

To see why it makes sense to exclude necessary beings and abstracta, imagine someone who posits things that are just like Cartesian souls except that they cannot exist without the abstract universal *thought* or without some necessary concretum other than God (perhaps a minor deity). It would be strange to say that these souls are not, therefore, substances in the sense that defines substance dualism.

All that matters for substance dualism is that the souls can exist without other contingent concrete things, in particular the physical bodies they animate. This is clear from the fact that the most widely recognised substance dualist after Descartes is Plato. And yet, on a common reading Plato posits abstracta without which Platonic souls could not exist, and perhaps also minor deities as well. Nobody ever doubts that Plato counts as a genuine substance dualist on this score.

It might be enough to exclude necessary beings from the domain of the independence definition without separately excluding abstracta. For it is widely thought that if abstracta exist at all, they must exist necessarily. But there is logical room for the view that abstracta exist contingently and that concrete things depend on them because concreta must instantiate abstract universals. So we must also exclude any abstract things that concrete things necessarily instantiate from the domain of the independence definition. For simplicity, it seems best to exclude abstracta generally.

It is not clear whether Descartes himself posits abstracta or necessary beings other than God, on which the concrete things he posits would necessarily depend. *Meditations* (AT VII, 64) implies that such things exist. *Principles* (AT VIII, A 27) appears to reverse this view. If Descartes does posit such things, then he implicitly excludes them from the domain of the independence definition. If not, then their inclusion or exclusion is left undetermined, and we can let our ordinary understanding of substance dualism guide us.

There is, then, no need to worry about the property-dependence objection insofar as it applies to abstract universals. It is concrete properties and parts that pose the problem. This is why opponents of concrete properties might see the part-dependence objection as more important than the property-dependence objection. (Fine-grained property-instancings of the

68 A Defence of the Independence Definition of Substance

sort that Nagel (1965) calls 'events' *will* plausibly create a parallel problem, however. These can be treated in the same way as concrete properties.)

The real problem, if there is a problem, is that no candidate substance could exist without some concrete properties or (for composites) parts. It is not possible to get around this problem by restricting the domain over which the independence definition quantifies to exclude concrete things. For this would empty the domain of members and the definition of content.

It might be supposed that we could meet the problem by excluding concrete *properties* and *parts* from the domain over which the independence definition quantifies. But this will make the independence definition reliant on our prior understanding of the distinction between substances and properties. It is not clear where this understanding would come from. Descartes himself seems to treat properties, explicitly at (AT XI B 24–5) and implicitly elsewhere, simply as things that do not satisfy the independence definition.

It is not surprising, therefore, that the property-dependence objection as it applies to concrete properties has been treated seriously. Even so, it is plausible that this objection, as well as the neighbouring part-dependence objection, arises from a simple misconstrual of the independence definition. Interpreters have been overly hasty, I suggest, to understand the definition in terms of the identity relation, and this has created an impression of a problem where there is none.

The independence definition says that a substance is something that can exist without anything else. Theorists habitually assume that this means that a substance can exist without anything *nonidentical* to it. This assumption is explicit in Hoffman and Rosenkrantz (1997, 2) and Lowe (1998, 138) and is clearly implicit in other works that take the property-dependence objection seriously. But in fact, phrases such as 'x without anything else' and 'x by itself' are not usually understood in this way.

Suppose somebody asks you what is on the table before you. You reply that there is just a coffee cup. When asked whether there is anything further, you reply 'no, the coffee cup is there by itself.' Your interrogator might object that your statement was false. For you have left out the left half of the cup and the handle, and its shape and size, supposing these are concrete properties: all these things are present on the table too.

The objection is, in a sense, correct. But only because your interrogator has misconstrued the ordinary meaning of the claim that the cup is present by itself. In the ordinary sense of the terms, it is no objection to the claim that the coffee cup is the only thing on the table that there are also things nonidentical to the cup there if they stand in the same sort of relationship to the cup as its parts and intrinsic properties.

A Defence of the Independence Definition of Substance 69

Likewise, if someone says that there is nothing in the cupboard but clothes, it is no objection that there are also sleeves, buttons, colours, and cuts. And if someone says that, for a time, Britain stood alone against Nazi Germany, it is no objection that the Nazis also had to reckon with East Anglia, Winston Churchill, and the 93rd Searchlight Regiment. At the risk of sounding like J. L. Austin, that is not how talk of things acting or existing by themselves ordinarily works. It is only in philosophical discussions of substance that anybody supposes otherwise.

Ordinarily, when we talk about something, x, 'on its own' or 'by itself' or 'without anything else,' we do not mean x without anything that is *non-identical* to x. It is advisable to reflect here on a lesson of the last half century of philosophy of mind already touched on in § 2.4.

Physicalism is the view that reality is exhausted by physical things, where 'physical things' are roughly the particles, fields, and forces picked out by the technical terminology of physics and mathematically describable systems thereof. Under the influence of Place (1956) and Smart (1959), it was long supposed that physicalism, so characterised, can be more precisely defined as the thesis that everything is *identical to* some physical thing. But after protracted debate, most philosophers have agreed that identity is too strong a relation for this job.

The problem with defining physicalism in terms of identity is that, intuitively, it seems that the sort of things physics does not explicitly describe (organisms, artifacts, minds, etc.) might be nothing over and above physical things, without being *identical to* anything identifiable using the vocabulary of physics (cf. Haugeland 1982). For this reason, philosophers have for long preferred to define physicalism in terms of 'supervenience,' 'grounding,' or, as I prefer, 'nothing over and above.'

This lesson should be taken to heart in considering the property-dependence objection. When we talk about x being present 'by itself' or 'on its own,' I suggest that we mean only that x is present without anything *over and above x*. This explains why the presence of the parts and concrete properties of the coffee cup do not conflict with the claim that the cup is there by itself. For the parts and concrete properties, though they are not identical with the cup, are subsumed by it. And if any relation other than identity is unproblematically sufficient for nothing-over-and-above-ness, subsumption is.

This also explains why the fact that a Cartesian mind cannot exist without any attributes or modes does not conflict with the fact that it can exist by itself. The attributes and modes are concrete properties of, and therefore subsumed by, the mind. They do not count as something other than it in the sense that would threaten its isolation.

70   *A Defence of the Independence Definition of Substance*

If we want to adopt an idiomatic reading of Descartes's independence definition, a reading that treats terms like 'by itself' or 'without anything else' as they are ordinarily treated, then we should remove the identity relation inserted by Hoffman and Rosenkrantz (1997, 2) and Lowe (1998, 138) and replace it with the nothing-over-and-above relation. The resulting reading can be expressed as follows:

> Substance = def. x is a substance if and only if, restricting our attention to contingent concrete things, the existence of x does not necessitate that there exists any y such that y is something over and above x.

This is my official formulation of the independence definition and the definition of substance that I adopt in what follows. I claim a number of advantages for this formulation, which I will briefly outline.

Firstly, like causal readings and Markie's (1994) hybrid reading, the formulation given here is immune to the property-dependence objection and to the neighbouring part-dependence objection. For on this formulation, the independence definition only requires that a substance could exist without anything over and above it, and the concrete properties and parts of things are subsumed by and hence nothing over and above them.

Secondly, the formulation proposed here achieves this whilst at the same time offering a twofold improvement on causal readings, including Markie's, in terms of textual fidelity. For as I argued in § 3.1, Descartes's language suggests metaphysical independence not causal independence, and as I have argued in this subsection, his language also suggests nothing-over-and-above-ness, not identity.

Third, unlike the revised independence definitions proposed by Lowe (1998) and Hoffman and Rosenkrantz (1997), this formulation stays close to Descartes's expression of the independence definition and retains the consequence that a nonphysical substance could exist without a body. This means that it is well-suited to the task of defining substance in the sense that is relevant to substance dualism.

Fourth, the formulation proposed here has a good claim to capture the intuitive idea of something that is capable of existing 'by itself' or 'on its own.' This is because it is arrived at by reflecting on what we ordinarily mean when we use these terms. As such, the definition of substance proposed here aligns with a salient pretheoretical category. This gives it an additional *prima facie* claim to be of metaphysical importance.

I note finally that I could perhaps put the definition in terms of grounding. However, as with definitions of physicalism, grounding brings in ideas

A Defence of the Independence Definition of Substance   71

about relative 'fundamentality' that seem to me unhelpful here. Grounding claims are also reputed to be more precise than 'nothing over and above' claims, but I am not convinced of this. Still, the reader is at liberty to substitute in their favourite grounding relation if they wish.

3.3.4 An Armstrongian Obstacle

It might be thought that the response to the property-dependence objection just given works for particular properties and parts, but that it does not work for concrete universals. For it is not obvious that a concrete universal can be nothing over and above its bearer in the way that a particular concrete property can. For example, the colour of the coffee cup, construed as a concrete universal, might also be present in the wallpaper. And it is plausible that something present in the wallpaper cannot be nothing over and above the cup.

Two responses are available. First, the theory of concrete universals already seems to require that these entities can be 'wholly present' in one place, despite also being present somewhere else (cf. Armstrong 1978, I, 108). If this is possible, then it is not clear why a concrete universal cannot be nothing over and above something in one place, whilst also being present elsewhere. For the claim that x is wholly present in location L intuitively entails that x is nothing over and above the things in L. This might seem incoherent, but it is arguably no addition to the apparent incoherence of being wholly present in multiple places.

Secondly, Armstrongians could stipulate that the extension of 'something over and above x' in the independence definition must be determined, not in the actual world, but in the counterfactual world where the candidate substance exists without anything that it is able to exist without. For even if the colour of the coffee cup, construed as a concrete universal, is *actually* something over and above the cup because it is also present in the wallpaper, it seems that it might *counterfactually* have been nothing over and above the cup. This is because the coffee cup could exist without the wallpaper or anything else that shares its colour.

It seems likely that one or other line of argument will allow Armstrongians to adopt the response to the property-dependence objection proposed here. If it did turn out that the property-dependence objection poses a unique problem for theories that posit concrete universals, it would be reasonable to suspect that the problem lies with concrete universals, rather than with the strong metaphysical independence definition. For the idea of something capable of existing by itself is intuitively coherent, whereas the idea of something capable of being wholly present in multiple places at the same time is independently dubious.

72 A Defence of the Independence Definition of Substance

3.4 Further Objections and Refinements

In this section, I consider five subsidiary objections to the definition of substance advanced here, four of which draw on Hoffman and Rosenkrantz (1997, 22, 44). (Weir (2021a) provides a more detailed defence of the independence definition against these and other objections.) Following this, I discuss whether we should add any additional criteria for substancehood or propertyhood beyond the independence definition. Along the way, I explain why we cannot posit Lockean substrata in addition to substances and properties as they are characterised here, an issue which becomes important in § 7.4.

3.4.1 Four More Objections from Hoffman and Rosenkrantz

Two of Hoffman and Rosenkrantz's further objections to the independence definition can be addressed without much argument. First, they object that the independence definition implies that if God exists, nothing else will be a substance, given that everything depends on God. This objection is anticipated at *Principles* (AT VIII 24) and it is addressed by excluding divine things from the domain of the independence definition as Descartes does, or by excluding necessary beings in general, as I have proposed.

Secondly, Hoffman and Rosenkrantz object that the independence definition has the consequence that things picked out by relational properties cannot be substances. For example, they say that the definition entails that a wife cannot be a substance because wives cannot exist without husbands. This objection conflates *de dicto* and *de re* modality. Any given wife might have existed even if her actual spouse had not.

A more important objection advanced by Hoffman and Rosenkrantz says that the independence definition entails that anything with essential origins is not a substance. They view this as a problem because, as Kripke (1972) argues, it is plausible that many things traditionally classed as substances have their origins essentially. It is plausible, for example, that it is part of the essence of a given animal that it has the parents it has.

In fact, proponents of independence definition need not concede that things with essential origins are not substances. The independence definition says a substance is something that could exist without anything else. It does not follow that a substance could exist without anything else *from the very start of its existence* or *for the entirety of its existence* or that it could have existed in a world where nothing else *had ever existed*, only that it could exist without anything else for some period. Things that have essential origins can satisfy the independence definition so long as they are capable of outlasting their origins.

A Defence of the Independence Definition of Substance 73

The most interesting subsidiary objection raised by Hoffman and Rosenkrantz says that a candidate substance cannot exist without a place or a time at which it exists. This objection suggests that no spatial or temporal thing, and hence no concrete thing, can count as a substance, minds, and bodies included. Whitehead (1969, 75) and Lowe (1998, 141) make the same point with respect to place.

Arguably, Descartes has the resources to address this problem within his system already. For Descartes appears to reject substantivalism about space and time. That is, Descartes appears to think that space and time are nothing over and above the spatial extension and temporal duration of substances. If so, then the fact that a spatial or temporal thing necessitates the existence of the space it takes up or the time for which it lasts does not threaten its status as a substance.

A drawback of responding to the problem in this way is that it makes attributing susbtancehood to spatial or temporal things hostage to the rejection of substantivalism about space and time. An alternative response is to take the view that space and time, if they are substantival, should be excluded from the domain over which the independence definition quantifies, along with necessary beings and abstracta. This response remains in the spirit of the sense of 'substance' that defines substance dualism, and so we can adopt it in what follows.

3.4.2 The Threat of Necessitism

A fourth objection, which does not appear in Hoffman and Rosenkrantz, says that the independence definition of substance relies on a further controversial assumption that it cannot so easily avoid: the thesis that at least some things exist contingently. This thesis is known as contingentism. Contingentism is the negation of necessitism, which says that everything that exists does so necessarily (see Williamson 2013, 1–5).

If necessitism is true, then the exclusion of necessary things from the domain of the independence definition will make the definition trivially true of everything. Moreover, removing this restriction will make the definition trivially false of everything apart from the totality of all things.

One way to respond to the threat of necessitism would be to specify that in the sense of 'necessitate' that is relevant to the definition, it is not sufficient for x to 'necessitate' that y exists, that at every possible world where x exists y also exists. Rather, 'necessitates' must be taken to mean something stronger, to the effect that the existence of y follows from something about the *nature of x specifically*. Perhaps this could be cashed out by saying that even amongst those *impossible* worlds that are possible apart

74 *A Defence of the Independence Definition of Substance*

from the nonexistence of y, there is no world where x exists and y does not exist. For this kind of use of impossible worlds, see Berto and Jago (2018).

In the context of Williamson's necessitism, however, there is a more straightforward response. Williamson's necessitism says that everything, including every concrete thing, necessarily exists, but not that they necessarily *concretely* exist. Rather, it says that those possible concreta that we ordinarily think of as not existing exist but not concretely. So, if Williamson's necessitism is right, we should just clarify that x is a substance if and only if x does not necessitate that there *concretely* exists some y such that y is something over and above x.

3.4.3 Additional Criteria

All the independence definition says about substances is that they can exist on their own. This might include scattered objects, such as the entity that comprises Descartes's mind and the Orion Nebula. There is a long tradition, however, that says that substances should be simple, unified things. In the extreme, this view says that substances must be mereological simples: things with no proper parts. Descartes himself sometimes seems to hold that substances must be simple, though elsewhere he accords substancehood to composites (AT VIII B 350; cf. Markie 1994, 71).

Likewise, all the independence definition tells us about properties is that they cannot exist on their own. This might also include scattered things, such as the entity that comprises the colour of a pillar box, and the shape of a desk; or even the colour of the pillar box, the shape of the desk, and a Cartesian soul, given that a metaphysically incomplete thing could comprise a metaphysically complete thing (cf. Williams 1953a, 7). It might accord better with ordinary usage to call these things groups of properties and/or substances.

A downside of adding a constraint on the simplicity of substances and properties is that it means that these categories lose their mutual exhaustivity. Apart from convenience, one advantage of having a use of 'substance' and 'property' on which these terms are exhaustive, is that it helps to clarify the question about whether there exist further entities, such as Lockean substrata, that must be combined with properties to yield a substance.

If by 'substance' and 'property' we just mean metaphysically complete and incomplete things respectively, then there is obviously no room for substrata in addition to these. For any candidate substratum we can ask: could it, or could it not exist on its own? If it could, it is a substance in its own right. If it could not, then it is just another property, albeit perhaps one of a special kind. (This view of substrata as properties is reflected in Alter and Pereboom's (2019) description of Aquinas's prime matter.)

A Defence of the Independence Definition of Substance 75

In fact, however, even stringent constraints on the simplicity of substances and properties are likely to make these two categories *and combinations thereof* exhaustive, thereby leaving no room for a third category of substratum. For any sensible constraint on the simplicity of substances will grant that if something is metaphysically complete, and it is sufficiently simple not to contain one or more substances within it, then it is itself a substance. And any sensible constraint on the simplicity of properties will grant that if something is metaphysically incomplete, and it is sufficiently simple not to contain one or more substances and/or properties within it, then it is itself a property. If so, it follows that everything that exists is either a substance, a property, or analysable without remainder into substances and properties.

There might be a case for having a broad use of 'substance' and 'property' that includes no constraint on simplicity, and a narrow sense that does. Fortunately, it is not necessary to decide on a convention here. For the arguments of the following chapters do not depend on the existence of scattered substances or properties. I only rely on the minimal assumptions stated in the previous paragraph, and even these are usually unnecessary.

In addition to saying nothing about the simplicity of substances, the independence definition says nothing about whether substances are continuants (things that persist through time) or occurrents (things with temporal parts, such as events and processes). But there is a traditional view, with roots in Aristotle (*Categories* 4a10) according to which substances must be continuants, not occurrents (cf. Crane 2001, 36).

According to one kind of ontology, every metaphysically complete occurrent will comprise metaphysically complete continuants. On this view, a splash, for example, will comprise a large number of metaphysically complete atoms, or similar, and inherit its completeness from these. For this kind of ontology, it does not matter whether we require that substances are continuants. Either way, if you posit metaphysically complete nonphysical things, you will be committed to nonphysical substances. That is all that matters in the following chapters.

According to a second kind of ontology, there can be metaphysically complete occurrents that do not comprise any metaphysically complete continuants. (This is one thing we might mean by a 'process ontology.') For proponents of this kind of ontology, there could be metaphysically complete nonphysical mental things, in addition to physical things, but no metaphysically complete nonphysical continuants.

There is an interesting question about whether we should count a position that posits metaphysically complete mental things, in addition to physical things, but no metaphysically complete nonphysical continuants as kind as substance dualism. I suggest that we should. For the thesis that there are metaphysically complete nonphysical mental occurrents remains closer to canonical examples of substance dualism than it is to canonical

76 *A Defence of the Independence Definition of Substance*

examples of property dualism. It retains, for example, the consequence that there exist mental things that could exist in a disembodied state. For this reason, I do not require that substances be continuants. It may be admitted, however, that a view on which the nonphysical substances are occurrents is a somewhat nonstandard form of substance dualism.

4 Four Theories of Mind and the Place of Russellian Monism

The contention of this book is that if you posit nonphysical properties, then you should also posit nonphysical substances and that you must therefore endorse substance dualism or idealism. As a final preparation for the main argument, this chapter reviews the main responses to the mind-body problem in light of the definition of substance that has been defended and explains why, for most people, physicalism, idealism, substance dualism, and property dualism will exhaust the options. This holds even when Russellian monism is taken into account. Property dualism is the only nonphysicalist alternative to substance dualism and idealism.

4.1 Physicalism and Idealism

From classical antiquity to modernity, most philosophers appear to have endorsed substance dualism. It is only in the twentieth century that property dualism becomes the standard form of dualism. In the ancient and Early Modern periods, substance dualism competed with materialism, the ancestor of present-day physicalism (not in the medieval period, so far as I can tell, notwithstanding the ambiguous case of universal hylomorphism). And from the turn of the eighteenth century, both positions faced increasing competition from idealism. This section defines the two monist positions: physicalism and idealism.

4.1.1 Physicalism

Physicalism is the claim that everything is physical, where 'physical' refers to the kind of things that are described by physics. Physicalism is often called 'materialism.' This is because physicalism is heir to the traditional materialism of Democritus, Lucretius, and Hobbes. Traditional materialism says that everything is *material*. That is, all that exists is matter characterised by shape, size, solidity, and locomotion. Traditional materialists

DOI: 10.4324/9781003378600-5

78 Four Theories of Mind and the Place of Russellian Monism

and physicalists agree on many questions about what exists. For example, they agree that there exist spatially extended objects, and they agree that there exist no Cartesian souls.

Physicalism is more liberal than traditional materialism, however. For physics describes things that do not answer to a traditional concept of matter, such as overlapping fields and volumeless particles. The success of modern physics has caused physicalism to supplant traditional materialism in present-day philosophy.

At present, the things described by physics include the fermions and bosons, the four fundamental forces, properties such as mass and spin, and mathematically describable systems of these things. Future physics might alter the list, but something resembling it is supposed to be exhaustive. The things that make it to the list are trivially physical in the sense that they are explicitly named in the technical vocabulary of physics.

Most physicalists recognise the existence of many things that are not trivially physical in this sense. These include natural things like plants and rock strata, social things like totem poles and symphonies, and mental things like thoughts and experiences. A question arises about how physicalists can claim that all that exists are the physical things and yet posit plants, totem poles, and so on.

The standard answer is that things that are not trivially physical stand in an intimate relation to the those that are such that the former count as no real addition to the latter. The leading candidates have been identity, supervenience, and grounding. (NB: Claims of the form 'a is trivially F' are intensional. Their truth or falsehood depends on the term used. For example, it is trivially true that the bachelor who authored *L'Ingénu* was unmarried, but it is not trivially true that Voltaire was unmarried. Hence the claim that e.g. a plant is not trivially physical does not rule out that it is identical with some trivially physical thing.)

Place (1956) and Smart (1959) made identity formulations of physicalism popular. But for the kind of reasons given by Haugeland (1982), it is now widely felt that the identity of all things with trivially physical things is a sufficient but not a necessary condition for physicalism. Haugeland (1982) helped make supervenience formulations of physicalism popular. But for the kind of reasons given by Horgan (1993), it is now widely felt that the supervenience of all things on trivially physical things is a necessary but not a sufficient condition for physicalism. Today, many theorists hope that a grounding formulation of physicalism will strike the right balance between identity and supervenience.

Throughout, theorists have used the term 'nothing over and above' as a suggestive placeholder for the relation that must hold between things that are not trivially physical and those that are for physicalism to be true (Smart 1959, 145; Nagel 1965, 339; Levin 1979, 22; Kripke 1980, 145,

Four Theories of Mind and the Place of Russellian Monism   79

fn. 74; Chalmers 1996, 41, 126, 133; Goff 2017, 43). For reasons touched on in § 2.4, I prefer to stick to 'nothing over and above.' But the arguments of this chapter and those that follow are intended to go through on any sensible formulation of physicalism, including the grounding formulations that are currently popular.

It is normal to add a further constraint that has not been mentioned yet, to the effect that physical things must be 'fundamentally nonmental' (cf. Wilson 2006, 92, fn. 1). This is usually taken to mean that physical things below a certain size and complexity must not be mental. I would prefer to use 'fundamentally nonmental' for any x such that x is nothing over and above some nonmental thing or things. And I would prefer to use 'fundamentally mental' for any x such that x is something over and above all nonmental things. But again, this will not matter in what follows.

This additional constraint means that 'physical,' is not a purely *referential* term but also has some *descriptive* content. The descriptive content is needed to avoid a situation in which a theory can count as physicalist simply by adopting a highly revisionary understanding of the things described by physics. (This is Strawson's (1994, 49–50) way of putting the point. In more recent works, he has campaigned for a purely referential understanding of 'physicalism' on the basis that physicalism as it is usually understood is too preposterous to be treated seriously. Strawson's earlier terminology better reflects established usage, however.)

4.1.2 Idealism

Idealism, in the sense that is relevant to this enquiry, is the converse of physicalism. It is the view that reality is exhausted by mental things, or that everything is mental. Idealism is paradigmatically attributed to Berkeley and Leibniz. Some thinkers in the historical schools of German and British Idealism, such as Fichte, Shelling, Hegel, and Bradley are also naturally understood as idealists. But the uppercase term 'Idealist' has no precise descriptive force when it names these figures, and there is no idealist doctrine that they all clearly share (cf. Hughes, 2021). I discuss idealism at length in Weir (2021c).

Since the critiques of Moore (1903) and Russell (1912), idealism has been confined to the periphery of analytical philosophy. As a result, there has not been a debate about how to define idealism, as there has respecting physicalism and, to some degree, dualism. But many of the same considerations apply. Hence, it is unsurprising that recent discussions of idealism tend to adopt a grounding definition:

> It is perfectly legitimate to regard Leibniz as an 'idealist' insofar as the fundamental beings of his ontology are non-extended, simples endowed

80 *Four Theories of Mind and the Place of Russellian Monism*

with a faculty of representation—a mental property. On this reading of 'idealism', it is essentially the thesis that the mental is that which grounds.

(Look 2013, 207, n. 35)

I will understand idealism broadly as the thesis that the universe is fundamentally mental, or perhaps that all concrete facts are grounded in mental facts. As such it is meant as a global metaphysical thesis analogous to physicalism, the thesis that the universe is fundamentally physical, or perhaps that all concrete facts are grounded in physical facts. The only difference is that 'physical' is replaced by 'mental'.

(Chalmers 2021, 591)

Just as I prefer a nothing-over-and-above definition of physicalism to a grounding definition, I also prefer the nothing-over-and-above definition of idealism. According to this definition, idealism is the claim that there is nothing over and above mental things. But readers can substitute in grounding if they prefer.

There is a *prima facie* puzzle about how to ensure that physicalism and idealism are incompatible. Suppose, for example, that every mental thing is nothing over and above some physical thing and vice versa. Is this physicalism, idealism, or both?

The reader might be tempted to answer that physicalism requires that mental things are less fundamental than trivially physical things, whereas idealism requires the opposite. If so, this might be considered a reason to prefer grounding to nothing-over-and-above definitions of physicalism and idealism after all. For the claim that one thing is grounded in another is usually taken to entail that the first is less fundamental than the second.

In fact, however, the distinction between physicalism and idealism cannot be captured by saying that, on physicalism, the mental things are less fundamental than the trivially physical things, whereas on idealism, the mental things are more fundamental. This can be seen by reflecting on identity theories.

Suppose that every mental thing is *identical* to some physical thing. Usually, this would be regarded as sufficient for physicalism (with the qualifications discussed in § 2.4). But suppose also that every physical thing is identical to some mental thing. The question about whether the resulting position is physicalism or idealism rearises. And this time, it cannot be answered by appeal to fundamentality because nothing can be more or less fundamental than itself.

Fortunately, there is a better explanation of the difference between physicalism and idealism that is available to proponents of the

Four Theories of Mind and the Place of Russellian Monism 81

nothing-over-and-above definition and the grounding definition alike. This solution can be arrived at by reflecting on the intuitive difference between the two positions.

To count as a physicalist, it is not enough that you say that mental things are nothing over and above the things described by physics. You must also be operating with an appropriately nonrevisionary understanding of the physical things. By contrast, insofar as your physicalist credentials are concerned, you can adopt a highly revisionary understanding of the mental things, as physicalists often do.

The opposite is true for idealism. To count as an idealist, it is not enough that you should say that physical things are nothing over and above mental things. You must also be operating with an appropriately nonrevisionary understanding of mental things. By contrast, insofar as your idealist credentials are concerned, you can adopt a highly revisionary understanding of the physical things, as idealists often do.

Hence, physicalists might take the view that conscious experiences are nothing over and above brain states because consciousness is just integrated information in the brain (cf. Tononi 2008). And idealists might take the view that physical objects are nothing over and above conscious experiences because physical objects are just perceptual phantasms (cf. Berkeley, *Principles*). But physicalists cannot take the view that physical objects are just perceptual phantasms, and idealists cannot take the view that conscious experiences are just integrated information in the brain (unless, of course, they understand *these* terms in some revisionary way).

These observations reflect the fact, already mentioned, that physicalism is not purely a referential claim. Physicalism does not merely claim that all that exists are the things referred to by the technical vocabulary of physics. Likewise, idealism does not merely claim that all that exists are the things referred to by mental terms. Idealism also carries some descriptive content about the referents of these terms.

The descriptive content of physicalism is usually expressed by saying that physical things cannot be fundamentally mental. Note, this does not mean that on physicalism, the trivially physical things must be *more* fundamental than mental things. It is usually taken to mean that physical things below a certain size and complexity must not be mental. In the definition I favour, it means that physical things are not something over and above the collection of all nonmental things.

A parallel constraint on idealism might say that for idealism to be true, the mental things *must be fundamentally* mental. That is not the only option, however. For we might think that idealism should allow that the mental things are fundamentally nonmental *so long as they are nonphysical*. The former option yields a slightly more exclusive, the latter a slightly more inclusive understanding of idealism.

82 *Four Theories of Mind and the Place of Russellian Monism*

The difference between these two specifications of idealism is subtle but might occasionally be useful. Suppose a theorist says that (i) the physical world does not exist – the technical vocabulary of physics fails to refer, (ii) the mental world really exists, (iii) the mental things are nothing over and above nonmental things – they are constituted by nonmental noumena perhaps, or the Absolute. Is this idealism? Intuitions are likely to vary. We might say that this is not idealism because the mental things are nothing over and above nonmental things. If so, we are adopting the exclusive descriptive constraint on idealism. Alternatively, we might say that this is idealism because it says that there exists nothing over and above nonphysical mental things. If so, we are adopting the inclusive descriptive constraint on idealism.

For most purposes, it does not matter which constraint we choose to adopt. Either way, physicalism is incompatible with idealism. For on either specification of idealism, the mental things will be something over and above the physical things that physicalism posits. In what follows, I employ the inclusive constraint. So defined, idealism says that there exists nothing over and above nonphysical mental things.

4.2 Substances and the Four Theories of Mind

I have claimed that of physicalism, idealism, substance dualism, and property dualism, property dualism is the only nonphysicalist position that does not posit nonphysical substances. § 4.2.1 explains why this is so and clarifies the relationship between the independence definition and these four positions. Following this, § 4.2.2 explains why for most theorists, these four positions will exhaust the available options.

4.2.1 The Four Theories and the Independence Definition

In § 2.3, I argued that the relevant definition of substance in the context of present-day philosophy of mind is Descartes's independence definition. I understand Descartes's independence definition as either a clarification or a modest extension of Aristotle's definition of substance at *Categories* (1a). It says that a substance is something that can exist by itself. More precisely, x is a substance if and only if, when we confine our attention to contingent concrete things, the existence of x does not necessitate the existence of any y such that y is something over and above x.

Something that satisfies the independence definition is metaphysically complete. Something that does not satisfy the independence definition is metaphysically incomplete. The things without which a metaphysically incomplete entity could not exist are its metaphysical complements. So y is a metaphysical complement of x, if and only if x could not exist without y or

Four Theories of Mind and the Place of Russellian Monism   83

some replacement for *y*. For example, it is plausible that the size of a desk, and the rest of the desk minus its size, are metaphysical complements.

Dualism is the thesis that in addition to physical things, there exist nonphysical mental things. If some of the nonphysical mental things are metaphysically complete, the result is substance dualism. If not, the result is property dualism. These options are mutually exhaustive. 'Substance *dualism*' might suggest that some of the physical things are *also* metaphysically complete (cf. Cucu and Pitts 2019, fn. 1). But for simplicity, I count as substance dualism any dualist position that posits nonphysical substances. I return to this in § 7.2.

Some theorists have suggested that it might be sufficient for 'substance dualism' that there exist some substances that are wholly physical, and some that have both physical and nonphysical properties (Francescotti 2001; Schneider 2012a). This is not how 'substance dualism' is usually understood, however. In one of the earliest works to use these terms, Levin (1979, 50–5e2) points out that we could use 'nonphysical substance' either for a substance with *some* nonphysical properties or for a substance that has only nonphysical properties. He recommends the second use and convention has followed.

It is useful to put this more precisely by saying that a nonphysical substance is something that is metaphysically complete in virtue of its nonphysical properties alone: it should be metaphysically complete when we consider only its nonphysical properties. Equivalently, a nonphysical substance must be strongly metaphysically independent of all physical things. This allows that a Cartesian mind, for example, can remain a nonphysical substance whilst having physical properties like belonging to someone 5'1" tall.

Property dualism is committed to the thesis that the nonphysical things that it posits are all metaphysically incomplete. This is equivalent to the claim that every nonphysical thing has a physical metaphysical complement. For if a nonphysical thing has only nonphysical metaphysical complements, together these will make up a nonphysical thing that is metaphysically complete.

It follows that property dualists must posit some metaphysically complete things that have both physical and nonphysical properties. So long as these things would not be metaphysically complete without their physical properties, they do not count as nonphysical substances. To distinguish these things from wholly physical and wholly nonphysical substances we could call them 'hybrid' substances, as Schneider (2012a) proposes. Property dualists are permitted to posit – indeed must posit – hybrid substances so defined.

I have claimed that idealism, as well as substance dualism, is committed to nonphysical substances. This is correct. For idealism says that there

84　*Four Theories of Mind and the Place of Russellian Monism*

exists nothing over and above nonphysical mental things. It follows that if idealism is true, then reality taken as a whole is a nonphysical thing that is metaphysically complete. For parallel reasons, physicalism entails that reality as a whole is a physical thing that is metaphysically complete.

It might be objected that reality as a whole is not sufficiently unified to count as a substance. However, I suggested in § 3.4 that at the very least, something that satisfies the independence definition and that does not itself comprise substances as parts should be considered sufficiently unified to count as a substance. So if reality as a whole is insufficiently unified to count as a substance, it must nonetheless be made up of substances. For idealists, these will be nonphysical substances, and for physicalists, they will be physical substances.

4.2.2 *The Exhaustivity of the Four Theories of Mind*

Physical things and nonphysical mental things exhaust the concreta most philosophers are tempted to posit. Insofar as we limit ourselves to these options, the four positions defined here are logically exhaustive. If you posit only physical things or only nonphysical mental things, then you are a physicalist or an idealist. If you posit both, and the nonphysical mental things are all metaphysically incomplete, you are a property dualist. If you posit both, and some of the nonphysical mental things are metaphysically complete, you are a substance dualist.

It follows that opponents of physicalism can only avoid positing nonphysical substances by endorsing property dualism, and they can only avoid the choice between substance dualism or idealism by rejecting nonphysical substances. For out of physicalism, idealism, property dualism, and substance dualism, property dualism is the only alternative to physicalism that does not posit nonphysical substances. Nonphysical substances have been unpopular since Ryle's (1949) attack on Cartesian 'ghosts.' So it is not surprising that present-day opponents of physicalism tend to endorse property dualism.

4.3 Paradigmatic Substance Dualists

In § 2.1, I suggested that paradigmatic substance dualists such as Plato, Augustine, and Descartes, and perhaps also Aristotle and Aquinas, are substance dualists in the sense I have defined. I pause in this section to substantiate this claim before considering the case of Russellian monism. If my earlier reading of Descartes is accepted, his qualification as a substance dualist is not in question, so I only comment on the other philosophers mentioned. Of course, this interpretive question deserves more focussed study elsewhere.

Four Theories of Mind and the Place of Russellian Monism 85

Plato does not have a concept of substance. Augustine does but he does not clearly define it (cf. *De Trinitate* XII, I, 1; II, VIII, 14). Both are committed to the claim that humans have souls that can survive death in a disembodied state, however. Plato's *Phaedo* and Augustine's *On the Immortality of the Soul* are devoted to this theme. It seems very likely that both Plato and Augustine understand the soul as something that is fundamentally mental, and therefore nonphysical. The question raised here is whether they understand souls as substances, in the sense characterised by the independence definition.

Plato and Augustine do not, to my knowledge, discuss this question directly. But there is an indirect case for an affirmative answer. For although many theorists hold that a person's mind could not exist without their body, few hold that it could not exist without other concrete contingent things, such as other minds or bodies. It follows that if Plato and Augustine hold that a person's mind could exist without their body, then we should expect them to think that it could exist without anything else at all and is therefore a substance.

This line of reasoning supports the standard view that Plato and Augustine are substance dualists. There is a debate about how to class Aristotle and Aquinas. Aristotle and Aquinas both posit a soul, or at least a part of the soul, that on a natural interpretation is something over and above physical things and that can survive without the body (cf. *De Anima* 413b 24–7; 429b 4–5; 430a17, 22–3; *ST*. 1.75). If so, the reasons for classing Plato and Augustine as substance dualists apply equally to Aristotle and Aquinas.

Some interpreters resist this interpretation of Aristotle on the basis that his claims about the separability of the intellect in *De Anima* apply only to the divine intellect described in *Metaphysics* Λ. If they are correct, then Aristotle probably is not a substance dualist in the sense defined here, where we are confining our attention to nondivine things. There seems to be no clear textual support for this interpretation, however, and I suspect that this is an example of the dualism-minimising trend in recent scholarship discussed in § 1.2.

Many interpreters resist the idea that Aquinas is a substance dualist. But there are no parallel doubts about Aquinas's commitment to the separability of the soul from the body. Rather, it is sometimes mentioned in this context that Aquinas holds that the disembodied soul is not *oneself* (cf. *Commentary on 1 Corinthians*, 21:33–4). But it *need not be* oneself to be a nonphysical substance, which is all substance dualism requires. (On the best interpretation of Aquinas, defended by Elanor Stump (2012), the disembodied soul is not identical to oneself, but does wholly *constitute* oneself whilst disembodied.)

It is also sometimes mentioned that Aquinas thinks that the disembodied soul is in an unnatural, incomplete state (ST Ia.75.4). But again, this does

86 Four Theories of Mind and the Place of Russellian Monism

not mean that it is not a substance, in the sense that defines substance dualism. Indeed, Descartes (AT VII 222) agrees with Aquinas on this point. Both compare a disembodied soul to a severed hand: something naturally incomplete, but not metaphysically incomplete.

As far as I can tell, there is no good reason to deny that Aquinas is a substance dualist. If there is some reason to think that anti-dualist interpretations of Aristotle are an example of unwarranted dualism-minimising of the sort discussed in § 1.2, then there is even more reason to think so with respect to Aquinas.

A further common feature of Plato, Augustine, and Descartes's theories is that the nonphysical substances they posit are subjects or selves. It is not surprising, therefore, that theorists tend to assume that substance dualism must posit nonphysical selves, or even that positing a nonphysical self, in addition to the body, is a sufficient condition for substance dualism (cf. Nida-Rümelin 2006; Loose et al. 2018).

As far as the definition advanced here is concerned, however, a follower of Hume or Nagarjuna might posit nonphysical substances that are subjectless perceptions or experiences. Something resembling this view might be helpful in accounting for Buddhist conceptions of disembodied survival and may be endorsed by Hume himself who says at § 4.5 of the *Treatise*, 'perceptions ... may exist separately, and have no need of any thing else to support their existence. They are, therefore, substances, as far as this definition explains a substance.'

At the same time, the definition I have defended permits views on which the self or subject of experience is nonphysical, but *not* a nonphysical substance because it is incapable of existing without physical things. Nida-Rümelin's (2006, 2010) position is an example. The self on such a view will count as a nonphysical property or as an insubstantial group or complex of nonphysical properties.

Both verdicts seem right. To assign the labels 'substance dualism' and 'property dualism' on the basis of whether positions posit nonphysical selves would make these terms atrocious misnomers. It is true that theories on which the nonphysical substances do not include selves will be unusual forms of substance dualism. But this is only because views that posit mental entities without selves are unusual generally. It might also be true that theories that posit metaphysically incomplete nonphysical selves are unusual forms of property dualism. But if this makes them closer to substance dualism, this is only because nonphysical selves are good candidates for nonphysical substances, not because selfhood logically entails substancehood.

In any case, on a plausible reading, Plato, Aristotle, Augustine, Aquinas, and Descartes are all substance dualists in the core sense that they posit nonphysical mental substances in addition to physical things. The same

Four Theories of Mind and the Place of Russellian Monism   87

reasoning applies to the many other thinkers, Western and non-Western, discussed in Chapter 1. It follows that when Ryle (1949, 1) says that the myth of the ghost in the machine 'hails chiefly from Descartes' or when Searle (2004) opens his book with a chapter on substance dualism entitled 'Descartes and Other Disasters,' they perpetuate a misleading impression that substance dualism is a Cartesian idiosyncrasy.

4.4 Russellian Monism

Insofar as we limit ourselves to positing physical things and nonphysical mental things, physicalism, idealism, substance dualism, and property dualism are logically exhaustive. Nonetheless, a further category requires attention: Russellian monism. This section argues that Russellian monism is not a fifth category on the same level as the other four. Rather, each of the four positions comes in a standard and in a Russellian monist version. For this reason, Russellian monist anti-physicalists can avoid theories that posit nonphysical substances only by endorsing property dualism. Russellian monists tend, in fact, to be Russellian monist property dualists even if they do not apply the name to themselves.

4.4.1 Defining Russellian Monism

Russellian monism is named after Russell (1927), but it is frequently attributed to Leibniz, and it enters recent philosophy in works such as Maxwell (1979) Lockwood (1989) Chalmers (1996), and Strawson (2003, 2006). Alter and Pereboom, (2019, § 1.1) define Russellian monism as the conjunction of three claims. First, physics describes the world only in terms of its spatiotemporal structure and dynamics. Second, there are categorical properties, often called 'quiddities' (i.e. 'whatnesses') that underlie the structural properties. Third, the quiddities underlying structural properties are 'relevant' to consciousness.

Intuitively, structural properties are relational properties that need something qualitative to relate. More precisely, Alter and Pereboom (2019) suggest that structural properties are either extrinsic, meaning relational properties, or 'relatively intrinsic' properties meaning intrinsic properties that are nothing over and above the extrinsic properties of the components of their bearers. This allows spatial properties like shape to count as structural since the shape of an object is nothing over and above the spatial relations between its parts. Categorical properties, on this view, are 'absolutely intrinsic.' They are intrinsic properties that are something over and above all extrinsic properties.

Having proposed these definitions, Alter and Pereboom substitute the term 'grounding' for 'nothing over and above' in order to be more precise.

88 *Four Theories of Mind and the Place of Russellian Monism*

As usual, I am not convinced that grounding is any more precise than nothing-over-and-above-ness here, and I consider the original nothing-over-and-above definition preferable.

Usually, the quiddities are 'relevant' to consciousness in the sense that although consciousness is something over and above the structural properties, it is nothing over and above those properties and their quiddities taken together. This is often expressed by saying that the quiddities together with the structural properties 'constitute' consciousness. The label 'Russellian monism' is also sometimes applied to theories on which the quiddities merely cause consciousness, which remains something over and above them. But this view is not in itself distinct from non-Russellian-monist dualism, as I have defined it, and so I do not count it as Russellian monism.

Russellian monism promises to unite the virtues of standard (i.e. non-Russellian monist) forms of dualism and physicalism (cf. Chalmers 2016a). Like dualism, it promises to explain why consciousness strikes us as something over and above the things described by physics. For it says that physics leaves out the 'deep nature' of the things whose structure it describes. And like physicalism, it promises to explain how consciousness is capable of acting causally on the physical world. For it says that consciousness is in fact nothing over and above the ordinary causes of physical effects, which physics only partially describes.

There is disagreement about how to categorise Russellian monism. Maxwell and Strawson call their position 'physicalism'; Chalmers (1996, 136–66) is undecided between 'property dualism,' 'idealism,' and 'neutral monism'; and many refrain from making a call on this question. This disagreement has two causes. The first is that Russellian monism is in fact compatible with all four of the responses to the mind-body problem distinguished in this chapter. The second is that most forms of Russellian monism are physicalist in a purely referential sense. I explain these causes of disagreement in the following two subsections, respectively.

4.4.2 *Russellian Monism Is Compatible With All Four Theories of Mind*

Russellian monist positions vary with the claims that they make about the quiddities underlying the things described by physics. It is often suggested that Russellian monist positions cannot be straightforwardly classed amongst the more familiar responses to the mind-body problem. But reflection on what follows on various specifications concerning the quiddities suggests that the familiar categories remain applicable.

If the quiddities are all fundamentally nonmental, the result is a physicalist version of Russellian monism, such as Montero's (2015). For on this kind of position, there exists nothing over and above the fundamentally

Four Theories of Mind and the Place of Russellian Monism   89

nonmental things referred to by the technical vocabulary of physics, and that is how we defined physicalism.

If some or all of the quiddities are fundamentally mental, the result is anti-physicalist Russellian monism. Because the Russellian monist's quiddities are by definition amongst the things referred to by physics, the *only* way they can fail to be physical is by being fundamentally mental. This contrasts with standard anti-physicalist positions where the non-physical mental things might be fundamentally nonmental things that are nonphysical because they are not amongst the things referred to by physics.

Anti-physicalist Russellian monism can be idealist or dualist. If all the quiddities are fundamentally mental, and there exists nothing over and above them, the result is idealist Russellian monism. This is the position often attributed to Leibniz (cf. Alter and Pereboom 2019 § 2.1; Look 2013, 207, n. 35; Weir 2021c). Importantly, idealist Russellian monists cannot posit spatial properties except insofar as these are nothing over and above the fundamentally mental things. So, idealist Russellian monists must adopt a revisionary understanding of space.

If some of the quiddities are fundamentally mental, but there also exist fundamentally nonmental things over and above them, the result is dualist Russellian monism. Dualist Russellian monism can be property dualist or substance dualist. If the fundamentally mental things are all metaphysically incomplete, the result is property dualist Russellian monism. If some of the fundamentally mental things are metaphysically complete, the result is substance dualist Russellian monism.

A property dualist Russellian monist might say, for example, that the quiddity underlying mass is fundamentally mental, but that the quiddity underlying charge is not. A substance dualist Russellian monist might say, for example, that the quiddities underlying rocks are fundamentally nonmental, but that the quiddities underlying brains are fundamentally mental, and that rocks and brains are substances.

Anti-physicalist Russellian monism is closely associated with panpsychism, the view that mentality is not confined to animate organisms but is significantly more widespread (cf. Strawson 2006). This is because it is widely accepted that animate organisms, including their brains, are made out of the same kind of things that make up what we usually think of as inanimate matter. It follows that if the quiddities of the things our brains are made up of are fundamentally mental, then so are the quiddities of the things rocks are made up of.

Panpsychist Russellian monism can still be substance dualist if the fundamentally mental substances are not found exclusively in the brains of animate organisms. Such a view might say, for example, that the quiddities underlying fermions are fundamentally mental, that the quiddities

90 *Four Theories of Mind and the Place of Russellian Monism*

underlying bosons are fundamentally nonmental, and that fermions and bosons are substances.

The panpsychist inference can be avoided by denying that our brains are made of the same kind of things as what we usually think of as inanimate matter. For example, perhaps when inanimate matter forms a brain, it 'fuses' into a radically new kind of entity whose underlying nature is different from that of the things that formed it as Mørch (2014) proposes. Mørch herself combines fusionism with panpsychism, but Carter (2018) has argued for a position close to Mørch's fusionism as a means to avoid panpsychism.

Russellian monism is, then, compatible with all four responses to the mind-body problem distinguished in this chapter. This explains, in part, why theorists have disagreed about how to class it. There is a tendency to ask where Russellian monism fits amongst the familiar positions. But for Russellian monism as it has come to be understood, and as Alter and Pereboom (2019) define it, this is a model example of a category error. Russellian monism is a move that proponents of any of the ordinary positions can make.

4.4.3 Russellian Monism and Referential Physicalism

The second cause of disagreement about how to categorise Russellian monism is that almost all Russellian monist positions count as physicalism in what Strawson (1994, 49–50) describes as a purely 'referential' as opposed to a descriptive sense of 'physicalism.' This has encouraged some theorists, including Strawson (2003, 2006) in more recent works, to class as 'physicalist' Russellian monist positions that are unambiguously anti-physicalist in the more familiar, partially descriptive, sense of 'physicalism.'

Things are physical in the referential sense if they are nothing over and above the things described by physics. Things are physical in the descriptive sense if they are nothing over and above the things described by physics, *and* they are fundamentally nonmental. So, physicalism in the referential sense is just physicalism without the prohibition of fundamentally mental things introduced in § 4.1. The fact that most Russellian monist positions are physicalist in this heterodox sense does not change the fact that those that posit fundamentally mental things must be idealist, property dualist, or substance dualist in the ordinary descriptive senses of these terms.

I have said that almost all versions of Russellian monism are physicalist in the referential sense. In fact, this is true of all versions of Russellian monism that do not posit anything over and above the (perhaps fundamentally mental) things referred to by the vocabulary of physics. This will include *all* versions of Russellian monism that have a claim to be genuinely monist. But it is also possible to imagine positions that satisfy Alter and

Four Theories of Mind and the Place of Russellian Monism 91

Pereboom's criteria for Russellian monism whilst positing some things over and above those referred to by physics.

4.4.4 Russellian Monist Property Dualists

In the introduction, I claimed that a major change in discussions of the mind-body problem since Wolff's (1751) *German Metaphysics* is that property dualism has supplanted substance dualism and idealism as the leading alternative to physicalism/materialism. The quotations listed in § 2.1 suggest that this claim would receive widespread assent. However, some would want to challenge it on the basis that property dualism is not obviously any less popular today than anti-physicalist forms of Russellian monism.

It should be clear from the account of Russellian monism presented in this section that the popularity of anti-physicalist Russellian monism is not in direct competition with that of property dualism. For anti-physicalist Russellian monism comes in property dualist as well as substance dualist and idealist forms. Furthermore, there is evidence that many leading anti-physicalist Russellian monists favour property dualist versions of the position. This would not be surprising given the unpopularity of nonphysical substances.

Descriptions of anti-physicalist Russellian monism often imply that the fundamentally mental things have properties, usually spatial properties, that are not themselves fundamentally mental. For example, this is the kind of position suggested by Strawson's (2003, 38, 29) proposal that reality has 'both experiential and non-experiential being' and that our 'ordinary concept of space … has correct non-structural descriptive content.' A different version of the position is suggested by Goff's (2017, 185) proposal that the fundamentally mental things have spatial properties with a nonphenomenal noumenal nature.

Both Strawson and Goff suggest that spatial properties are something over and above the fundamentally mental properties of their bearers; they differ on whether the spatial properties answer to our pretheoretical concepts of them. Goff (2017, 185) also proposes that consciousness might be an 'aspect' of 'consciousness+,' which combines consciousness and a noumenal and presumably nonspatial '+' component. This too suggests a property dualist form of Russellian monism.

Officially, Strawson rejects the view that his position is a version of property dualism as opposed to substance dualism, giving the following reason:

'Property dualism,' applied to intrinsic, non-relational properties, is strictly incoherent (or just a way of saying that there are two very

92 Four Theories of Mind and the Place of Russellian Monism

different kinds of properties) insofar as it purports to be genuinely distinct from substance dualism, because there is nothing more to a thing's being than its intrinsic, non-relational propertiedness.

(Strawson 2003, 27)

Strawson implies here that the distinction between property dualism and substance dualism has to do with whether something's 'intrinsic, nonrelational being' has more to it than its 'propertiedness.' This suggests that Strawson has in mind a distinction that understands 'substances' as substrata of the sort characterised in § 2.3, or perhaps one that takes 'substance' in the everyday sense of 'kind of stuff.'

Both of these senses of 'substance' are irrelevant to the distinction between property dualism and substance dualism. The important distinction is between things that do and do not satisfy the independence definition: things that are and are not metaphysically complete. Insofar as he does not posit fundamentally mental things that are metaphysically complete, Strawson is, in the relevant sense, a property dualist. (McPherson (2006, 72–89) and Coleman (2016, 43) also class Strawson as a property dualist.)

Goff also rejects the characterisation of his view (at least the consciousness+ version) as property dualist. He does so on the basis that consciousness+ properties are supposed to be 'unified properties' (pers. comm. 15 March 2019). However, it is not clear how the unity of the consciousness aspect and the '+' aspect could invalidate the label of 'property dualism' without also undermining the duality implied by 'consciousness+.' This disagreement seems to me, therefore, to be merely terminological.

Chalmers (1996) is ambivalent between standard property dualism and Russellian monism. Unlike Strawson and Goff, Chalmers does not specify that the Russellian monist position he envisages would include both fundamentally mental and fundamentally nonmental properties. But this would cohere with Chalmers's (1996, 55) description of the position as a 'property dualist' one which 'retains an essential duality between the properties that physics deals with directly and the hidden intrinsic properties that constitute phenomenology.'

Something revealed by this discussion is that it is difficult to ascertain for certain whether any proponent of anti-physicalist Russellian monism is committed to a property dualist version of this position because they tend not to be explicit about the metaphysical completeness of the things they posit. I only claim that those anti-physicalist Russellian monists who are committed to property dualism will be vulnerable to the main argument of the next three chapters and that this appears to include many prominent Russellian monists. If there are anti-physicalist Russellian monists who reject property dualism, they are already committed to nonphysical substances, and this deserves to be given much greater fanfare.

Four Theories of Mind and the Place of Russellian Monism   93

4.4.5 Neutral Monism

Russellian monism is often associated with the term 'neutral monism.' I conclude this chapter by commenting on what neutral monism would involve. Neutral monism is supposed to be neutral about whether reality is ultimately physical or ultimately mental. This could be because reality is both physical and mental or because it is neither. As Stubenberg (2018, § 1) points out, the first view does not seem to differ from dualism. So, it makes sense to reserve 'neutral monism' for views on which reality is neither physical nor mental.

How we understand neutral monism depends on how generous we are about what counts as physicalism. I have defined physicalism as any view that says there exists nothing over and above the things described by physics subject to the minimal descriptive criterion that these things are fundamentally nonmental. Some theorists defend more stringent criteria. If you adopt more stringent criteria on what counts as physical, it will make sense to reclass as neutral monist some positions that I class as physicalist.

For example, it is sometimes argued that to count as physical, things must not have quiddities that help constitute consciousness, even if the quiddities are fundamentally nonmental. On this view, it would be natural to reclass Montero's (2015) Russellian monism as neutral monist on the basis that it entails that reality is made up of fundamentally nonmental things described by physics that are nonetheless not physical.

Likewise, how we understand neutral monism depends on how generous we are about what counts as idealism. In § 4.1.2, I adopted the inclusive constraint which requires only that the mental things posited by idealists should be nonphysical, not that they must be fundamentally mental. If you adopt the more exclusive constraint on which the mental things must be fundamentally mental, it will make sense to reclass positions that only satisfy the inclusive constraint as neutral monist on the basis that they entail that reality is made up of fundamentally nonmental things that are also nonphysical. A Neoplatonic or Vedic view on which material things are illusory, and mental things are nothing over and above a fundamentally nonmental One or Brahman might count as neutral monist in this sense.

The relatively generous specifications of 'physical' and 'mental' that I have adopted leave correspondingly little room for neutral monism. To count as neutral monist, a position would have to posit only things that are through and through nonmental and that are not described by physics either. Clear examples are hard to find. Two-worlds transcendental idealism might count, depending on the ontological status of the phenomenal world. So might the Madhyamika emptiness doctrine, supposing mental and physical things are kinds of *svabhava*.

94 *Four Theories of Mind and the Place of Russellian Monism*

It might also be possible to articulate a version of neutral monism by driving a wedge between two senses of 'mental' so that the things described by physics can turn out to be too mental to count as physical, but not mental enough to count as mental. It seems to be in this sense that Russell is sometimes considered a neutral monist. However, where we use 'mental' univocally, no such position can be coherently formulated.

5 The Strangeness of Property Dualism

The first half of this enquiry defined the available responses to the mind-body problem and filled in some of the history of this problem. Since the early twentieth century, that history has been characterised by a striking shift away from nonphysical substances despite increasing support for nonphysical properties. The second half will argue that if you posit nonphysical properties in response to the mind-body problem, then you should also posit nonphysical substances. The flagship argument enters in § 5.5. The intervening sections explain informally why property dualism is a strange position given the insights that motivate it and present two auxiliary arguments.

5.1 The Knowledge Argument and the Conceivability Argument

Although I have described in detail the metaphysical differences between responses to the mind-body problem, I have only mentioned in passing why anyone would want to accept any of them. The dialectic of the last few decades has centred on the case for and against physicalism. The leading argument for physicalism says that it is the only position that can accommodate mental causation. I summarised that argument in § 1.4. The leading objection to physicalism says that it cannot accommodate consciousness.

'Consciousness' here means phenomenal consciousness. Chalmers (1995) distinguishes phenomenal consciousness from other things that get called 'consciousness' but which pose no special problem for physicalism. Something has phenomenal consciousness if it has an 'inner life,' if there is 'something it is like' to be that thing in the terminology established by Nagel (1974).

There exists a widespread and persistent intuition that phenomenal consciousness, henceforth 'consciousness,' is not physical. Several arguments attempt to articulate this intuition. The most influential are the knowledge argument (Jackson, 1982; Robinson 1982, 4) and the conceivability

DOI: 10.4324/9781003378600-6

96 *The Strangeness of Property Dualism*

argument (Chalmers 1996, 2010). (I comment briefly on two other arguments against physicalism about consciousness, the explanatory gap argument and the transparency argument, in § 7.5.)

The knowledge argument starts with a well-known thought experiment: a scientist, Mary, learns everything physical science has to say about colour perception. However, Mary has never seen colour (other than black and white) for herself. Jackson reasons that when Mary first sees colour:

> She will learn something about the world and our visual experience of it. But then it is inescapable that her previous knowledge was incomplete. But she had all the physical information. Ergo there is more to have than that, and Physicalism is false.
>
> (Jackson 1982, 130)

The knowledge argument concludes that consciousness is something over and above physical things on the basis that Mary learns something new about the world when she first consciously experiences colour.

The conceivability argument starts from the premiss that the physical facts about the world do not a priori entail the existence of consciousness. This is often supported by zombie thought experiments (Chalmers 1996, 94–9). A zombie twin is a physical duplicate of an actual conscious human, without any conscious experiences: an organism just like the actual one except that it is 'all dark' on the inside. Zombies seem to be conceivable. If so, premiss one appears to be true. Premiss one can also be supported by the Mary thought experiment.

The second premiss of the conceivability argument says that if the physical facts about the world do not a priori entail the existence of consciousness, then they do not necessitate the existence of consciousness either. This is usually supported by appeal to some general form of modal rationalism, the thesis that conceivability is a reliable guide to possibility (see § 6.2 for detail on this). It follows from these premisses that the physical facts do not necessitate the existence of consciousness. If so, it seems that consciousness must be something over and above physical things. (I return to this final step in § 6.4.)

Stated in this way, the knowledge argument and the conceivability arguments are simple. Much of the serious philosophical work gets done responding to objections. The main objection to the conceivability argument is an objection to the modal rationalism of premiss two. I discuss this objection at length in § 6.2.

In the rest of this chapter, I consider what kind of view these arguments motivate if they are successful. In particular, I raise some intuitive doubts about the common practice of treating these as arguments for property dualism as opposed to substance dualism or idealism. This practice has

The Strangeness of Property Dualism 97

played a significant role in reinforcing the idea that nonphysical substances have no role to play in present-day philosophy of mind. And yet it has rarely been subjected to serious scrutiny.

5.2 Zombies Plus Experiences

The usual response to the knowledge argument and the conceivability argument is to posit nonphysical phenomenal properties but to resist any suggestion that there exist nonphysical substances. However, it is not clear that such responses are coherent. The intuitive problem here can be seen by reflecting on the standard property dualist position. (As I explain in § 7.3, the most important claims made in this and the next chapter also apply to Russellian monist versions of property dualism, but some are more relevant to standard versions.)

Standard property dualist views say that the world is largely as physicalists picture it: it is a vast spatiotemporal manifold, populated by physical particles, properties, fields, and forces, and complex systems of these things. Breaking with physicalists, however, property dualists add that some of those systems, including human organisms, also have nonphysical phenomenal properties.

A conscious human being, on this picture, can be thought of as a composite of a philosophical zombie and some phenomenal properties. There is a sense, of course, in which the physical component is not a zombie when the phenomenal properties are present. Equally, however, there is a sense in which the physical component, considered in itself, in abstract from any phenomenal properties it might have, remains a zombie. In this sense, property dualism says that everyone has a zombie just as everyone has a skeleton.

In addition to the zombie part, however, property dualism says that conscious humans also have nonphysical phenomenal properties. To borrow Searle's (2002) metaphor, the nonphysical phenomenal properties ornament the zombie (or the zombie's brain as Searle prefers to suppose) like frosting on a cake.

Searle's comparison is intuitively apt. However, this reveals something strange about property dualism. For as Searle (2002, 63–4) points out, the frosting on a cake would usually be considered not a property of the cake, but something else on top of it that might naturally be taken for a separate substance. (The *Port Royal Logic* would call being iced a 'substantial mode' (Arnauld and Nicole 1662, 32). These 'represent true substances applied to other substances as modes and manners' and include 'being clothed' and 'being armed.')

In pointing this out, Searle touches upon the intuitive problem with property dualism. He goes on to argue that the commitments of property

98 The Strangeness of Property Dualism

dualists imply substance dualism. As I explain in a moment, the way Searle reaches this conclusion involves an important error. But the initial intuition is fertile and can be developed in several more promising directions.

Searle's argument goes as follows. First, he observes that we would not describe the uncontroversial properties of a brain, such as its weight, shape, or colour, as something over and above it. On this basis, he reasons that for one thing to be something over and above a second thing just is for it to be a separate substance. He concludes that property dualism is incoherent:

> This conception requires that consciousness be a separate thing, object, or non-property type of entity. ... Ironically, the very dualism of the property dualist picture makes it impossible to state the theory without implying a version of substance dualism.
>
> (Searle 2002, 63–64)

If Searle is right, then property dualism affirms a contradiction by conjoining the claim that consciousness is something over and above physical things and the claim that consciousness is not a nonphysical substance.

Searle's reasoning is flawed. For it is based on the assumption that if property dualism is true, then the phenomenal properties must stand in the same kind of relation to the brain (or whatever the physical bearer is) as its weight, shape, or colour. It is easy to see why Searle might think this, but it misses something important.

In the context of property dualism, 'brain' is ambiguous. It might mean the brain, *including* any nonphysical phenomenal properties that it might have: the brain construed as what Schneider (2012a) calls a 'hybrid substance.' Alternatively, it might mean the brain considered in abstract from any phenomenal properties it might have: the zombie brain—the wholly physical thing that the phenomenal properties crown.

In the first case, property dualists *will not* say that phenomenal properties are something over and above the brain, any more than its shape or weight. For the property dualist claim is that phenomenal properties are something over and above physical things, not that they are (incoherently) something over and above physical things *and* their phenomenal properties.

Searle makes it clear that by 'brain' he means an entity that the phenomenal properties are supposed to be something over and above. It follows that Searle has in mind what I am calling the zombie brain. But *in that case*, he is wrong to suppose that property dualists are committed to the claim that the phenomenal properties stand in the same relation to the brain as its shape or weight. This is because the (zombie) brain is something that includes physical properties, such as shape and weight, but excludes the phenomenal ones. Rather, property dualists are committed to the claim that the phenomenal properties stand to the (zombie) brain as the

The Strangeness of Property Dualism   99

shape of the brain stands to *the brain minus its shape* (or, if you like, '*brain-minus-its-shape*').

This distinction undermines Searle's argument. For whilst the shape of the brain might be nothing over and above the brain, it is trivially something over and above the brain minus its shape. And yet for all that, it does not seem to be, either intuitively or in the strict sense I have defined, a separate *substance* from the brain minus its shape. For the shape, taken by itself, appears to be metaphysically incomplete. (To be shaped, as *the Port Royal Logic* confirms, is not a 'substantial mode.')

Searle is wrong, therefore, to suggest that for one thing to be something over and above a second thing just is for it to be a separate substance. It follows that there is nothing straightforwardly incoherent in the claim that whilst consciousness is something over and above the brain, it is a property of the brain and not a separate substance. To this extent, property dualism does make sense.

Even so, Searle is right that the intuitive aptness of the cake-and-frosting metaphor reveals something odd about property dualism. This is because, in a couple of respects, the relationship between the phenomenal properties and the brain seems unlike *even* the supposedly parallel relationship between the shape of the brain and the brain minus its shape. This insight can be developed in several ways.

5.3 The Symmetry Argument

I now propose a more promising argument for the view that property dualists must posit nonphysical substances that arises out of the same intuition as Searle's. I call this the 'symmetry argument.' It will be followed by the compresence argument and the parity argument. I present the symmetry argument and the compresence argument partly because it is plausible that they bring out, in a different way, the same underlying problem that is best expressed by the parity argument. The parity argument will carry the serious dialectical weight.

5.3.1 Zombies and the Symmetry Principle

The intimate relation between the shape of a brain and the brain minus its shape is reflected in the fact that the brain minus its shape strikes us, intuitively, as a fragmented being: something radically deficient, whose ontological career requires backup. More precisely, the brain minus its shape appears to be metaphysically incomplete, because of the missing property – there is a gap that needs to be filled for it to exist.

In sharp contrast, neither the zombie brain without its phenomenal properties nor the zombie taken as a whole strikes us as deficient in this way.

100 *The Strangeness of Property Dualism*

Rather, zombies seem like metaphysically complete things. Furthermore, the conceivability argument seems to support this: if zombies are possible, this must be because the physical properties of zombies do not stand in need of nonphysical phenomenal complements.

This helps explain why it seems correct to say that the property dualists' phenomenal properties stand to the zombie brain as frosting to a cake, whereas this comparison does not seem apt for the relationship between the shape of the brain and the brain minus its shape. Intuitively, the brain without its phenomenal properties, like the cake without its frosting, remains metaphysically complete.

It is tempting to say that if a zombie is metaphysically complete, then there is *no room* for additional phenomenal properties to be added—it is saturated as it is. To make this intuition into an argument, we might conjecture that metaphysical complementarity is a symmetric relation. That is, if x would be metaphysically incomplete without y, then y would be metaphysically incomplete without x. I call this the symmetry principle.

The symmetry principle would explain why it is that when, for example, we distinguish the size of a desk from the rest of the desk minus its size, we get two metaphysically incomplete things. Equipped with this principle, we might argue as follows:

(i) Physical things are metaphysically complete.
(ii) Metaphysical complementarity is a symmetric relation.
(iii) Therefore, if there are nonphysical things, there are nonphysical substances.

Anyone who accepts the conceivability argument for standard forms of property dualism is under pressure to accept (i), though for reasons I discuss in § 6.4, this is not entirely straightforward; and (ii) is intuitively appealing and gains abductive support from its explanatory power. If (i) and (ii) are true, then no nonphysical thing could have a physical metaphysical complement. Hence, as (iii) says, nonphysical things will have to be nonphysical substances if they exist at all.

5.3.2 *Relational Properties and Asymmetrical Metaphysical Complementarity*

It might be that the symmetry argument is ultimately successful. If so, however, the symmetry principle (ii) requires some refinement in light of apparent counterexamples. The weight of an object, for instance, seems metaphysically incomplete. Weight is not something that could exist all by itself. And yet it is plausible that heavy objects are metaphysically complete without their weights.

For example, if a Bösendorfer piano were the only object in existence, it would lack weight. For there would be no other body to provide a gravitational field. If so, the relationship between the weight of an object and the object minus its weight is one of asymmetrical metaphysical complementarity.

Cases like weight threaten the symmetry argument. Still, it might be that weight is an exception to (ii) only because it is a relational property. If so, we could reformulate the symmetry argument so that it applies to nonrelational properties only. This would still include nonphysical phenomenal properties as they are usually understood. It is hard to find clear counterexamples to (ii) where relational properties are excluded. For this reason, the symmetry argument might undermine standard forms of property dualism after all. (I comment on the threat posed by the symmetry principle to Russellian monist property dualism in § 7.3.)

The symmetry argument is probably redundant, however. For even without the symmetry principle, a zombie does not seem, intuitively, like the right kind of thing to combine with nonphysical phenomenal properties. And this intuition can be used to drive arguments that do not rely on the symmetry principle. The symmetry argument should play at most an auxiliary role in expressing the problem with property dualism.

5.4 The Compresence Argument

This section presents a second argument for the view that property dualists must posit nonphysical substances. Like the symmetry argument, the compresence argument aims to bring out the intuitive strangeness of property dualism captured by Searle's frosting image. Again, I think the underlying problem is best captured by the parity argument of the next section, and only present the compresence argument briefly, and relatively informally.

5.4.1 The Laws of Compresence

Metaphysicians have often been struck by the way in which properties, unlike parts, seem to intermix or blend with one another, their 'interfusion and compenetration' as Williams (1953b, 188) calls it. For example, the shape and size of an object, or the pitch and timbre of a sound seem to run through one another in such a way that, although we can distinguish them intellectually, we cannot point – literally or in some analogical manner – to one as opposed to the other.

Importantly, this close relationship does not seem to obtain whenever two properties belong to the same substance. For example, there is a sense in which the shape of the stem of a flower, and the colour of the head, both belong to the same flower, and yet intuitively, they remain unmixed. This

102   *The Strangeness of Property Dualism*

appears to be because they belong to the same substance only by belonging to different parts of that substance.

If two properties belong to the same substance only because they belong to different parts of that substance, I say that they are 'loosely compresent'; in other cases, they are 'strictly compresent.' Two components of a substance count as different parts if and only if they are nonoverlapping and metaphysically complete. This terminology can be used to express an argument against property dualism anticipated by Schneider (2012a).

Schneider, along with Searle, is one of the relatively few metaphysicians who have subjected the coherence of property dualism to serious scrutiny. Schneider's main argument is limited, in my opinion, by the fact that she relies on Lowes' heterodox definition of substances. However, Schneider (2012a) raises a further challenge to property dualism that does not have this drawback and that can be developed into a new argument:

> Why is it that physical and mental properties can be compresent with one another? After all, not every property can be compresent in the same bundle as every other. Consider any property and its negation, or consider properties that cannot be coinstanced as a matter of law (e.g., a particle's both having mass and traveling at the speed of light).
> (Schneider 2012a, 68)

It is true that not every property can be compresent with every other. However, to turn this observation into an argument requires greater precision. For *almost* every property can be loosely compresent with every other if we are sufficiently permissive about mereology: even mass and lightspeed travel.

There seem to be major restrictions on strict compresence, however. For example, red and green can be compresent, in the sense that a flower can have a red head and a green stem. But it is plausible that this is the only way that red and green can be compresent: something cannot be both red and green all over. This seems to be because red and green are different determinates of the same determinable.

There also seem to be cases where properties cannot be strictly compresent because they are determinates of incompatible determinables. For example, whilst shape can be strictly compresent with size, and pitch with timbre, intuitively, shape cannot be strictly compresent with timbre.

Admittedly, a Bösendorfer can have both a shape and a timbre in the sense that it produces sounds of a certain timbre. Intuitively, however, nothing can have both shape, in the sense that a physical object has shape, and timbre, in the sense that a sound has timbre, unless it is a composite of an object and a sound. (I consider the objection that sounds are physical waves, and therefore do have shape, in a moment.)

The Strangeness of Property Dualism 103

5.4.2 *The Compresence Principle*

Returning to property dualism, there is no intuitive problem with physical and nonphysical phenomenal properties being loosely compresent. There is no reason why something massive like a brain and something phenomenal like a pain should not be or belong to different parts of a composite. But it is not clear that physical and nonphysical phenomenal properties can be strictly compresent.

To see this, picture a zombie on the one hand and a nonphysical phenomenal state on the other, such as the conscious experience of sunlight glimmering on a body of water. Then try to picture these things coalescing in the way that strictly compresent properties do. This is difficult to achieve.

It is not clear what such coalescing would consist in. At best, it is possible to think of the conscious experience as occurring where the zombie is; to tell yourself that it is present in the same region. But this is not enough. For the shape and size of an object are not just in the same region. Rather, they interfuse and compenetrate, as Williams puts it, so that the shape is a shape of that size, the size a size of that shape. Trying to frame an idea of physical and nonphysical phenomenal properties doing this is like trying to frame an idea of something that is both four feet across and C-sharp major. The properties appear immiscible.

It should be emphasised that this problem arises only if we assume, with property dualists, that phenomenal properties are nonphysical things that answer to our pretheoretical concepts of them. There is no parallel problem for physicalist positions on which phenomenal properties are functional or neurological states. Neither is there any problem for substance dualist or idealist positions. For on these positions, physical and phenomenal properties are not strictly compresent to start with. This is a special problem for property dualism.

I call the claim that physical and nonphysical phenomenal properties cannot be strictly compresent the compresence principle. Using this principle, we can formulate the compresence argument:

(i) Physical and nonphysical phenomenal properties cannot be strictly compresent.
(ii) If anything has physical properties and nonphysical properties, these properties belong entirely to different parts of that thing.
(iii) Therefore, if anything has physical and nonphysical properties, it is a composite of a physical and a nonphysical substance.

Like the symmetry argument, the compresence argument has intuitive force. And, unlike the symmetry principle, (i) has no counterexamples that

104 *The Strangeness of Property Dualism*

are not question-begging. Admittedly, if (i) is warranted, this is only on the basis of our intuitive grasp of physical and phenomenal properties. However, this is equally true of the arguments (like those described in § 5.1) that motivate property dualism in the first place.

It might be that (i) expresses the *only* case where properties cannot be strictly compresent because they are determinates of incompatible determinables. This need not contradict the claim that shape and timbre are also an example. For shape and timbre seem immiscible only where we treat timbre as a qualitative characteristic that answers, roughly, to our pretheoretical grasp of it. If we use 'timbre' to name an aspect of the vibrations that cause auditory experience, it becomes plausible that something can have both shape and timbre.

The example of shape and timbre might be clarified, therefore, by saying that it is timbre construed as the qualitative property presented in experience that seems incompatible with shape: phenomenological timbre, the timbre of the *Lebenswelt*. Property dualists are likely to say that phenomenological timbre just is a nonphysical phenomenal property, making this an instance of (i) after all.

It would be interesting if (i) were the only case where properties cannot be strictly compresent because they are determinates of incompatible determinables. For this would seem to vindicate, in an adapted form, Descartes's (AT VIII, 1, 25, 32) contention that thought and extension are the sole principal attributes. (An alternative view, which remains Cartesian in spirit, would say that physical and phenomenal are in fact the incompatible determinates of some especially elevated determinable such as *concretum* or *being*.)

I think that the compresence argument is sufficiently forceful to deserve serious consideration. However, as I have noted, it is a dialectical weakness of the argument that it relies on the intuitive force of the compresence principle, a force some might not feel. Richard Holton, for example, tells me that he judges that he can form an idea of physical properties interfusing with phenomenal properties as property dualists envision them. He gives the example of the sensation of pain propagating through one's hand.

Try as I might, I cannot sympathise. If one's hand is taken as an item not of physics but of *phenomenology*, then I certainly have an idea of an object whose fleshiness is at the same time alive with conscious feeling, and I regard this as vital to the phenomenology of embodiment. But property dualism is supposed to attribute nonphysical phenomenal properties to physical things of the sort posited by physicalists: it is the hand as it is described by physics, and not as it is presented in experience, that has to bear the phenomenal pain. I find that impossible to make sense of.

5.4.3 The Significance of the Symmetry Argument and the Compresence Argument

Both the symmetry argument and the compresence argument bring out the intuitive strangeness of property dualism. Once you take seriously the idea that conscious experience is something over and above physical things, it requires an effort of will to take the view that it is, nonetheless, a property of physical things.

It is therefore odd that the knowledge argument and the conceivability argument are usually treated as arguments for property dualism; especially so given that, as I explained in § 2.2, serious objections to nonphysical substances in recent metaphysics are scarce. Because of this, the symmetry argument and the compresence argument might be enough on their own to warrant the reintroduction of nonphysical substances into present-day responses to the mind-body problem.

However, there is a further way of developing the intuitive case against positing nonphysical properties without nonphysical substances that should be especially dialectically forceful. It is to this third line of argument that I turn in the next section, and on which I focus in the next chapter.

5.5 The Parity Argument

Both the symmetry argument and the compresence argument put pressure on property dualists. At the very least, it is incumbent on proponents of property dualism to explain why these arguments fail. These include both theorists like Kim (2005), who endorse property dualism and forcefully reject substance dualism, and theorists like Jackson (1982, 1986) and Chalmers (1996, 2010) who endorse property dualism whilst withholding assent from or distancing themselves from nonphysical substances.

Still, there is dialectical room for property dualists to resist the symmetry argument and the compresence argument by rejecting the symmetry principle or the compresence principle. There is a third line of argument that, I claim, leaves little dialectical room for revolt, at least for property dualists who accept the soundness of the conceivability argument. (As I explain in § 7.5, this should and does include most property dualists.) The third argument says that if you accept the conceivability argument then, by parity of reasoning, you must accept a cousin of Descartes's disembodiment argument, with the conclusion that there are nonphysical substances.

I call this the parity argument. The advantage of the parity argument is that it does not rely on any novel principle. Instead, it aims to show that the existence of nonphysical substances follows directly from the explicit commitments of property dualists. In this section, I give a first approximation of the parity argument and distinguish two kinds of objections that property dualists might make. I present the argument in detail in the next chapter and explain why the objections do not seem promising.

106 *The Strangeness of Property Dualism*

5.5.1 Phenomenal Properties Seem Complete

Like the symmetry argument and the compresence argument, the parity argument attempts to bring out the intuitive strangeness of property dualism. The symmetry argument focussed on the fact that the physical component of a conscious human, like Searle's cake, does not seem to need the phenomenal component (the frosting) to exist. The parity argument focusses on the fact that the phenomenal component, like Searle's frosting, does not seem to need the physical component (the cake) either.

Arguably the term 'component' implies substancehood. If so, it should be understood loosely here. The important intuition is that phenomenal properties do not depend on physical properties any more than physical properties depend on phenomenal properties: conscious experiences do not strike us as metaphysically incomplete for want of cerebral matter. Adopting the language of the conceivability argument, the phenomenal facts about the world do not 'a priori entail' the existence of anything physical.

It is worth noticing the difference this creates between phenomenal and physical properties on the one hand and the pairs of properties that usually go together on the other. Typically, when a pair of properties can be strictly compresent, they do not merely fit well, they actually require one another as a matter of conceptual necessity. You cannot have pitch without timbre, or timbre without pitch, likewise shape and size.

Conceptually at least, this is not the case for physical and phenomenal properties. Physical properties do not seem incomplete in the absence of phenomenal properties, and phenomenal properties do not seem incomplete in the absence of physical properties. You can tell from the armchair that a timbre must be of some pitch and volume, but not that a pain must have some extension or mass.

If physical and phenomenal properties can be strictly compresent in the same substance, it is natural to expect that they should stand in the same kind of conceptual relationship as other properties that are capable of doing so. The fact that they disappoint this expectation makes the picture to which property dualists are committed suspiciously inelegant. This is plausibly regarded as a sign that something has gone wrong.

A sign is not an argument. But the fact that the phenomenal properties do not seem to a priori entail the existence of physical properties can also be turned into a powerful deductive argument against positing nonphysical properties without nonphysical substances, at least insofar as the motivation for positing nonphysical properties includes the conceivability argument.

5.5.2 The Phenomenal Disembodiment Argument

As I formulated it earlier in this chapter, the conceivability argument begins with the premiss that the physical facts about the world do not a priori

The Strangeness of Property Dualism   107

entail the existence of consciousness. It infers, via modal rationalism, that the physical facts do not necessitate the existence of consciousness. This formulation captures the important elements of Chalmers's (1996, 2002, 2006, 2010) classic presentations.

Proponents of the conceivability argument conclude that consciousness is something over and above physical things. However, there is a further conclusion that we might draw. If the physical facts do not necessitate the existence of conscious experience, it seems to follow that the physical things, taken together, could exist by themselves and hence that physical reality is a substance or has substances as parts.

The reasoning by which this inference is drawn is fairly direct. If reality comprises physical things and phenomenal things and the existence of the physical things does not necessitate the existence of the phenomenal things, then the physical things, taken together, seem to be metaphysically complete. If the restriction on simplicity criteria suggested in § 3.4 is obeyed, then the fact that physical reality is metaphysically complete entails that it is a physical substance, or that it is made up of physical substances.

Suppose, for now, that the existence of physical substances is indeed a collateral outcome of the conceivability argument. This is not in itself a problem for property dualists (though I have already indicated how it might create trouble in combination with the symmetry principle). But the fact, if it is a fact, that this conclusion follows from the conceivability argument is a serious problem.

This is because it will then be possible to formulate a disembodiment argument for the existence of *nonphysical* substances by transposing references to the physical and the phenomenal in the conceivability argument. The resulting argument, which forms the core of the parity argument, will go as follows:

(i) The phenomenal facts do not a priori entail the existence of anything physical.

(ii) If the phenomenal facts do not a priori entail the existence of anything physical, then they do not necessitate the existence of anything physical.

(iii) Therefore, the phenomenal facts do not necessitate the existence of anything physical.

This is a disembodiment argument because (i)–(iii) concern the existence of mental things in the absence of physical things. In effect, (i) says that we can conceive of the phenomenal facts obtaining in the absence of anything physical, and (ii) and (iii) reason that this is therefore possible. This argument differs from Descartes's disembodiment argument in two respects, however.

108 *The Strangeness of Property Dualism*

Firstly, when Descartes delivers his disembodiment argument (e.g. AT VII 78), his main purpose is to show that mind and body are distinct. The substancehood of the mind is at most a secondary issue. Secondly, Descartes' formulation focuses on the subject of experience, picked out by the first-person pronoun, 'I,' whereas the present argument speaks impersonally of the phenomenal facts.

The first difference is one of emphasis. Descartes is not writing for property dualists, and so his foremost concern is the distinctness of mind and body, rather than the substancehood of minds. The second difference is more important. For one objection to Descartes's argument is that indexicals such as 'I' introduce a gap between conceivability and possibility. This objection to Descartes's personal disembodiment argument does not apply to the impersonal phenomenal disembodiment argument introduced here.

5.5.3 The Parity Argument

The phenomenal disembodiment argument is not the parity argument. Rather, the parity argument is a Matryoshka argument that contains the phenomenal disembodiment argument within it. It goes as follows:

(i) If you accept the conceivability argument, you must accept the phenomenal disembodiment argument.
(ii) If you accept the phenomenal disembodiment argument, then you must accept the existence of nonphysical substances.
(iii) Therefore, if you accept the conceivability argument, then you must accept the existence of nonphysical substances.

This is a valid hypothetical syllogism. So, if (i) and (ii) are true, then proponents of the conceivability argument must accept the existence of nonphysical substances. This would be tremendously significant for present-day philosophy of mind. For on the one hand, many present-day theorists accept the conceivability argument (Bourget and Chalmers's (2022, 12) data suggest the figure is about 24.4%). But on the other hand, nonphysical substances are widely scorned, as the quotations in § 2.1 illustrated.

The critical question, then, is whether (i) and (ii) are true. I explain why (i) and (ii) seem to be correct in the next chapter. It happens that Goff (2010, 2012, 2014) defends roughly premiss (i) of the parity argument in developing an objection to Russellian monism and analytic functionalism. I make use of Goff's discussion in defending this premiss in § 6.1.2. It is clear that Goff would reject (ii) of the parity argument, however. In § 6.4, I explain why the kind of objection Goff is likely to raise against (ii) fails.

6 Parity of Reasoning Demands Nonphysical Substances

There is something strange about property dualism as a response to the mind-body problem when it is looked at closely. Chapter 5 set out three strategies for arguing that the strangeness of property dualism is due to its incoherence: the symmetry argument, the compresence argument, and the parity argument. The symmetry argument and the compresence argument suggest that property dualism distorts the ordinary relationship between properties and their bearers in a way that is at best counterintuitive. The parity argument suggests that the commitments of a leading argument for property dualism, the conceivability argument, entail that there are nonphysical substances. This chapter defends the parity argument in detail.

6.1 If Zombies Are Conceivable, Then Ghosts Are Conceivable

Premiss (i) of the parity argument says that if you accept the conceivability argument, you must accept the phenomenal disembodiment argument. Like the conceivability argument, the phenomenal disembodiment argument has two premisses: an epistemic premiss of the form 'φ does not a priori entail χ', and a conditional premiss of the form 'if φ does not a priori entail χ then φ does not necessitate χ.' The only difference is that the phenomenal disembodiment argument reverses references to the physical and the phenomenal in φ and χ.

Proponents of the conceivability argument should accept premiss one of the phenomenal disembodiment argument because it is supported by parallel and equally compelling thought experiments to those that support premiss one of the conceivability argument. Proponents of the conceivability argument should accept premiss two of the phenomenal disembodiment argument because it follows from the modal rationalism that supports premiss two of the conceivability argument. I now explain this in detail.

DOI: 10.4324/9781003378600-7

110 *Parity of Reasoning Demands Nonphysical Substances*

6.1.1 Zombies Are Conceivable

Premiss one of the conceivability argument says that the physical facts about the world do not a priori entail the existence of conscious experience. Chalmers (2010, 108, 142) suggests that this can be put more precisely by saying that it is conceivable that P and not Q, where P is the conjunction of all microphysical truths about the world, specified in the language of microphysics, and Q is an arbitrary phenomenal truth, such as the truth that you are now beholding this text, or simply the fact that someone is conscious.

This restriction of P to the microphysical truths presupposes that macroscopic physical things are nothing over and above the microscopic things. This is not obviously correct. It conflicts with some views of quantum entanglement, for example. Neither is this restriction necessary, however. Instead, we can think of P as the conjunction of physical truths specified in the language of physics, with the now-familiar requirement that this should exclude truths that involve the existence of fundamentally mental things.

Premiss one of the conceivability argument is supported by thought experiments. The leading example is the zombie-world scenario. It seems that we can coherently conceive of an exact physical duplicate of the actual world without any of the conscious experiences. Premiss one can also be supported, indirectly, by the Mary scenario, and for some specifications of Q, by other scenarios (cf. Chalmers 1996, 99–106).

What seems conceivable can turn out to be inconceivable on further reflection. For example, initially, it seems that different answers to complex mathematical problems could be true. But persistent reflection reveals that only one option is possible. For this reason, Chalmers (2002, 2–4) suggests that premiss one should be understood as the claim that the physical facts do not entail the existence of consciousness even on 'ideal a priori reflection' where this is a priori reflection that cannot be defeated by better a priori reflection.

In Bourget and Chalmers's (2022, 12) latest survey, 981 philosophers surveyed accept or lean towards the view that zombies are conceivable (including those who favour the view that zombies are possible), compared to just 264 who accept or lean towards the view that they are inconceivable. So, insofar as sustained a priori reflection by humans is a guide to ideal a priori reflection, there should be widespread agreement that the zombies thought experiment supports premiss one of the conceivability argument.

Premiss one of the conceivability argument is rejected by a minority who say that adequate a priori reflection on the physical facts is enough, on its own, to reveal the facts concerning conscious experience. Proponents of this view typically endorse analytical functionalism, the thesis that phenomenal properties are, as a matter of conceptual necessity, functional

Parity of Reasoning Demands Nonphysical Substances   111

properties (Putnam 1967; Shoemaker 1975) or the realisers of functional properties (Lewis 1966; Armstrong 1968). However, analytical functionalism is deservedly unpopular.

6.1.2 Ghosts Are Conceivable

Premiss one of the phenomenal disembodiment argument can be supported by equally compelling thought experiments. This premiss says that the phenomenal facts about the world do not a priori entail the existence of anything physical. In parallel with Chalmers (2010), we might put this more precisely by saying that it is conceivable that 'Q and not P,' where Q is the conjunction of phenomenal truths, specified in phenomenal language, and P is an arbitrary physical truth.

In defending premiss one of the phenomenal disembodiment argument, it is useful to make use of Goff's (2010, 2012, 2014) concept of a ghost. Ghosts are the phenomenal equivalent of zombies: a ghost is 'a creature whose being is exhausted by its being conscious, by there being something that it is like to be it' (Goff 2010, 123). Someone's 'ghost twin' is a purely phenomenal duplicate of that person:

> My ghost twin is a creature that has qualitatively identical conscious experience to me – what it is like to be my ghost twin is exactly the same as what it is like to be me – but whose nature is exhausted by its conscious experience.
>
> (Goff 2010, 124)

Premiss one of the phenomenal disembodiment argument can be supported by a ghost-world thought experiment that parallels the zombie-world thought experiment. The ghost world is a phenomenal duplicate of the actual world that is populated entirely by ghosts: a world like ours but where idealism is true. If the ghost world is conceivable, premiss one of the phenomenal disembodiment argument is true.

To capture the idea that the ghost world contains only ghosts, we can add a 'that's-all' clause, T, to 'Q and not P' in the formal expression of premiss one of the phenomenal disembodiment argument. Chalmers (2010, 143) proposes the same addition to the conceivability argument to capture Jackson's (1998, 26) idea that the zombie world should be a *minimal* physical duplicate. So, the official version of premiss one says that 'Q and not P, and T' is conceivable.

It is likely that anyone who accepts that the zombie world is conceivable will accept that the ghost world is conceivable. For these claims reflect the same philosophical spirit. They arise out of the same kind of reflection, based on the same trust in our pretheoretical physical and phenomenal concepts.

112 *Parity of Reasoning Demands Nonphysical Substances*

Furthermore, the conceivability of the ghost world seems to follow from Descartes's observation that you can coherently doubt that there exists anything beyond your own conscious states, whilst continuing to affirm the existence of those conscious states. Goff defends the conceivability of ghosts on these grounds:

> The arms and legs you seem to see in front of you, the heart you seem to feel beating beneath your breast, your body that feels solid and warm to the touch, all may be figments of a particularly powerful delusion. You might not even have a brain. ... [Nonetheless] you know for certain that you are a thing that has an experience as of having arms and legs, a beating heart, a warm, solid body.
>
> (Goff 2010, 124)

Chalmers (1996) endorses roughly the same view when he says,

> It is compatible with our experiential evidence that the world we think we are seeing does not exist; perhaps we are hallucinating, or we are brains in vats. This problem can be seen to arise precisely because the facts about the external world do not supervene logically on the facts about our experience.
>
> (Chalmers 1996, 75)

If it is true that you can coherently doubt the existence of anything beyond your conscious states, it seems to follow that your ghost twin is conceivable. If so, the ghost world is presumably conceivable too.

The main objection to the conceivability of the zombie world comes from analytical functionalism. The same is true of the ghost world. If it is a conceptual truth that phenomenal properties are functional properties, the ghost world should be inconceivable after all because it contains functional properties without realisers. Theorists who accept the conceivability of the zombie world standardly reject analytical functionalism, however, and so they will not see this as an obstacle to the conceivability of the ghost world. (Goff (2012) uses the conceivability of ghosts to argue against analytical functionalism.)

For these reasons, it seems that proponents of the conceivability argument should accept premiss one of the phenomenal disembodiment argument. At the very least, to refuse to do so without some explanation as to why these cases differ would seem to betray a double standard.

There is no reason to suppose that proponents of the conceivability argument will expose themselves to this criticism. The above quotations suggest that Chalmers and Goff would accept premiss one of the phenomenal disembodiment argument. The same is likely to be true of many others.

Parity of Reasoning Demands Nonphysical Substances 113

As Goff says, few people read Descartes's *Meditations* 1 and 2, and think 'I don't know where he's going with this. ... I can't get into Descartes' mind-set at all!' This is because most people find that ghosts are conceivable.

It seems likely, therefore, that premiss one of the phenomenal disembodiment argument, like premiss one of the conceivability argument, will be relatively uncontroversial, all the more so amongst proponents of the conceivability argument. The next two sections focus on showing that proponents of the conceivability argument must accept premiss two of the phenomenal disembodiment argument as well. I consider one final way of resisting premiss one of the phenomenal disembodiment argument in § 7.4.

6.2 Modal Rationalism and Zombies

Premiss two of the conceivability argument says that if the physical facts do not a priori entail the existence of consciousness, then they do not necessitate the existence of consciousness. In Chalmers's symbolism, if P and not Q is conceivable, then P and not Q is possible. This is an expression of modal rationalism, the claim that, in some cases at least, conceivability is a reliable guide to possibility.

Modal rationalism is controversial and so too, for this reason, is premiss two of the conceivability argument. Hence, whilst 60.9% of philosophers accept or lean towards the claim that zombies are conceivable, Bourget and Chalmers (2022, 12) report that only 24.4% accept or lean towards the claim that zombies are metaphysically possible. The other 36.5% implicitly reject modal rationalism.

The main objection to premiss two of the conceivability argument says that the fact that a physical duplicate of our world must include the conscious experiences could be an a posteriori necessity of the kind identified by Kripke (1972) and Putnam (1973). Proponents of the conceivability argument take great care to respond to this objection and to explain why the modal rationalism they endorse remains plausible.

The best-known response to this objection is Chalmers's (2006, 2010) appeal to two-dimensional semantics. More recently, Nida-Rümelin (2007) and Goff (2014, 2017) have defended a simpler but closely related approach that appeals to the 'transparency' of phenomenal concepts. For reasons I explain in a moment, the two approaches come to the same thing as far as the parity argument is concerned.

6.2.1 The Two-Dimensional Strategy

The main insight of the two-dimensional response is that the intensions of some terms are determined by empirical factors. 'Water' is a classic example. It is usually accepted that 'water' rigidly designates the natural kind

114 *Parity of Reasoning Demands Nonphysical Substances*

H_2O (cf. Kripke 1972). That is, the term 'water' refers to H_2O across all possible worlds. If so, the statement 'water is H_2O' expresses a necessary truth. Even so, intuitively, in the unlikely scenario that we discover that the liquid we have been calling 'water' is actually XYZ, we will say that water is not H_2O after all, but XYZ.

This is odd. How can we say that water is necessarily H_2O and yet that we are ready to call XYZ water, should the circumstances develop in the right way? Two-dimensional semantics offers an explanation: our use of 'water' is, in a sense, deferential. That is, we defer to empirical reality to determine the necessary and sufficient conditions for counting as 'water' and therefore what counts as water in counterfactual scenarios. To do so, however, we must first pick out the actual stuff whose empirical essence completes the meaning of the term.

It follows that there are two layers in the meaning of 'water,' which explain the divergence of our intuitions about how to use 'water' in hypotheses about the actual world and in descriptions of counterfactual worlds. The function from how the world actually is to the extension of 'water' in the actual world is the term's 'primary intension.' The function from the empirical nature of the thing that satisfies the primary intension to the extension of 'water' in counterfactual worlds is its 'secondary intension.'

Reflection on hypotheses about how the actual world is suggests that the primary intension of 'water' picks out roughly the clear drinkable liquid that predominates in lakes, rivers, and oceans. So, the primary intension of 'water' is approximated by the description 'clear liquid in lakes and rivers.' Reflection on counterfactual worlds suggests that the secondary intension of 'water' picks out whatever natural kind satisfies the primary intension of 'water' in the actual world: if water is actually H_2O, then water is H_2O in all counterfactual worlds.

'Water' is one of many terms that appear to have primary intensions that determine their actual extension and secondary intensions that pick out the same thing across all possible worlds. Sentences, in turn, derive primary and secondary intensions from those of their nonlogical terms. For example, the primary intension of 'water is H_2O' is roughly captured by 'the clear liquid in lakes and rivers is H_2O,' and the secondary intension of 'water is H_2O' is roughly captured by 'H_2O is H_2O' (supposing we are right about the actual nature of water).

Two-dimensional semantics suggests that wherever the primary and secondary intensions of a claim differ, there will be a gap between conceivability and possibility. For a priori reflection, however ideal, will not be a reliable guide to the possibility of the secondary intension of a claim, in the absence of the empirical data needed to discern what the secondary intension of that claim is. If you need empirical data to know that 'water is H_2O'

Parity of Reasoning Demands Nonphysical Substances   115

expresses the same proposition as 'H$_2$O is H$_2$O' rather than the same proposition as 'XYZ is H$_2$O,' then you are not in a position to know a priori that 'water is H$_2$O' expresses a true proposition.

However, this limitation on modal rationalism is a blessing in disguise. For it suggests that it is not any deficiency of reason in discerning possibility from impossibility that prevents us from knowing a priori some statements that express necessary truths. It is merely that we do not know what contingently belongs in the extension of the primary intension of terms such as 'H$_2$O.' If so, then our inability to know a priori that water is H$_2$O turns out to be an example of our ordinary inability to know contingent truths a priori.

Two-dimensional semantics is therefore a false friend to opponents of modal rationalism. It places a constraint on our ability to know a priori that some claims express necessary truths. But in doing so, it removes the main objection to the thesis that modal rationalism is otherwise true. For what holds of the 'water is H$_2$O' example plausibly holds for all Kripkean a posteriori necessities. If so, there remains no threat to our long-held suspicion that we can know necessary claims a priori, *once we know what propositions they express*.

Two-dimensional semantics, then, suggests that the leading objection to modal rationalism is only relevant to claims whose primary and secondary intensions differ. If this is correct, then the only way that objection could undermine premiss two of the conceivability argument is if the primary and secondary intensions of P or Q differ. Either this will be because the primary and secondary intensions of phenomenal terms differ or because the primary and secondary intensions of physical terms differ.

The first option is implausible. For phenomenal terms are intuitively one-dimensional, or 'semantically neutral,' as Chalmers puts it. That is, we seem to use phenomenal terms to refer to exactly those qualities by which we determine their actual extension. 'Pain' is a classic example. Intuitively, nothing could count as pain without feeling painful in the way that something can have the chemical structure of water without filling lakes, and nothing could feel painful without being pain in the way that XYZ might fill lakes without being water. We do not seem to use 'pain' for an empirically determined essence.

Besides which, proponents of the conceivability argument can simply stipulate that they are using phenomenal terms for those qualities by which we actually identify their referents. Or, they can introduce a different term for those qualities, referring to them as the 'feelings' or 'modes of presentation' of phenomenal states, and run the conceivability argument for these instead, as Chalmers (1996, 149; 2010, 153) suggests. Either way, premiss two of the conceivability argument appears to be safe from the objection that phenomenal terms have different primary and secondary intensions.

116 *Parity of Reasoning Demands Nonphysical Substances*

The second option is that premiss two is false because the primary and secondary intensions of physical terms differ. This would mean that terms like 'mass,' 'charge,' and so on rigidly designate some underlying essence such that (1) a physical duplicate of the actual world that excludes the hidden essence does not necessitate the existence of consciousness, but (2) a physical duplicate of the actual world that includes the hidden essence does necessitate the existence of consciousness.

Proponents of the conceivability argument usually accept that this is a coherent possibility. However, they point out that the result is not regular physicalism but Russellian monism (e.g. Chalmers 2010, 152). Proponents of the conceivability argument typically accept that *either* the argument is sound *or* Russellian monism obtains. It is not clear whether the argument permits any kind of Russellian monism or anti-physicalist kind only. This depends on whether *any* fundamentally nonmental thing could a priori entail the existence of consciousness. Chalmers is open to this possibility; Strawson (2006, 24) dismisses it out of hand.

6.2.2 *The Transparent Concepts Strategy*

Two-dimensional semantics provides an independently motivated framework that seems to vindicate the conceivability argument, despite the existence of Kripkean a posteriori necessities. However, Nida-Rümelin (2007) and Goff (2014, 2017) point out that it is possible to adopt largely the same line of defence by focussing on our intuitions about phenomenal concepts and ignoring the wider semantic picture. Because Nida-Rümelin does not set out the application to the conceivability argument, I follow Goff's (2017) exposition.

Goff (2017, 74) proposes that some concepts are 'transparent' in the following sense: a concept C of a referent E is transparent if and only if what it is for E to be part of reality is a priori accessible to anyone who possesses C in virtue of possessing C. Goff suggests that the concept of sphericity is a plausible example:

> For the property of sphericity to be instantiated is for there to be something with all points on its surface equidistant from its center; if you possess the concept of sphericity, and you're clever enough, you can work that out from the armchair.
>
> (Goff 2017, 15–16)

Goff argues that direct phenomenal concepts are also transparent. A direct phenomenal concept is a phenomenal concept of a conscious state such that the content of the concept is wholly based on attending to that state

Parity of Reasoning Demands Nonphysical Substances 117

(cf. Chalmers, 2003). For example, the concept you form of a shade of red by looking at something that colour is a direct phenomenal concept.

Goff's (2017, 107–8) case for thinking that direct phenomenal concepts (henceforth just 'phenomenal concepts') are transparent is based on the plausibility of the claim he calls 'Revelation.' Revelation is the thesis that when you attend to a phenomenal state and form a phenomenal concept of it, you know exactly what it is for someone to be in that state, and you know with something close to certainty that you are in that state. Revelation suggests that phenomenal concepts are transparent.

Goff provides two reasons for believing Revelation. Firstly, he suggests that 'calm and careful meditation' on the doctrine reveals it to be true. Secondly, he proposes that Revelation is the best explanation for the near certainty with which we are able to know introspective truths. More recently, Michelle Liu (2021) has provided empirical support for the thesis that Revelation is part of our ordinary, implicit conception of experience. Arguments for Revelation deserve independent treatment. But the intuitive appeal of the thesis is obvious. Plausibly, if you know anything at all, you know what your current experiences are like, just by having them.

Transparent concepts are closely related to semantically neutral terms. If you are using a term to express a transparent concept, then it seems that your use of that term must be semantically neutral. For if you are using the term to express a transparent concept, then you do not need to defer to empirical reality to determine its secondary intension: you already know what it is for the referent to be a part of reality.

Likewise, if your use of a term is semantically neutral, then it seems that you must be using it to express a transparent concept. For if you are able to identify the extension of that term across possible worlds, then you must know what it is for the thing or things in the extension to be a part of reality.

Even if the connection between transparent concepts and semantically neutral terms is not as tight as this in all cases, it seems likely that the transparency of phenomenal concepts is the intuitive root of the judgement that phenomenal terms are semantically neutral. It is also plausible that phenomenal terms express transparent concepts because we use them to name the qualities by which we identify their actual extensions.

Proponents of phenomenal transparency can ignore the semantic theory and defend premiss two of the conceivability argument directly. For they can take the view that Kripkean a posteriori necessities like 'water is H_2O' are cases that comprise one or more terms that express opaque (i.e. non-transparent) concepts. For example, 'water' expresses an opaque concept, because you can have the concept without knowing that for water to exist is for H_2O to exist. This parallels the claim that the primary and secondary intensions of 'water' differ.

118 *Parity of Reasoning Demands Nonphysical Substances*

Proponents of phenomenal transparency can take the view that the main challenge to modal rationalism is only relevant to claims whose terms express opaque concepts. If so, modal rationalism remains plausible for claims expressed by transparent concepts. This is Goff's (2017, 100) 'Transparency Conceivability Principle.'

The defence of premiss two of the conceivability argument then follows the same structure as it does on the appeal to two-dimensional semantics. If premiss two is false, this must be because either phenomenal or physical terms express opaque concepts. Proponents of phenomenal transparency hold that phenomenal concepts are transparent. So, if premiss two is false, this must be because physical concepts are opaque concepts of things whose underlying nature necessitates the existence of consciousness. This is Russellian monism.

Theorists who defend premiss two of the conceivability argument by appeal to two-dimensional semantics or phenomenal transparency still need some justification for endorsing modal rationalism about primary intensions, or about transparent concepts. For otherwise the fact that a physical duplicate of our world must contain conscious experiences might be what Chalmers calls a 'strong necessity': a necessary a posteriori truth that cannot be explained away in the way that Kripkean examples can.

However, once the objection raised by Kripkean examples has been defeated, our original intuition that modal rationalism is true arguably becomes the deciding factor, at least in the absence of clear counterexamples (cf. Chalmers 2010, 170–84). Goff (2017, 123–4) provides some further arguments for accepting modal rationalism about claims expressed using transparent concepts. Cleeveley (2022) does the same for semantically neutral terms.

Elsewhere, I mean to add a defence of modal rationalism about semantically neutral terms/those that express transparent concepts of my own. In short: semantic knowledge is knowledge of intensions, intensions are functions over possible worlds, therefore (however mysteriously, and whether we like it or not) semantic knowledge just is modal metaphysical knowledge. But since my object here is not to defend the conceivability argument but to argue that those who accept the conceivability argument must accept the phenomenal disembodiment argument, I need not enter into this issue here.

In addition to allowing us to ignore wider semantics, Goff (2017, 100–1) suggests that it is an advantage of the phenomenal-transparency approach that it avoids the implication that all terms have primary intensions. Goff sees this feature of two-dimensional semantics as a drawback because it rules out terms that express 'radically opaque' concepts that reveal 'no significant properties' of their referents and because of this 'do not have primary intensions' (Goff 2017, 91, 100).

It is not clear that this is a genuine drawback, however. For it is hard to see how a term could lack a primary intension whilst retaining a meaning.

Parity of Reasoning Demands Nonphysical Substances 119

This idea is reminiscent of Carnap's (1932) example of the person who claims that the word 'teavy' has a meaning, but cannot say for any hypothesis about how the world is, what things are teavy:

> If the person who uses the word says that all the same there are things which are teavy and there are things which are not teavy, only it remains for the weak, finite intellect of man an eternal secret which things are teavy and which are not, we shall regard this as empty verbiage.
>
> (Carnap 1932, 64)

Still, the transparency approach is simpler, and I favour its terminology in what follows. Everything I say about terms that express transparent concepts is intended to apply to terms that are semantically neutral.

6.3 Modal Rationalism and Ghosts

This section explains why proponents of the conceivability argument must accept premiss two of the phenomenal disembodiment argument. I also explain why the phenomenal disembodiment argument, unlike the conceivability argument, leaves no room for physicalist Russellian monism. This means that the phenomenal disembodiment argument delivers a stronger conclusion than the conceivability argument on the basis of the same commitments about modal rationalism, even before we consider nonphysical substances.

6.3.1 Modal Rationalism and Phenomenal Disembodiment

Premiss two of the phenomenal disembodiment argument says that if the phenomenal facts do not a priori entail the existence of anything physical, then they do not necessitate the existence of anything physical. More precisely, if Q and not P is conceivable, then Q and not P is possible, where Q is the conjunction of the phenomenal truths, and P is an arbitrary physical truth.

The commitments of the conceivability argument suggest that there are only two ways in which premiss two of the phenomenal disembodiment argument could be false. Either because phenomenal terms express opaque concepts or because physical terms express opaque concepts.

Proponents of the conceivability argument cannot reject premiss two on the grounds that phenomenal terms express opaque concepts. For this would undermine premiss two of the conceivability argument as well. So, if proponents of the conceivability argument can reject premiss two of the phenomenal disembodiment argument, this must be on the grounds that physical terms express opaque concepts.

120 *Parity of Reasoning Demands Nonphysical Substances*

However, if you accept premiss one of the phenomenal disembodiment argument, and you reject premiss two because physical terms express opaque concepts, then this must be because physical concepts are opaque concepts of things whose underlying nature is necessitated by the phenomenal facts. This is an expression of Russellian monism. So, as with the conceivability argument, the objection to premiss two on the basis that physical terms express opaque concepts results in Russellian monism.

So, if you accept that either the conceivability argument is sound, or that Russellian monism is true on the basis that phenomenal concepts are transparent, then you must accept the same in the case of the phenomenal disembodiment argument as well. At this stage, however, an important disanalogy between the two arguments emerges, which reveals the superior firepower of the phenomenal disembodiment argument.

As we have seen, it is possible to reject premiss two of the conceivability argument on the basis that physical concepts are opaque concepts of things whose underlying nature *necessitates* the existence of consciousness. Likewise, it seems that one can reject premiss two of the phenomenal disembodiment argument on the basis that physical concepts are opaque concepts of things whose underlying nature *is necessitated by* the phenomenal facts. The result, in both cases, is Russellian monism, but the direction of necessitation is reversed.

The difference in the direction of necessitation means that whilst the physical-opacity response makes room for physicalist Russellian monism in the case of the conceivability argument, it only leaves room for anti-physicalist Russellian monism in the case of the phenomenal disembodiment argument. For the physical-opacity response, in the case of the phenomenal disembodiment argument, says that the underlying nature of the physical things is necessitated by the phenomenal facts. Equivalently, the physical opacity response to the phenomenal disembodiment argument says that physical concepts refer to things that survive in the ghost world. As I specified in § 6.1, following Goff, the nature of things in the ghost world is exhausted by their conscious experience. So, if the physical concepts are concepts of things that survive in the ghost world, it follows that the things they pick out are fundamentally mental.

If this is true of all physical concepts expressed by the terms in P (the conjunction of the physical facts expressed in the technical vocabulary of physics), then idealist Russellian monism follows. If it is only true of some of the physical concepts expressed by P, then dualist Russellian monism follows. Physicalist Russellian monism, including the position Chalmers calls 'panprotopsychism,' is ruled out by the commitments of the conceivability argument as deployed in the phenomenal disembodiment argument.

Strikingly, this means that the opacity of physical concepts cannot be used to challenge premiss two of the phenomenal disembodiment argument

Parity of Reasoning Demands Nonphysical Substances   121

after all. For that premiss says that if the phenomenal facts do not a priori entail the existence of anything physical, then they do not necessitate the existence of anything physical. If we are using 'physical' in the descriptive sense in which it appears in the definition of physicalism, then the consequent of this conditional is compatible with the claim that the phenomenal facts necessitate the existence of things that are 'physical' in a merely referential sense, whilst in fact being fundamentally mental.

It follows that, whereas the modal rationalism appealed to by proponents of the conceivability argument implies that either premiss two of the conceivability argument is true, or that Russellian monism obtains, the same commitments imply unambiguously that premiss two of the phenomenal disembodiment argument is true. Proponents of the conceivability argument must accept that if the phenomenal facts do not a priori entail the existence of anything physical, then they do not necessitate the existence of anything physical either.

6.3.2 *Premiss (i) of the Parity Argument Is True*

I have already explained in § 6.1 why proponents of the conceivability argument must accept premiss one of the phenomenal disembodiment argument. I have now explained in § 6.3 why they must also accept premiss two of the phenomenal disembodiment argument. If so, then proponents of the conceivability argument must accept the phenomenal disembodiment argument, as premiss (i) of the parity argument claims.

6.4 Phenomenal Disembodiment and Nonphysical Substances

Proponents of the conceivability argument, then, must accept the phenomenal disembodiment argument. One consequence, I have claimed, is that proponents of the conceivability argument must reject physicalist forms of Russellian monism. That is a significant conclusion in itself. However, premiss (ii) of the parity argument says that there is a further consequence that is more significant still: if you accept the phenomenal disembodiment argument then you must accept the existence of nonphysical substances.

It is likely that premiss (ii) of the parity argument will initially elicit dissent. For, as I explain in a moment, (ii) seems to conflict with an important restriction on modal rationalism that proponents of the conceivability argument tend to endorse. Having explained this, I will explain why (ii) of the parity argument does not in fact rely on any modal rationalism beyond that which proponents of the conceivability argument must accept. If so, premiss (ii) of the parity argument is also secure, and we should judge the argument sound.

122 *Parity of Reasoning Demands Nonphysical Substances*

6.4.1 *The Intuitive Case for Premiss (ii)*

Premiss (ii) of the parity argument is a claim about what follows from the conclusion of the phenomenal disembodiment argument. It is therefore a claim about what follows from the thesis that the phenomenal facts do not necessitate the existence of anything physical, that Q and not P is possible.

Premiss (ii) of the parity argument expresses the idea that, just as the conclusion of the conceivability argument seems to entail that there exist physical substances, the conclusion of the phenomenal disembodiment argument seems to entail that there exist nonphysical substances. For if reality comprises physical things and phenomenal things, and the existence of the phenomenal things does not necessitate the existence of the physical things, then the phenomenal things, taken together, are metaphysically complete. It follows that either phenomenal reality is itself a nonphysical substance or (inclusive) it is made up of nonphysical substances.

Pending some objection, premiss (ii) of the parity argument seems appealing. Because the threat posed by the phenomenal disembodiment argument to property dualism has gone unrecognised, objections in the literature are scarce. However, property dualist responses to existing disembodiment arguments such as Descartes's and Kripke's suggest an important challenge to premiss (ii) of the parity argument, which I introduce step by step in the next four subsections. I set out an optional response in § 6.4.6 which I believe is successful, but which proponents of the conceivability argument could consistently reject. I present a better response in § 6.4.8 which proponents of the conceivability argument must, in my judgement, accept.

6.4.2 *Descartes's and Kripke's Disembodiment Arguments*

As I mentioned in § 5.5, Descartes's is a *personal* disembodiment argument in the sense that it starts from the thesis that *my* existence (including my current conscious states) does not a priori entail the existence of anything physical: it is conceivable that I do not have a body. From this, the argument infers that I could in fact exist without anything physical. The argument concludes that I am distinct from my body.

The most influential disembodiment argument since Descartes's is Kripke's (1972), advanced over the final twelve pages of 'Naming and Necessity.' In fact, Kripke outlines several different arguments, all of which aim to undermine versions of the identity theory. The relevant argument here is Kripke's (1972, 336–7) disembodiment argument against the token-identity theory.

Unlike Descartes's argument, Kripke's focusses on phenomenal and physical things described impersonally: a particular pain '*A*' and the particular

Parity of Reasoning Demands Nonphysical Substances   123

brain state with which *A* is reputed to be identical, '*B.*' The argument begins with the premiss that we can conceive of pain *A* existing without brain state *B*. It infers that pain *A* could in fact exist without brain state *B*. The argument concludes that *A* and *B* are not identical. (Instead of conceivability, Kripke talks about what 'seems possible' but this is a fair reconstruction nonetheless.)

Descartes restricts his modal rationalism to claims about things of which we have a 'clear and distinct idea.' This can be seen as an anticipation of Nida-Rümelin and Goff's transparency approach to ruling out a posteriori necessities (cf. Goff 2014, 10). Kripke employs what is usually seen as the 'blueprint' for the two-dimensional semantic strategy (García-Carpintero and Macià 2006, 2).

It might be a collateral consequence of Descartes's and Kripke's arguments that there exist nonphysical substances. However, the details would have to be filled in to show that this follows. Whether or not they entail the existence of nonphysical substances, these arguments resemble the phenomenal disembodiment argument sufficiently that we might expect some objections to Descartes's and Kripke's arguments to be relevant to the phenomenal disembodiment argument as well.

6.4.3 Objections to Descartes and Kripke

Chalmers (1996, 2010) and Goff (2010, 2014, 2017) reject Descartes's argument. Chalmers (1996) also rejects Kripke's argument. For reasons I will explain, their objections do not directly apply to the phenomenal disembodiment argument, but they do point to an objection to premiss (ii) of the parity argument: the claim that if you accept the phenomenal disembodiment argument, then you must posit nonphysical substances.

Chalmers (2002, 195–6; 2010, 199–200) rejects Descartes's argument because it could be an a posteriori necessity that I am embodied. If so then the second premiss of Descartes's argument would be false. If Chalmers's objection is consistent with the commitments of the conceivability argument outlined in § 6.2, this must be because the claim that 'I am embodied' contains terms that express opaque concepts.

Although Chalmers does not specify the guilty term, it is probable that he has in mind the indexical 'I.' If this is right, then Goff (2010, 2014, 12) makes the same objection to Descartes's argument when he says,

> A gap between conceivability and possibility can open up when one introduces indexical reference into one's conception. This is why we cannot infer from the conceivability to the possibility of my ghost counterpart.
>
> (Goff 2010, fn. 9)

124 *Parity of Reasoning Demands Nonphysical Substances*

Goff is distinguishing here between his ghost twin and his ghost *counterpart*. A ghost twin is a phenomenal *duplicate* of a conscious human. A ghost counterpart is *that person*, in some possible world, existing as a ghost (Goff 2010, 24).

This is the classic objection to Descartes's disembodiment argument (cf. Swinburne 2018, 139). It is not obvious that it is successful. For even if some uses of indexicals express opaque concepts, it is not obvious that the term 'I,' used of oneself, does so. Nida-Rümelin (2012) and Swinburne (2018) argue for the contrary view. (Swinburne talks of 'informative designators' rather than semantically neutral terms, or terms that express transparent concepts, but the idea is largely the same.)

Still, even if 'I' does not in fact express an opaque concept, proponents of the conceivability argument are clearly not guilty of any *inconsistency* in taking the view that it does. It follows that Descartes's disembodiment argument does not pose the same threat to the consistency of property dualists' commitments that I claim for the phenomenal disembodiment argument.

Unlike Descartes's argument, Kripke's focusses on phenomenal and physical things described impersonally. Despite this, a neighbouring objection can be directed at Kripke's argument. This is because Kripke focusses, not on physical and mental things of a given character, but on a particular brain state, and a particular pain, *'that very sensation'* as Kripke (1972, 335) calls it (Kripke's emphasis). Chalmers (1996, 147–8) objects that as a result, Kripke's argument relies on 'intuitions about what counts as *that very thing* across possible worlds, and such intuitions are notoriously unreliable' (Chalmers's emphasis).

Once again, if Chalmers's objection is compatible with the commitments of the conceivability argument, then there must be some term in Kripke's argument that expresses an opaque concept. The obvious suspect is the demonstrative 'that' in *'that very sensation.'* If the indexical 'I' can introduce a gap between conceivability and possibility, then it would not be a surprise if demonstratives could do so too.

This is the classic objection to Kripke's argument (cf. Feldman 1974; McGinn 1977; Chalmers 1996, 148). Again, it is not obvious that it is successful. For even if some uses of demonstratives express opaque concepts, it is not obvious that the term 'that' used of the pain one currently feels does so. One might think that this is a case of knowledge by acquaintance *par excellence* that leaves no room for conceptual opacity to creep in.

However, proponents of the conceivability argument will not be guilty of any inconsistency in taking the view that demonstratives, used in this way, express opaque concepts, so long as the conceivability argument does not itself rely on the contrary claim. If so, Kripke's argument, like Descartes's,

Parity of Reasoning Demands Nonphysical Substances 125

does not pose the same threat to the consistency of property dualists' commitments that I claim for the phenomenal disembodiment argument.

6.4.4 Reconciling the Objection With the Conceivability Argument

The objections directed at Descartes's and Kripke's arguments say the same thing. The objection is that the claims about conceivability upon which these arguments rest do not just use phenomenal and physical terms. Instead, they combine phenomenal and physical terms with singular terms such as 'I' or 'that.' These terms are suspected of expressing opaque concepts because our intuitions about identity across worlds are 'notoriously unreliable.' So, proponents of the conceivability argument can reject modal rationalism about these claims.

If proponents of the conceivability argument can consistently reject Descartes's and Kripke's disembodiment arguments on this basis, this must be because the claims about conceivability on which their argument rests do not use the objectionable terms. That is, they must not use 'I' or 'that,' or other terms that fix the reference of our descriptions to actual things when we are describing counterfactual scenarios. (Uses of 'that' that do not fix the reference to actual things, but to some counterfactual thing already described are permissible.)

This reveals a feature of the conceivability argument that is not usually made explicit. When the argument refers to the physical and phenomenal facts, P and Q, these must not be taken to include, essentially, any of the actual physical or phenomenal things. P and Q characterise how a world is physically, and phenomenally, but they do not say that any of the *actual* physical or phenomenal things are present.

This explains why proponents of the conceivability argument emphasise that zombies are physical duplicates of actual humans, rather than the actual humans themselves without their conscious experiences. But even when talking about zombies, proponents of the conceivability argument sometimes slip into language that implies that we are talking about actual humans in nonactual worlds (e.g. Chalmers's (2010, 142) use of the phrase 'the individual in question is a zombie in a physically identical world').

It is crucial to the conceivability argument that its premises concern the conceivability and possibility of a physical *duplicate* of the actual world without conscious experience. Otherwise, proponents of the conceivability argument could not consistently reject Descartes's and Kripke's disembodiment arguments on the basis that our intuitions about identity across possible worlds are unreliable. (This is why I said in § 5.3 that it is not totally straightforward that the conceivability argument entails that physical things are metaphysically complete. The response I give in this section, if it is successful, will also vindicate that claim, however.)

126 *Parity of Reasoning Demands Nonphysical Substances*

6.4.5 *Is There a Threat to the Parity Argument?*

There are two ways that the objection to Descartes's and Kripke's disembodiment arguments might threaten the parity argument. Firstly, this objection might apply directly to the phenomenal disembodiment argument. In that case, proponents of the conceivability argument could consistently reject the phenomenal disembodiment argument after all, *contra* (i) of the parity argument. Secondly, the objection might pose a threat to (ii) of the parity argument. If either alternative obtains, then proponents of the conceivability argument can consistently avoid positing nonphysical substances after all. Neither alternative obtains, however, as I now explain.

The first question is whether the objection to Descartes's and Kripke's argument also applies to the phenomenal disembodiment argument. The answer is that it does not. For the *raison d'etre* of the phenomenal disembodiment argument is that it mimics the conceivability argument, only swapping references to the physical and the phenomenal. If the conceivability argument avoids terms like 'I' and 'that' which fix the reference to an actual thing, then the phenomenal disembodiment argument does so too.

If this is not obvious from the statements of the phenomenal disembodiment argument given earlier, this is because it is not obvious in the statements of the conceivability argument on which it was based. However, I now stipulate that just as the conceivability argument is based on the conceivability of a physical duplicate of our world without the conscious experiences, so the phenomenal disembodiment argument is based on the conceivability of a phenomenal duplicate of our world, without the physical things.

It follows that the objection that Chalmers and Goff direct at Descartes's and Kripke's disembodiment arguments does not apply to the phenomenal disembodiment argument. If you accept the conceivability argument, then parity of reasoning really does require that you accept the phenomenal disembodiment argument as well, as I argued in § 6.3 and as premiss (i) of the parity argument states. And at the very least, this rules out physicalist Russellian monism including 'panprotopsychism.'

It might be thought, however, that the response advanced on behalf of the phenomenal disembodiment argument here poses a serious threat to premiss (ii) of the parity argument: the claim that if you accept the phenomenal disembodiment argument, then you must accept the existence of nonphysical substances.

The conclusion of the phenomenal disembodiment argument says that the phenomenal facts do not necessitate the existence of anything physical. Q and not P (plus the 'that's all' clause T) is possible where Q is the conjunction of phenomenal facts, and P is an arbitrary physical fact: a ghost world is possible. I have suggested that this entails that there are nonphysical

Parity of Reasoning Demands Nonphysical Substances 127

substances. For if there exist nonphysical things that do not necessitate the existence of physical things, then the nonphysical things, taken together, are metaphysically complete, and therefore constitute and/or comprise one or more nonphysical substances.

Proponents of the conceivability argument can raise the following objection. Now that I have clarified the phenomenal disembodiment argument, it is clear that its conclusion only entails that a phenomenal *duplicate* of the actual world could exist without anything physical. It does not follow from this that the *actual* phenomenal things could do so. If so, then the phenomenal disembodiment argument at most entails that nonphysical substances are possible, not that any such things actually exist.

Property dualists who are committed to the conceivability argument might urge that by breaking rank with Descartes's and Kripke's argument, the phenomenal disembodiment argument fails to demonstrate what it sets out to show. Property dualists might add that the only way to resolve this would be to adjust the phenomenal disembodiment argument, making it an argument about the conceivability of the actual phenomenal things existing without the actual physical things, like Descartes's and Kripke's arguments, which would make it vulnerable to the objections that Goff and Chalmers make to those arguments after all.

6.4.6 *An Optional Response*

This objection fails. If the conceivability argument shows that consciousness is nonphysical as property dualists claim, then the phenomenal disembodiment argument shows that there are nonphysical substances. It does not have to be adjusted to bring it into conformity with Descartes's and Kripke's arguments.

I explain why in a moment. First, it is worth pausing to consider what would follow if we did adjust the phenomenal disembodiment argument to make it an argument about the conceivability of the actual phenomenal things existing without the actual physical things. For although it is true that property dualists could *consistently* reject the resulting argument, it is not clear that they could *reasonably* do so.

This is because it is possible to argue that the usual obstacles to identifying *the very same* thing across possible worlds will not arise in the present case. There is reason to think that we can in fact reidentify the actual phenomenal things across possible worlds. To put it in Goff's terminology, there is reason to think that we can in fact transparently conceive of ghost *counterparts*, not merely of ghost *twins*.

To see why this is plausible, it is sufficient to reflect on cases where our ability to identify things across possible worlds runs into trouble. For it

128 *Parity of Reasoning Demands Nonphysical Substances*

quickly emerges that these are typically cases where we are not conceiving of those things under transparent concepts to begin with.

A classic example is Kripke's (1972, 332–3) suggestion that it seems possible that a given table should turn out to have been made out of ice from the River Thames. The lesson seems to be that when we take ourselves to be conceiving of a world where the table is made of ice, we are not really doing so. Rather, we are conceiving of a world that contains a different table which we misidentify as the original.

It seems obvious, however, that if we seem to be able to conceive of the table being made of ice, this is because we are not conceiving of it under transparent concepts to start with, even before indexical terms such as 'this table' are introduced. For if we were, then we would be conceiving of a table made of wood. Rather, we must have been thinking of the table under opaque concepts which could perhaps be approximated by 'a table-shaped Mahogany-looking object in such and such lecture room at Princeton University.' This is essentially what Kripke (1972, 333) himself affirms when he says that in judging that the table could turn out to be made out of ice, what we are really imagining is 'a table looking and feeling just like this one and placed in this very position in the room.'

This kind of problem cannot arise in the ghost-world case. If we have transparent concepts of phenomenal properties, as proponents of the conceivability argument claim, then we cannot be mistaken about the identity of things in the ghost world because we are overlooking the nature of the originals. If we are mistaken about their identity, it seems that this must be because they are brutely nonidentical to the actual things that they duplicate. This is a different kind of case to that of Kripke's ice table.

Brute differences in identity might well be possible. There is at least some intuitive attraction to this idea. For example, call the uppermost iron atom in the spire of the Burj Khalifa 'K.' Is there a possible world exactly like ours, except that K is a different but exactly similar iron atom, with an exactly similar history? It is not clear. But at least, there seems to be nothing to prevent this. There is at least some appeal to the idea that K's identity is a further fact over and above all its other characteristics: the kind of thing that proponents of Vaisheshika call a 'vishesha' or Scotists a 'haecceity,' i.e. 'thisness.'

If some kind of haecceitism, so defined, is true, then we cannot be confident that anything in the ghost world is identical to anything in the actual world, even if phenomenal concepts are transparent. In the same way, we cannot be sure that the uppermost iron atom in the Burj Khalifa in an exact duplicate of our world is K.

On the other hand, it is plausible that once we have ensured that everything else about the imaginary iron atom is like K, once there is nothing else in its nature to prevent it from being K, we can simply *stipulate*

Parity of Reasoning Demands Nonphysical Substances   129

that it is *K* that we are conceiving. Or at least, it is plausible that we can do so as long as we obey whatever a priori constraints there are on identity, such as the indiscernibility of identicals.

If so, then it is not clear what is supposed to prevent us from successfully conceiving of actual phenomenal things existing in a ghost world after all. Once we have ensured that nothing else in the nature of these things prevents them from being identical to the originals, we can simply stipulate that they *are* the originals.

If proponents of the conceivability argument do not have a response to this reasoning, then they will be under pressure to accept the phenomenal disembodiment argument even after it has been adjusted to make its premisses focus on the actual phenomenal things. The same probably holds of Kripke's argument and perhaps Descartes's argument as well. (Whether this defence succeeds in the case of Descartes's argument also depends on questions about the meaning of 'I,' which I outline in § 7.2.)

It seems, then, that property dualists might have to accept the phenomenal disembodiment argument even when it has been adjusted to make it an argument about actual things. If so, then they must accept the existence of nonphysical substances. I do not pursue this claim further, however. For even if it is correct, it still makes the parity argument dialectically weaker than is necessary.

6.4.7 *Modality and Duplication*

For the reason just given, I think it might well be unreasonable for proponents of the conceivability argument to reject the phenomenal disembodiment argument, even when it has been adjusted to make it depend on our ability to reidentify things across possible worlds. If it can be done, however, it is preferable to leave the phenomenal disembodiment argument in its original form and to defend premiss (ii) of the parity argument directly. This can indeed be done, I will argue, by appealing to the following principle: exact duplicates do not differ in their modal characteristics. The advantage of appealing to this principle, as I explain in a moment, is that the conceivability argument seems to depend on it no less than the parity argument.

If the principle just stated is true, then all that is required to show that there exist nonphysical substances is that there exist possible duplicates of actual nonphysical things that are metaphysically complete. And this is what the phenomenal disembodiment argument in its unaltered form purports to show.

The new principle is intuitively plausible. To see this take an object such as a glass bottle and consider: could an exact duplicate of this thing, an atom-for-atom replica, have modal differences merely in virtue of its

130 *Parity of Reasoning Demands Nonphysical Substances*

nonidentity to the original? For example, could there be an exact duplicate of this glass bottle that differs only in that, despite having the same atomic structure and so on, it is metaphysically incapable of shattering?

The answer is intuitively no. If the duplicate could not possibly shatter, whereas the original could, this must be due to some difference between them. Modal characteristics do not plausibly float free from the categorical nature of things. Intuitively then, exact duplicates share their modal characteristics.

Importantly, this is intuitively true of *full* duplicates only. The same does not hold of *partial* duplicates. It is implausible that there could exist an exact duplicate of the glass bottle that is metaphysically incapable of shattering. But there is no reason why there could not exist a duplicate with respect to shape, size, and colour only that is incapable of shattering; a plastic copy for example.

It is also worth noting that if the principle is true, then a full duplicate of a metaphysically incomplete thing will be metaphysically incomplete too and must therefore be accompanied by some complement. There might be room for the modal characteristics of a duplicate of a metaphysically incomplete thing to differ from those of the original *because* its complement is not an exact duplicate of the complement of the original.

For example, the shape, size and colour of the plastic bottle can be thought of as an exact duplicate of a metaphysically incomplete component of the original glass one. Because this duplicate has plasticity as a complement rather than glassiness, there is room for certain kinds of modal differences: the original could survive if all the plastic in its world vanished, whereas this is not true of the duplicate.

Finally, it seems obvious that exact duplicates *will* differ in those modal properties that follow a priori from the nature of identity. Suppose, for example, we name the original glass bottle G and an atom-for-atom duplicate D. G will have the modal characteristic that it cannot exist in a world without G. D will lack this characteristic. Instead, D will have the parallel characteristic that it cannot exist in a world without D.

This third constraint can also be put by saying that, for any modal truth about G, the exact same will hold of D where you replace all references to G with references to D. But differences will emerge if you replace some but not all of the references to G. For D stands in the same modal relations to *itself* that G stands in to itself.

Partial duplicates, and duplicates of metaphysically incomplete things, might well differ modally from the originals. For categorical differences in the part or complement that is not duplicated make room for ordinary non-brute modal differences. But it remains plausible that full duplicates of metaphysically complete things do not have brute modal differences: modal differences that are totally invisible to ideal a priori reflection.

Parity of Reasoning Demands Nonphysical Substances   131

This principle is plausible. I do not insist that it is true, however. All I claim is that if the principle is true, then the phenomenal disembodiment argument entails the existence of nonphysical substances, and if the principle is false, then the conceivability argument does not disprove physicalism, as I will now explain.

6.4.8 Premiss (ii) of the Parity Argument Is True

The first premiss of the conceivability argument says that the physical facts do not a priori entail the existence of consciousness. The second premiss says that if so, then the physical facts do not necessitate the existence of consciousness. Proponents of the conceivability argument conclude that the physical facts do not necessitate the existence of consciousness and hence that consciousness is something over and above physical things. This final step usually goes unexamined, but it deserves close attention.

The claims about conceivability upon which the conceivability argument depends must not concern the *actual* physical or phenomenal things. For otherwise, the argument would be vulnerable to the same objection that its proponents direct at Descartes's and Kripke's disembodiment arguments. Borrowing Goff's terminology: the zombie world that the conceivability argument shows to be possible is a world of *zombie twins* not *zombie counterparts*. The immediate conclusion of the argument is that zombie twins are possible.

Proponents of the conceivability argument infer that physicalism is false, that our own conscious experiences are something over and above our physical characteristics. But it seems reasonable to ask: why should the fact that our zombie twins are possible tell us anything about our own metaphysical nature? To put the question vividly: call your zombie twin Z. The conceivability argument purports to show that Z is possible. It seems to follow that if there are worlds where Z is conscious, those must be dualist worlds. But why should this tell us anything about you or the actual world, given that you are not Z?

This question is never (to my knowledge) pressed against proponents of the conceivability argument. It is plausible that this is because it has an obvious answer: Z and Z's world is an exact physical duplicate of you and your world. So if the former does not necessitate the existence of consciousness, then neither does the latter.

According to this answer, we can reason from the modal characteristics of the duplicates, back to the modal characteristics of the originals, and thence to the metaphysical nature of the originals. This is intuitively plausible. And it does not require that we rely on our ability to identify '*the very same things*' across possible worlds, as Descartes's and Kripke's disembodiment arguments require.

132 *Parity of Reasoning Demands Nonphysical Substances*

But this reasoning does rely on the assumption that identity alone does not make a difference to the modal characteristics of exact duplicates. For otherwise, we could not reason from the modal characteristics of the zombie world back to the modal characteristics of the actual physical things.

To see the trouble this would create for the conceivability argument, suppose that identity alone can make a difference to modal characteristics. In that case, physicalists might object to the argument as follows (using Scotistic language for convenience). Just because *your physical characteristics* plus *Z's haecceity* do not necessitate the existence of consciousness, opponents of the conceivability argument might say, it does not follow that your physical characteristics plus *your haecceity* do not do so. Just because physical *duplicates* of the actual world can lack consciousness, it doesn't follow that physical *counterparts* can.

If there is a genuine *non sequitur* here, then we have no reason to suppose that your conscious experiences are anything over and above your physical characteristics. Perhaps for you to have your current conscious states consists in nothing more than *this very* physical body having the physical properties it does.

Proponents of the conceivability argument have not been troubled by this objection. It does not appear amongst those catalogued by Chalmers (2010, 112–23) for example. Neither does it appear amongst the standard objections raised by physicalists. This makes sense. For proponents of the conceivability argument can reply that the objection relies on ridiculous brute modal differences between exact duplicates. The objection requires that the actual physical things differ in their modal characteristics from their duplicates in the zombie world. It is hard to see what could account for such differences. The physical things in the zombie world are *ex hypothesi* metaphysically complete things that the physical things in the actual world fully duplicate, haecceities aside. Modal differences between the two would seem totally arbitrary.

Indeed, such brute modal differences are arguably even less plausible than the standard cases of 'strong necessity' which proponents of the conceivability argument reject. For although strong necessities might not follow a priori from the categorical nature of things, they could at least covary with the categorical nature of things. They might be just as orderly and lawlike as ordinary modal truths. Such strong necessities seem comparatively plausible next to the new variety: necessary truths that are not merely invisible to reason equipped with transparent concepts but that also vary from one exact duplicate to the next. If you reject strong necessities of the first kind, you should certainly reject the truly Herculean necessities upon which the present challenge to the conceivability argument depends.

Proponents of the conceivability argument can plausibly take the view that an objection that appeals to the possibility of modal differences that

Parity of Reasoning Demands Nonphysical Substances   133

are due to identity alone rests on too bizarre a picture of modality to be taken seriously. This response is likely to be widely accepted, even amongst opponents of the conceivability argument. For once again, the objection under consideration never seems to get raised.

So the conceivability argument is probably safe from objections that appeal to modal differences between exact duplicates arising from identity alone. But if the conceivability argument *is* safe from such objections, then so is the parity argument. If so, the prospects for property dualism look unfavourable.

If property dualists reject premiss (ii) of the parity argument on the basis that the actual phenomenal things might have different modal characteristics to those in the ghost world, they will be guilty of relying on the very picture of modality that, I have argued in this section, undermines the conceivability argument. For all that premiss (ii) of the parity argument requires is that, if a ghost duplicate of the actual world is metaphysically complete, then so are the phenomenal things in the actual world that it duplicates: the mere difference in identity does not affect this. I do not see any way for proponents of the conceivability argument to get around this.

7 The Consequences of the Parity Argument for Nonphysical Substances

In Chapter 6, it was claimed that the parity argument presents a powerful case for the thesis that theorists who posit nonphysical properties in response to the mind-body problem should be prepared to posit nonphysical substances as well. It might be thought that if the parity argument were as powerful as has been claimed, it would not have been overlooked by property dualists, and so it must go wrong somewhere. §§ 7.1–7.3 explain why the parity argument has been overlooked. These sections also draw out some wider consequences of the argument. § 7.4 and § 7.5 address two final lines of objection to the parity argument.

7.1 Five Reasons Why the Parity Argument Goes Unnoticed

Premiss (i) of the parity argument says that if you accept the conceivability argument, then you must accept the phenomenal disembodiment argument. Premiss (ii) says that if you accept the phenomenal disembodiment argument, then you must accept the existence of nonphysical substances. Premiss (i) was defended in §§ 6.1–6.3, premiss (ii) in § 6.4. If both premisses are true then proponents of the conceivability argument must abandon property dualism and accept the existence of nonphysical substances.

If the parity argument *is* successful, it might be thought surprising that it should have gone unnoticed. For the parity argument is closely related to well-known disembodiment arguments and to the conceivability argument itself. This section explains why this is not so surprising after all.

One obvious reason why the threat posed by the parity argument should have been overlooked is that the weight of resistance to property dualism has been expected, and has in fact come, from physicalists. For example, Jackson (2003, fn.1) reports receiving too many papers, letters, and emails seeking to convince him to give up property dualism to recall which caused him to succumb. It would be surprising if he received as many communications urging him to take a further step and posit nonphysical substances as well.

DOI: 10.4324/9781003378600-8

The Consequences of the Parity Argument   135

The predominance of physicalism has encouraged property dualists to devote most of their attention to contesting physicalist arguments, whilst according much less attention to substance dualism and idealism. So too has the widespread idea that theories that posit nonphysical substances are known to be hopelessly flawed. This idea enters analytical philosophy with Ryle (1949) and Wittgenstein (1953) and seems to have persisted through inertia after the arguments that gave it its original thrust lost general assent.

The idea that theories that posit nonphysical substances need not be taken seriously has been reinforced by the suspicion, expressed by physicalists such as Dennett (1991, 37), that proponents of nonphysical substances have ulterior motives. In particular, it is suspected, with some justification that, for some, the appeal of nonphysical substances is more religious than philosophical, despite the energetic opposition to substance dualism by recent Christian thinkers. And dismissing the idea of nonphysical substances accords, more generally with our intellectual culture's abhorrence of the idea of the soul, discussed in Chapter 1.

For two reasons, then, property dualists have not spent much time worrying about whether their position is secure against objections from substance dualists and idealists. This can be seen in the time and effort that property dualists accord to addressing physicalist positions. It can also be seen in the tendency of property dualists to pass over defences of traditional anti-physicalist positions such as Plantinga (1970) or Swinburne (1986, 2013, 2019) without serious engagement. There is, therefore, no reason to suppose that property dualists have been on the lookout for objections like the symmetry, compresence, and parity arguments.

A third reason why the parity argument might have gone unnoticed, and one that has reinforced the presumption that nonphysical substances need not be taken seriously, is the prevailing confusion about the idea of substance. As I noted in Chapter 2, it is very odd that there should be a widespread consensus that we should not posit nonphysical substances when nobody is confident about how 'substance' should be understood in this context. Nonetheless, that has been the situation in philosophy for some time.

One way in which this lack of clarity has held back discussion is by leaving unchecked a tendency to suppose that 'substance' must mean something like 'substratum' in the Lockean sense introduced in § 2.3: an extra ingredient that must be combined with something's properties for it to exist. One of the less profitable contributions of British empiricism has been a centuries-long tradition of encouraging this confusion.

For example, Bertrand Russell frequently says things like 'most of us, nowadays, do not accept "substance" as a useful notion' (1948, 70) without mentioning that he has in mind only a very specific idea of substance – an

136 *The Consequences of the Parity Argument*

idea that can only claim third place amongst historically important usages and that has little or no connection to the traditional Aristotelian and Cartesian definitions. As a result, readers who reject substrata suppose they must also reject theories that posit nonphysical substances in response to the mind-body problem.

The resulting confusion is neatly illustrated in the following passage from Campbell's (1990) book *Abstract Particulars*:

> In terms of the traditional alternative views of the mind-body relation, Trope Dualism is closest to Attribute Dualism. It is, indeed the purest version of attribute dualism, as it recognizes the attributes, both physical and nonphysical, without postulating any further, single, underlying substance.
>
> (Campbell, 1990, 165)

Campbell contrasts a dualism of 'attributes' with a dualism involving the 'underlying substance,' saying that trope dualism is emphatically of the former variety. This is misleading in two ways.

Firstly, as I argued in § 2.3.2, the idea of substances as underlying substrata is not the relevant one when we are distinguishing the traditional alternative views of the mind-body relation. For the paradigm substance dualist, Descartes, firmly rejects such things. Descartes even expresses this by saying that there is no real distinction between the substance *mind* and the attribute *thought*. Neither does the second most iconic substance dualist, Plato, so much as hint at a substratum theory. Underlying substrata are not relevant here.

Secondly, as I observed in § 2.4.5, in the sense of 'substance' that *is* relevant in this context, tropes as Campbell understands them typically *are* substances. For Campbell (1983, 186; 1990, 3, 3, 21, 89) claims that most 'tropes' could exist by themselves. Hence Campbell's 'trope dualism' is in fact no less a form of substance dualism than Descartes's. (Obviously, if this is correct, the problem is with the prevailing terminological confusion rather than with Campbell's book.)

A fourth reason why the parity argument might have gone unnoticed is the close association of nonphysical substances, and substance dualism in particular, with the idea of nonphysical selves or subjects expressed by the first-person pronoun 'I.' This association has become so close that theorists are sometimes tempted to *define* substance dualism as the kind of dualism that posits nonphysical selves (see Nida-Rümelin 2006; Loose et al. 2018; and perhaps Zimmerman 2010, 119–20, 134).

This, in combination with the lack of clarity over substance already mentioned, has obscured the fact that the difference between substance dualism and property dualism is essentially a *modal* one. This alone goes a

The Consequences of the Parity Argument   137

long way towards explaining why the parity argument should have gone unnoticed. For the basic strategy of that argument is to capitalise on the connection between the modal commitments of the conceivability argument and the modal nature of the independence definition of substance.

The fact that the difference between substance dualism and property dualism has been left so unclear also makes it less surprising that property dualists have sometimes treated disembodiment arguments like Kripke's and even Descartes's as potential allies rather than as threats (e.g. Chalmers 1996, 146–6; 2010, 199–200). And because we are not obliged to defend at length our reasons for rejecting arguments that would only help our cause, this might in turn explain the ease with which property dualists have accepted physicalist objections to Kripke and Descartes that are in fact, according to the argument of § 6.4.6, unavailable to them.

A fifth and final factor that helps explain why the potential of the parity argument has not previously been noticed is the growing tendency for proponents of the conceivability argument to favour Russellian monism, along with the idea that Russellian monism confounds the ordinary distinctions between responses to the mind-body problem. This results in a sense that Russellian monist positions do not share borders with neighbouring positions and threats on unpatrolled borders are naturally overlooked.

These final two topics, the association between nonphysical substances and selves, and the relationship of the arguments of Chapters 5 and 6 to Russellian monism, deserve closer attention. I devote the next two sections to these themes, respectively.

7.2 Nonphysical Substances and the Individual Soul

It might be thought that it is a weakness of the parity argument that it exerts pressure on property dualists to posit nonphysical substances, not necessarily nonphysical selves or souls. For this means that the resulting position might, in this respect, remain closer to familiar property dualist positions than it does to classic substance dualist or idealist positions. I have partially addressed this concern already in § 4.3. It is important to note, however, that the parity argument, if it is successful, actually pushes property dualists closer to classic substance dualist or idealist positions than I have so far shown.

Because I based the phenomenal disembodiment argument on the conceivability argument, I presented it as an argument about the conceivability of a ghost *world*. If follows from the argument, expressed in this way, that the phenomenal world taken as a whole is metaphysically complete, and hence that there exists at least one nonphysical substance. It need not follow that there exist *multiple* nonphysical substances, however. If not,

138 *The Consequences of the Parity Argument*

the result will be a fair distance from classic substance dualism or idealism as they are ordinarily understood.

However, instead of focussing on a ghost world, we could run a parallel argument that focusses on a phenomenal duplicate of an individual human without anything else, a 'lonely ghost' to use Goff's (2012) term. If the ghost world is conceivable, then it seems that lonely ghosts will be too. For as philosophers since Descartes have often observed, the phenomenal facts about a given person do not seem to a priori entail the existence of anything physical *or the existence of any other mind*.

Rather than pressing property dualists to posit at least one nonphysical substance, this version of the parity argument will press them to posit at least one nonphysical substance per conscious individual. This is intuitively close to what many classic substance dualist and idealist positions say: it looks very much like a revival of the idea that sentient beings have immaterial souls.

What the parity argument *will not* force proponents of the conceivability argument to do is to concede that the referent of the pronoun 'I' is identical to any one of these nonphysical substances. For example, it will remain possible that although each human comprises a physical body and a substantial nonphysical mind or soul, 'I' refers to the union of the two, as Aquinas proposes. The parity argument obliges those property dualists who reject idealism to adopt a position that is as paradigmatically substance dualist as Thomas Aquinas's (on the reading of Aquinas suggested in § 4.3) but not necessarily the numerical identification of self and soul advocated by Plato and Descartes.

It is worth mentioning a second respect in which the parity argument does not, on its own, press property dualists to go beyond Aquinas. Whilst the argument, if it is successful, requires that dualists should posit nonphysical substances, it does not require that they posit *physical* substances.

This means that the argument leaves room for idealism, as well as substance dualism. But it also leaves room for a third position that rarely gets discussed. This position will say that although the nonphysical phenomenal things are metaphysically complete substances, the physical things are not. So what exists are nonphysical substances, some of which have some inessential physical properties.

This position is reminiscent of Aquinas's philosophical anthropology because, whilst Aquinas is committed to the claim that the soul can exist without the body, he is not committed to the claim that the body can exist without the soul. (This parallel should not be pressed too far, however. For Aquinas does posit things other than human bodies that are naturally regarded as physical substances insofar as *their* forms are not souls.)

As I said in § 4.2, until now, I have counted any dualist position that posits nonphysical substances as substance dualism. There is a case, however,

The Consequences of the Parity Argument 139

for classing the position described here as a kind of inverse property dualism. The position is equidistant between substance dualism and idealism in the same way that standard versions of property dualism are equidistant between substance dualism and physicalism.

Just as standard property dualism can claim to be property dualist but 'substance physicalist,' because the nonphysical properties all belong to physical things like zombies that are substances in their own right, the present position can claim to be property dualist but 'substance idealist.' It too is a departure from Wolff's trichotomy of materialism, substance dualism, and idealism, but a departure in the opposite direction.

Although the parity argument leaves room for this position, it is not obvious that the wider considerations raised in this enquiry do so, however. For this inversion of property dualism, like the original, involves asymmetrical metaphysical dependence. This makes it vulnerable to an inversion of the symmetry argument of § 5.3, which combines the symmetry principle with the premiss that the *nonphysical* things are metaphysically complete. For this reason, the thesis that the viable positions are those of Wolff's trichotomy remains attractive on a definition of 'substance dualism' that requires that there exist physical substances.

It is also clear that this third position is only open to proponents of the conceivability argument who reject the transparency of physical concepts. For if you accept that the physical concepts are transparent, then the conceivability argument itself entails that the physical world is metaphysically complete.

This brings out one of many important differences between the position of Russellian monist property dualists, who reject the transparency of physical concepts, and that of standard property dualists, who do not, or who at least do not have to do so. Before addressing some final objections to the parity argument, it might be useful to consider in greater detail its relationship to Russellian monist positions.

7.3 The Parity Argument and Russellian Monism

As I explained in § 4.4, as far as one can tell from descriptions of the position, many anti-physicalist Russellian monists are committed to property dualist versions of the view. That is, they take the view that the fundamentally mental things to which our physical vocabulary refers are not wholly mental, but also have some 'nonexperiential being' as Strawson (2003, 38) puts it, perhaps in the form of spatial properties, or the mysterious '+' component of Goff's (2017, 185) 'consciousness+.'

I did not say for certain that any present-day Russellian monist is committed to property dualist Russellian monism because they tend not to be explicit about their commitments concerning metaphysical completeness.

140   *The Consequences of the Parity Argument*

I only said that if they are, then they will be vulnerable to the main argument of this enquiry. If not, then they are already committed to nonphysical substances, no less than Plato, Aquinas, or Descartes.

The Russellian monist stratagem brings out an additional respect in which the parity argument is more powerful than the symmetry argument of § 5.3 and the compresence argument of § 5.4. For the symmetry argument will only go through if we have an adequate grasp of physical properties to tell that zombies are metaphysically complete. And the compresence argument will only go through if we have an adequate grasp of physical properties to tell that these do not mix with phenomenal properties in the way that strict compresence requires. (Though, as I have noted, if the parity argument is successful, then an inversion of the symmetry argument becomes available, which does not rely on our grasp of physical things.) Russellian monists can object that these arguments are inconclusive because we do not know the nature of physical properties. Perhaps if we were truly acquainted with them, we would find that physical properties stand in the same kind of conceptual relation to phenomenal properties as shape does to size or pitch to timbre.

Whatever the merits of that objection might be, there is no parallel objection to the parity argument. If the parity argument is sound, then proponents of the conceivability argument, Russellian monist or otherwise, must accept that the actual phenomenal things are nonphysical substances.

Russellian monists can, of course, combine this conclusion with the thesis that physical concepts are opaque. This opens up two possibilities depending on the referents of the physical concepts. The first is Russellian monist idealism. The second is Russellian monist substance dualism.

The first option says that the physical concepts all refer to phenomenal things of the sort that survive in the ghost world. The result is idealist Russellian monism. If it is combined with the view that it is only macroscopic things like humans that are conscious, the result will resemble Berkeley's idealism; if it is combined with the view that other things, such as microscopic cells or particles are conscious, it will resemble Leibniz's idealism. Either way, the result is thoroughly idealist. For it entails that our world *is a ghost world*. Like all versions of Russellian monism, the resulting position remains physicalist in the purely referential sense described in § 4.1 and § 4.4.3 but it does so only on pain of adopting a highly revisionary understanding of physical things.

The second option says that some of the physical concepts refer to fundamentally nonmental things of the sort that do not survive in a ghost world. These might include Strawson's spatial characteristics or Goff's '+' component of 'consciousness+.' The result is substance dualist Russellian monism on which our physical concepts refer to some physical things and some nonphysical substances.

The physical things, according to dualist Russellian monism will be physical in the strict sense specified in § 4.1: they will be fundamentally nonmental things referred to by the technical terms of physics. The non-physical substances will be strongly metaphysically independent of the physical things. If the physical things are not metaphysically complete, the result is the position equidistant between substance dualism and idealism described in § 7.2. If the physical things are metaphysically complete, as seems more probable in light of the inverse symmetry argument, the result is orthodox but Russellian monist substance dualism.

There is a tendency to see Russellian monism as a panacea that, if it is tenable, removes the long-standing puzzles about the mind-body relation and allows us to circumvent the traditional catalogue of responses. In § 4.4 I argued that Russellian monists must in fact choose between the familiar positions no less than their non-Russellian monist colleagues. If the parity argument is successful then Russellian monists who are motivated by the conceivability argument must choose a position that posits nonphysical substances.

7.4 The Transcendence of the Ego

In § 6.1, I explained why it is plausible that proponents of the conceivability argument should accept premiss one of the phenomenal disembodiment argument. Informally, the premiss says that we can conceive of an exact phenomenal duplicate of the actual world with nothing else in it, a ghost world in Goff's terminology. Formally, the premiss says that Q and not P, and T is conceivable where Q is the conjunction of phenomenal truths, P is an arbitrary physical truth, and T is a 'that's all' clause.

The reason for thinking that proponents of the conceivability argument should accept premiss one of the phenomenal disembodiment argument is that thought experiments about ghosts seem to be just as compelling as thought experiments about zombies. A secondary reason is that our ability to follow Descartes's method of doubt in *Meditations* 1 and 2 seems to prove that we are able to conceive of ghosts. Goff (2010, 2012, 2014) has defended the conceivability of ghosts on the basis of these claims at length.

It is probable that most proponents of the conceivability argument will indeed accept premiss one of the phenomenal disembodiment argument. But there exists a possible loophole that I now consider. The loophole consists in the possibility that, although we can conceive of a phenomenal duplicate of the actual world without anything that answers to our physical concepts, we cannot conceive of it without anything nonphenomenal *at all*. For the existence of phenomenal consciousness a priori entails *some* nonphenomenal being.

142   *The Consequences of the Parity Argument*

7.4.1 *A New Threat to the Parity Argument*

The nonphenomenal being that is a priori entailed by the phenomenal facts, on this proposal, would have to be something very inconspicuous. It must be something so faint that we are able to overlook its presence in the ghost world even as we, of conceptual necessity, imagine it there; something so muted and indistinct that it is capable of escaping our notice whilst nonetheless undermining the ghost world thought experiment as I have described it, by contravening the 'that's all' clause.

I consider candidates for this nonphenomenal intruder in the ghost world in a moment. First, it is worth reflecting on how its existence would affect the phenomenal disembodiment argument, and hence the parity argument. There are two possibilities. The first possibility is that the intrusive entity is something whose nature we fully grasp, as we do the conscious experiences that necessitate it. In that case, with minor adjustments, the phenomenal disembodiment argument, and hence the parity argument, will go through unaffected. For we can simply revise Q so that it includes both phenomenal facts and facts about this new kind of entity.

The second possibility is that the nonphenomenal being is something whose nature we only partly grasp (we must do so partly, or its existence could not follow a priori from the phenomenal facts). Equivalently, on this second view, what we fully grasp is just the metaphysically incomplete tip of what could be an ontological iceberg lurking beneath the surface of the ghost world: something whose existence could confound attempts at drawing modal inferences, however closely related conceivability and possibility might be.

On this second possibility, the phenomenal disembodiment argument, and hence the parity argument, will no longer have the force I have attributed to them, at least in their present form. For the possibility will arise that the extra nonphenomenal element, though it does not answer to our ordinary physical concepts, is itself the fundamentally nonmental essence of some physical thing: perhaps *this thing* is the interior nature of the body. If so, the argument that property dualists must posit nonphysical substances will be inconclusive after all.

The issue broached in this section – whether the phenomenal facts a priori entail the existence of any nonphenomenal being over any above the phenomenal things – is, then, of great significance for the parity argument, and hence for the status quo of present-day philosophy of mind. In the following two subsections, I consider two candidates for the additional nonphenomenal entity: a 'substratum' and a 'transcendental ego.' I do not regard either as a serious threat to the parity argument, but the latter is independently interesting and merits more consideration than I can give it here.

7.4.2 Substrata

There can be no specific threat to the parity argument here unless we can find a plausible candidate for the nonphenomenal being whose existence is a priori entailed by our conscious experiences. Furthermore, we can rule out candidates that were excluded from the domain of the independence definition in § 3.3 and § 3.4, including necessary beings, abstracta, and also space and time if these turn out to be substantival. For a nonphysical mind that depends on these things may nonetheless count as a substance in the sense that defines substance dualism.

In his reply to the compressed version of the parity argument in Weir (2021b), Goff (2021b, 319–21) grants that the argument is sound so long as we suppose that substances are bundles of properties. But he suggests that the argument may be unsound if substances are composites of properties and a 'substratum.' I explain in this subsection why I do not consider substrata a serious candidate for the nonphenomenal entity that might pose a threat to the parity argument.

As we saw in § 2.3, Locke, perhaps inadvertently, popularised the idea that 'substance' refers to a mysterious propertyless thing that is needed to 'support' a substance's properties. The Lockean idea of a substratum, so conceived, is very different to the Aristotelian-Cartesian idea of a substance. Aristotle and Descartes's favourite examples of substances are ordinary propertied objects such as humans, horses, minds, and bodies, not mysterious propertyless entities underlying these things.

Locke expresses scepticism about the coherence of the idea of a propertyless substratum. More recent philosophers, such as Russell (1948, 211) and Mackie (1976, 77) have followed suit. The association of the idea of a substance with the idea of a substratum is one reason why many contemporary philosophers regard the idea of substance itself as suspect. Justin Broackes (2006) attempts to rescue the traditional idea of substance from its association with propertyless substrata (cf. Weir 2021a, 2023).

It should be clear that, in terms of the definitions proposed in Chapters 2 and 3, the idea of a propertyless substratum is indeed incoherent, supposing the substratum is meant to be a third kind of entity, and not either a property or a substance in its own right. For as I pointed out in § 3.4, insofar as 'substance' and 'property' refer to metaphysically complete and incomplete entities, respectively, there is no room for a third kind of entity that must be combined with properties to yield a substance. The two categories are logically exhaustive.

Still, it might be thought that we need to posit something to play the role assigned to substrata even if that thing is, insofar as the criterion of metaphysical completeness is concerned, either a substance or a property. And it might be suggested that substrata, so conceived, still threaten to undermine

144   *The Consequences of the Parity Argument*

the parity argument. Whilst I am not convinced that we ought to posit substrata of any kind, this possibility merits consideration.

Gustav Bergman (1947, 1967) argues that we must posit a substratum to contribute particularity to an entity whose properties are presumed to be universals. Substrata on this view are also known as 'bare particulars' (cf. Armstrong 1978, 1997; Sider 2006; Bailey 2012). C. B. Martin (1980) proposes that we must posit a substratum to bind together properties that could otherwise exist independently. It is implausible that particularity or bindedness can exist by itself. So these are not good candidates for substances. But both might be considered nonphenomenal properties of substances.

It is not clear that a substance needs a particularising or binding 'substratum' in addition to its other properties. I reject, with Arda Denkel (1992), Martin's suggestion that without a substratum to bind them, properties would be separable. For it seems to me that the need of properties for one another – of shape for size or pitch for timbre – arises out of the nature of the properties, and not from some further thing. But I do not think that theories that posit substrata, so conceived, will pose a threat to the parity argument anyway.

Theories that posit a particularising or binding 'substratum' may be tolerated on two conditions. Firstly, insofar as the criterion of metaphysical completeness is concerned, that 'substratum' had better be regarded as a property and not, incoherently, as a third kind of entity, neither substance nor property. Secondly, we must posit one such 'substratum' per item that, insofar as its other properties are concerned, appears to be metaphysically complete.

For example, insofar as their other properties are concerned, the size of the desk and the desk minus its size each appear to be metaphysically *incomplete*. So it is acceptable to posit just one particularising or binding substratum for both – for the whole desk, that is. By contrast, insofar as their other properties are concerned, the upper left draw of the desk and the desk minus the draw each appear to be metaphysically complete. So we must posit one particularising or binding substratum for each, insofar as we posit such entities at all.

It must not, on pain or absurdity, turn out that whilst my desk can survive without its upper left draw, a perfect duplicate of my desk cannot survive without its upper left draw, not because somebody has nailed it down or glued it shut, but purely because the two 'share the same substratum.' To entertain such a possibility would not only be unprincipled and bizarre but would, moreover, necessitate general scepticism about the separability of any pair of objects.

I assume that readers will recognise the absurdity of the kind of situation I am ruling out. Nonetheless, they might ask: if there are binding or

The Consequences of the Parity Argument   145

particularising 'substrata' at all, how do we *know* that these are not inconsistently distributed so that perfect physical or phenomenal duplicates may differ in their modal properties solely because of the arbitrary dispensation of these 'substrata'?

In answer, I would say that if it is correct to posit binding or particularising 'substrata' at all, it is because we abstract these properties from complete entities by 'selective attention,' or 'partial consideration' (cf. Heil 2003, 171–3). The particularity of the desk and the binded-ness of its properties are not extra ingredients, over and above the arrangement of physical properties. Rather, they are features *of* that arrangement revealed under selective attention. It is for this reason that we would be sure that any physical duplicate of my desk will be capable of existing without its upper left draw. For the same reason, we can know that any phenomenal duplicate of my ghost twin will be capable of existing without a physical body.

I do not insist that the proposed explanation of how we know that 'substrata' are not arbitrarily distributed is correct. I do urge that theories on which substrata may be arbitrarily distributed are too absurd to pose a serious challenge to the parity argument. So far as I know, no serious proponent of substrata supposes that these entities may be distributed in such an unprincipled manner. We must not allow prejudice against nonphysical substances to lead us to apply a different standard when it comes to our ghost counterparts.

7.4.3 Transcendental Egos

To pose a threat to the parity argument the nonphenomenal thing whose existence is a priori entailed by conscious experience must be some contingent, concrete substance or property. For the reasons given in the previous subsection, it cannot be a 'substratum.' This narrows down the candidates considerably. But there remains one candidate whose special place in the history of the mind-body problem makes it especially worthy of consideration.

The obvious candidate is something resembling what Kant calls the 'transcendental ego.' Kant's use of this term, and its subsequent use in the phenomenological tradition, is fraught with interpretive difficulties. However, the central idea is that the transcendental ego is a nonempirical thing, about which we know nothing except that it must exist for there to be conscious experiences.

Taking inspiration from this idea, I stipulate that in this section, 'transcendental ego' will name a subject of experience that meets two conditions. Firstly, its existence is a priori entailed by the existence of experience. Secondly, its full nature is not something that we grasp under transparent concepts.

146 *The Consequences of the Parity Argument*

These conditions reflect the traditional use of the term 'transcendental ego' that begins with Kant. But interpretive work is not needed here. For any understanding of the transcendental ego that fails to satisfy either condition will pose no threat to the parity argument and will therefore be irrelevant to this chapter. And any understanding that satisfies both conditions will be of interest.

It is worth emphasising how specific the notion of a transcendental ego must be in order for it to pose a threat to the parity argument. No threat is posed by the simple observation that conscious experiences must have a subject or by the hypothesis that the subject may be something over and above the experiences. It is only the view that consciousness a priori entails the existence of a subject whose nature we do not fully grasp under transparent concepts that poses a threat.

Nonetheless, at least some theorists, such as Husserl (1913), can be interpreted as arguing that we must posit transcendental egos so defined. Others, such as Sartre (1936–7) argue that no such things exist. On the Sartrean view, the subject of conscious experience is nothing over and above the conscious experiences themselves. Priest (2000) examines the contention between Husserl and Sartre on this point.

Insofar as the arguments of this enquiry carry weight, the question of whether we must posit a transcendental ego in the sense specified turns out to be of considerable importance to present-day responses to the mind-body problem and deserves greater attention than it has been given. For, perhaps surprisingly, if we decide in favour of transcendental egos, then this seems to open up room for a coherent kind of property dualism.

On the kind of property dualism that results, the nonphysical phenomenal properties of a given subject will be incapable of existing without their transcendental ego, which will itself be, or be in part, the fundamentally nonmental physical thing that underlies some of our physical descriptions – maybe it is the noumenal entity underlying the empirical body or brain. The transcendental ego will thus provide the hook that tethers nonphysical experiences to the physical world.

7.4.4 The First Response to Transcendental Egos

The objection from transcendental egos is both the most powerful and the most interesting objection to the parity argument, and it is the natural next topic of enquiry if that argument is otherwise accepted. It is impossible to do full justice to the objection here. Nonetheless, there are at least two reasons to think that the significance of the parity argument remains largely intact, despite the availability of the objection from transcendental egos.

The first reason is that, even if there is logical space to posit a transcendental ego, the number of present-day anti-physicalists who occupy this

The Consequences of the Parity Argument 147

space is likely to be small. Most theorists say little of pertinence to the question of transcendental egos, but those who do seem to divide into two groups.

In the first group are theorists like Priest (1991, 2012), Nida-Rümelin (2012), and Swinburne (2019) who do seem to believe that consciousness a priori entails the existence of a subject that is something over and above its experiences, but who hold that we have a transparent grasp of the nature of this subject. In the second group are theorists like Strawson (2008) and Goff (2017) who deny that conscious experiences necessitate the existence of a subject that is something over and above the experiences. Both groups reject transcendental egos of the sort that would threaten the parity argument.

It might seem surprising that many theorists should endorse the view I attribute to Strawson and Goff, on which conscious experiences need not by undergone by a subject that is something over and above them. For this might be mistaken for the counterintuitive view, sometimes attributed to Hume and Buddhism, on which there could exist conscious experiences that are undergone by no subject at all.

That is not the view that I am attributing to Strawson and Goff, however. Rather, I am attributing to them the Sartrean view that the existence of the subject consists in the existence of its experiences. This position is not especially counterintuitive. Strawson (2008, 82) expresses it in the claim that the subject and content of an experience are identical. Goff (2017, 178) does so in the claim that 'subjecthood is a determinable of which each conscious state is a determinate ... [and] that if one grasps the essence of a given determinate one thereby grasps the essence of the determinable of that determinate.' Descartes (AT VIII, A 28–30) does so in his claim that minds are not really distinct from the principal attribute of thought.

Strawson (2003, 28) actually anticipates the objection to the parity argument under consideration in this section when he suggests that 'experience (experiential content) is impossible without a subject of experience' and that 'a subject of experience cannot itself be an entirely experiential (experiential-content) phenomenon.' However, Strawson immediately expresses doubt about this claim and rejects it when he (2008) returns to the issue later.

So even if the existence of a transcendental ego creates a way around the parity argument, it is probable that most actual opponents of physicalism will be unable to take advantage of this fact. For opponents of physicalism tend to be committed to the nonexistence of transcendental egos of the sort required, either because they believe that the subject of experience is nothing over and above its experiences or because they believe that the subject, though something over and above the experiences, is something whose nature we grasp under transparent concepts.

148   *The Consequences of the Parity Argument*

7.4.5 The Second Response to Transcendental Egos

The first reason to think that the parity argument retains most of its significance despite the availability of the objection from transcendental egos is that many opponents of physicalism are committed to the nonexistence of transcendental egos. A second reason is that if we do posit transcendental egos, there is reason to think that they should be regarded as nonphysical things alongside their phenomenal properties. If so, the fact that conscious minds need transcendental egos will not threaten their status as nonphysical substances.

By definition, we know little or nothing about transcendental egos. So the case for regarding them as physical or nonphysical will be indirect. It is not clear what indirect argument could be given for viewing transcendental egos as physical. By contrast, there is a promising source for an indirect argument for viewing transcendental egos as nonphysical to be found in familiar observations about the unity of consciousness.

It is often observed that there seems to be a superlatively sharp boundary between the experiences undergone by one subject and those undergone by another. This idea surfaces repeatedly in the history of philosophy but it is customary to quote William James's vivid image when introducing it:

> Take a sentence of a dozen words, and take twelve men and tell to each one word. Then stand the men in a row or jam them in a bunch, and let each think of his word as intently as he will; nowhere will there be a consciousness of the whole sentence.
>
> (James 1890, 160)

All we know about transcendental egos is that they are the subjects of experience. The unity of consciousness suggests that these subjects must themselves be unitary, sharply bounded things.

The thesis that conscious experiences are radically unitary is sometimes used to argue directly against physicalism (e.g. Hasker 1995, 1999). The usual strategy combines the claim that conscious experience is highly unitary with the observation that this is not true of macroscopic physical things such as human organisms, to draw the conclusion that either the conscious experiences or the subject of experience is nonphysical. Alison (1989) attributes an argument in this vicinity to Kant himself.

It is not clear that unity arguments pose an independent threat to physicalism. For physicalists can respond that phenomenal concepts do not reveal the nature of conscious experiences, degree of unity included. Bayne's (2010, 289) treatment of the unity of consciousness as a 'virtual' phenomenon is an example of this response. On the other hand, if the transparency of phenomenal concepts is accepted, other challenges to physicalism such as the knowledge argument and the conceivability argument become available.

The Consequences of the Parity Argument 149

Arguments from the unity of consciousness do, however, put considerable pressure on proponents of the conceivability argument to see the subject of experience as a highly unitary thing. For proponents of the conceivability argument are committed to the transparency of phenomenal concepts. This is what leads to at least some versions of the 'combination problem' for Russellian monism (cf. Goff 2009, 2017 165–216; Mørch 2014; Chalmers 2016b). It is probable that the same fact can also be used to argue that proponents of the conceivability argument who posit transcendental egos should regard these as nonphysical.

In outline, such an argument would go as follows. Premiss one: the transcendental ego, if there is such a thing, is a superlatively unified entity. Premiss two: physical candidates for the subject of experience, such as the human organism or its brain, are all disunified entities. Therefore the transcendental ego, if there is such a thing, is distinct from any physical candidate for the subject of experience.

The prospects for responding to the objection from transcendental egos by appeal to a unity argument require more detailed consideration elsewhere. It is probable, however, that some of the details could be borrowed from existing arguments such as that of Zimmerman (2010, 137–44).

Zimmerman advances a unity argument for the claim that property dualists should embrace 'substance dualism.' Zimmerman is not working with the strict sense of 'substance' that I am using, however. Rather, he argues that property dualists should accept a position like Nida-Rümelin's (2006) on which the nonphysical properties belong to a nonphysical self. In § 4.3, I argued that such a position does not necessarily merit the title of 'substance dualism.' But Zimmerman's argument might be combined with the parity argument to yield a case for thinking that property dualists must embrace substance dualism as I define it that is immune to the objection from transcendental egos.

The parity argument, then, retains its significance even in the face of objections that appeal to the existence of a transcendental ego. For property dualists are unlikely to posit transcendental egos in the first place. And those who do will be under pressure to see these as nonphysical things that do not threaten the status of minds as nonphysical substances. This topic deserves greater attention than it has received here, however, especially if it has the contemporary significance that the parity argument suggests.

7.5 No Property Dualism Without the Conceivability Argument

A final way property dualists might hope to avoid positing nonphysical substances is by abandoning the conceivability argument. For as I mentioned in § 5.1, the conceivability argument is not the only argument that has been advanced for property dualism. The knowledge argument has

150   *The Consequences of the Parity Argument*

had comparable influence. So has the explanatory gap argument (cf. Levine 1983; Chalmers 1995, 2010, 105–6). Furthermore, Goff (2017) argues convincingly for a pure 'transparency argument' against physicalism.

Unlike the conceivability argument, these alternative arguments, as they are usually expressed, do not depend on modal rationalism. Instead of arguing that consciousness is nonphysical on the basis of a modal gap between consciousness and physical things, they argue for this conclusion on the basis of an epistemic, explanatory or conceptual gap only. For this reason, the presuppositions of these arguments are unlikely to entail the existence of nonphysical substances in the direct way that the presuppositions of the conceivability argument do.

Perhaps then, there is room for theorists to endorse property dualism, either in a standard or a Russellian monist form, on the basis of one of these arguments, whilst remaining invulnerable to the parity argument. If so, the significance of the parity argument will be less than I have suggested.

Initially, this seems like a serious threat to the significance of the parity argument. But in fact, for two reasons, the upshot for the parity argument is minimal. The first reason is that it seems that the vast majority of opponents of physicalism are in fact committed to the soundness of the conceivability argument. If so, property dualism without the conceivability argument is unlikely to be a popular position. The second reason is that the theoretical room for endorsing property dualism without the conceivability argument is narrower than one might suppose.

7.5.1 *The Influence of the Conceivability Argument*

The contemporary influence of arguments in philosophy is hard to gauge. Nonetheless, the available evidence suggests that the overwhelming majority of present-day opponents of physicalism accept the conceivability argument, even if some put greater emphasis on other arguments.

This is clearly true of the main property dualists discussed in this enquiry. Strawson (2003, 47) endorses a version of the conceivability argument involving zombies. Kim (2005; 169) endorsees a version involving inverted spectra. Jackson (2003) reverses his adherence to property dualism, but in doing so, he explicitly withdraws his assent from both the conceivability argument and the knowledge argument. Chalmers's (1996, 2010) and Goff's (2017) versions of the conceivability argument were discussed in § 6.2.

There is evidence that this pattern is replicated more widely. As I said in § 6.2, Bourget and Chalmers (2022, 12) report that 24.4% of philosophers accept or lean towards the metaphysical possibility of zombies. It is reasonable to take this as the figure for proponents of the conceivability argument. This is probably a low estimate. For some Russellian monists, like

The Consequences of the Parity Argument   151

Strawson (2003), are likely to have answered that zombies are impossible on the basis that physical terms rigidly designate fundamentally mental things.

This compares to 52.9% who accept or lean towards the impossibility of zombies. Physicalism is supposed to be the clear front-runner in the metaphysics of mind. For this reason, it would be surprising if the 52.9% of philosophers who reject the possibility of zombies included a large number of opponents of physicalism. And one assumes that *anyone* who accepts the metaphysical possibility of zombies will identify as an opponent of physicalism. It follows that the overwhelming majority of the 32.1% of respondents who identify as opponents of physicalism accept the conceivability argument.

If this is right, then the significance of the parity argument is secure whether or not there is theoretical room for property dualism without the conceivability argument. Indeed, *even if* there were many opponents of physicalism in addition to the 24.4% mentioned, an argument that shows that the commitments of 24.4% of philosophers lead to nonphysical substances would already be highly significant.

7.5.2 *The Unity of Arguments from Consciousness*

The case for the significance of the parity argument need not depend on these figures alone, however. The numbers suggest that the conceivability argument and other anti-physicalist arguments are seen as standing or falling together. So do Jackson's (2003) comments on why he revised his position on dualism. Reflection on the relationship between the commitments of the arguments suggests that this is right: if the conceivability argument is flawed, so too are the other leading anti-physicalist arguments. If so, the parity argument will exert pressure on property dualists generally, not just those who rely directly on the conceivability argument.

Although the knowledge argument, the explanatory gap argument, and the transparency argument do not depend on modal rationalism, there is good reason to think that these arguments do depend on the assumption that phenomenal concepts are transparent (or that phenomenal terms are semantically neutral, or similar). Chalmers (2010, 105–6) and Goff (2017, 74–5, 106–32) explain why. If so, positions that accept one of these arguments whilst rejecting the conceivability argument will be unattractive for reasons I now explain.

If it is true that these arguments depend on the transparency of phenomenal concepts, it follows that their proponents can only reject the conceivability argument, and hence the parity argument, if they are willing to posit strong necessities. Strong necessities, again, are the brute a posteriori necessities that cannot be accounted for in the way that Kripkean examples can.

152 *The Consequences of the Parity Argument*

For the reasons given in § 6.4, we should include here a posteriori necessities resulting solely from differences in identity between exact duplicates.

There is logical room for property dualists to reject the conceivability argument on the basis that it is a strong necessity that conscious experiences could not exist without some of the physical things that exist. But it is hard to see why anyone would occupy this logical space given the wider theoretical pressures.

It is generally accepted that strong necessities are counterintuitive. They should not be posited without reason. Even most physicalist opponents of the conceivability argument try to avoid relying on strong necessities. There are two main strategies. A priori physicalists take the view that sufficient a priori reflection will show that the physical facts necessitate the existence of consciousness after all. A posteriori physicalists (typically) take the view that phenomenal concepts are not transparent (cf. Goff 2017, 115–20, 129).

Although physicalists tend to avoid strong necessities, they do at least have some reasons to take such postulates seriously. For physicalists can appeal to the causal-closure argument as grounds for thinking that conscious experiences *must* be nothing over and above, and hence necessarily accompanied by, physical things. Together, the causal-closure argument, the conceivability of zombies, and the thesis that phenomenal concepts are transparent create theoretical pressure to accept that there are strong necessities.

Property dualists, by contrast, abandon any advantages that strong necessities might have for physicalists when they take the view that consciousness is something over and above physical things. This being so, it is hard to see what reason property dualists could have to suppose that there are nonetheless inexplicable necessities linking phenomenal and physical things. These bizarre postulates, which are resisted by physicalists to whom they would be extremely theoretically useful, would be theoretically useless to property dualists. (This is so, at least, pending an argument, as opposed to a prejudice, against positing nonphysical substances.)

It seems, therefore, that it is not mere partisanship that causes most opponents of physicalism to accept the conceivability argument. Once you have accepted one of the other arguments on the basis of the transparency of phenomenal concepts, the theoretical pressure to accept the conceivability argument becomes overwhelming. If so, the parity argument retains its full force, at least until a serious objection to nonphysical substances emerges. As I explained at the start of Chapter 2, such objections have so far been lacking.

It is worth observing, finally, that it is not clear that an appeal to strong necessities could get one back to a recognisable property dualist picture anyway. For it is conspicuous that, usually, when properties belong to a

The Consequences of the Parity Argument   153

substance, they also stand in a certain kind of conceptual relation to the other properties of that thing. The properties seem to mix or interpenetrate. I discussed this in § 5.4 and subsequent sections.

A property dualist who is determined to avoid admitting the existence of nonphysical substances might posit that conscious experiences strongly necessitate physical things. But the resulting picture will not be one where phenomenal properties belong to brains in the way that shape or size or weight do. Rather, the relation between the mind and the body will continue to look just like it does on a traditional substance dualist view, except that the occult magnetism of a strong necessity binds these things together.

This is not the kind of position 'property dualism' connotes. Indeed, if the nonphysical minds or souls on this view do not count as substances as characterised by Descartes's independence definition, they will remain excellent candidates for substances in the sense suggested by Aristotle's *Categories* (1a). For the minds or souls will not intuitively 'exist in' or be 'said of' bodies in anything like the way that properties usually are. Having gone that far, it is hard to see what the attraction of insisting on the strong necessities could be.

Conclusion

I have argued that, given the commitments that typically motivate their position, theorists who posit nonphysical properties in response to the mind-body problem must also posit nonphysical substances, as characterised by the Aristotelian-Cartesian independence definition of substance. They are likely to see this as unfortunate. For nonphysical substances have been unfashionable since the early twentieth century.

Contemporary hostility to nonphysical substances is a point of convergence for several intellectual trends. These include the lasting influence of Ryle (1949) and Wittgenstein (1953), the naturalistic aspirations of present-day metaphysics, and wider antipathy directed both at the idea of the soul and at any idea associated with Descartes. Cartesianism, as John Cottingham says, 'has become the ultimate philosophical bête noire':

> Both in the theory of knowledge and the philosophy of mind, late-twentieth-century philosophers tend to define their position in stark opposition to what they see as deeply flawed Cartesian paradigms. ... Descartes, the 'father of modern philosophy,' has been comprehensively disowned by his putative offspring.
>
> (Cottingham 1994, 2)

Cottingham said this of the late twentieth century a couple of decades ago. But attitudes towards Descartes and Cartesian metaphysics remain largely the same today.

It is not obvious that opponents of physicalism *should* see the conclusion of this enquiry as unfortunate. For as I explained in Chapter 2, the idea that nonphysical substances are especially theoretically troublesome, compared to nonphysical properties, does not appear to be well founded.

Furthermore, the idea that nonphysical substances are a peculiarly Cartesian invention is false. As I argued in Chapter 4, Descartes's theory of mind belongs to the same tradition as Plato, Aristotle, Augustine, and Aquinas. Similar ideas can be found in Homer, the Bible, the Epic of

DOI: 10.4324/9781003378600-9

Conclusion   155

Gilgamesh, and in countless traditions the world over, including the classics of Confucian, Daoist, Hindu, Jain, and Islamic philosophy mentioned in § 1.2.

This is no coincidence. Developmental psychologists have argued that from early childhood, 'we implicitly endorse a strong substance dualism of the sort defended by philosophers like Plato and Descartes' (Bloom 2007, 149). The evidence suggests that soul-body dualism is a 'cognitive default' (Bering 2006, 454).

As I have made clear, I think that the positive implications of this enquiry the idea of the soul should be taken at face value. The arguments against physicalism about consciousness appear to be sound. And anyone who accepts those arguments should be prepared to posit nonphysical substances resembling immaterial souls. We may find this conclusion embarrassing, but it is really no more embarrassing than the alternatives.

Those who sympathise with this conclusion must consider how we might best make sense of the place of nonphysical substances in the world. A particularly important question, in this context, is *when* in the natural history of species, and in the gestation of individual organisms, immaterial substances come into existence. This question is disconcerting because it seems strange that the radical discontinuity involved in the coming to be of an immaterial substance should occur at any point during a physical process that appears continuous and gradual.

The discontinuity between the existence and nonexistence of an immaterial substance is an advantage for substance dualism and idealism, insofar as it reflects the apparently fundamental divide between the interiority of one person's mind and that of another person or the exteriority of the physical world. But this advantage becomes a challenge when we begin to integrate philosophy of mind with natural history and biology.

A useful starting point, in responding to this problem, is the observation that the empirical world investigated by natural science is dependent on the phenomenology that constitutes it. This need not mean embracing idealism. For there may be nonmental noumena beneath the empirical surfaces. But the appearance of continuity and graduation in the empirical world might be misleading given the nature of the underlying noumena mental or nonmental. It is against the backdrop of the empirical world construed as fundamental that the existence of nonphysical substance looks so strange.

If we do adopt this starting point, we are likely to end up with a position on which the mind or soul is not an item in the body or something that floats above it like a cloud, but the space in which one's own body and other bodies are encountered (cf. Priest 2012). Heraclitus hints at such a view when he says, 'You will not find the boundaries of soul by travelling in any direction, so deep is the measure of it' (Burnet 1920, 102). Your

156 *Conclusion*

phenomenal states might be thought of, on this view, as a film that clings to the exterior of the noumenal world. Or, if you prefer, the soul is like a torch that blazes the unseen world into light.

These are only metaphors. For our understanding of film and fire are of empirical things. But they are metaphors that might be helpful in displacing worse metaphors, that we often take for granted – such as the idea that you are a moist robot representing physical objects to yourself by means of computational processes.

These speculations must be developed on another occasion. And for those readers who find them outrageously extravagant, I emphasise again that the primary purpose of this enquiry has not been to argue in favour of nonphysical substances, only for the conditional claim that if you oppose physicalism for the ordinary reasons, then you should be prepared to posit nonphysical substances. This is a claim about where a certain, fairly common, kind of rational reflection leads. Its truth is independent of whether that kind of reflection is epistemically valuable.

I conclude by noting one way in which this enquiry should be of interest beyond metaphysical discussions about the mind-body problem. This is in connection with the interdisciplinary project of understanding why humans think about the mind-body relation in the way that we do.

There is growing interest in the 'meta-problem of consciousness' (cf. Chalmers 2018). This is the problem of explaining why it is that humans persistently intuit that consciousness is nonphysical. The cultural and psychological data suggest that at its core this is in fact the problem of explaining why humans persistently intuit that consciousness characterises nonphysical *substances*.

The philosophical literature on the meta-problem does not usually try to explain the impulse to see the mind as something not just nonphysical but also substantial, i.e. capable of existing without the body and without other minds. The psychological literature offers a number of proposals. These usually attribute the impulse to see the mind as a nonphysical substance to selective pressures in the human social environment (cf. Bering 2006).

There is, however, a conceptual side to this story that philosophy must supply. The present enquiry can be seen as identifying some elements of that story. In particular, the foregoing arguments suggest that the attraction of the idea that minds are nonphysical substances is closely tied to the distinctive nature of phenomenal concepts and to our intellectual resistance to brute necessities.

These factors might help explain the prevalence of substance dualism in early infancy and across cultures. If so, this will not only help to fill in the evolutionary psychological picture, but it will also help guide our development of that picture. It will follow, for example, that cognitive systems that

Conclusion 157

arose later in our evolutionary history than phenomenal consciousness and modal reasoning cannot play the principal role in accounting for the prevalence of substance dualism. This is likely to be true of cognitive systems developed in response to selective pressures in the human social environment. Existing evolutionary psychological explanations of common-sense dualism may therefore need rethinking.

If it is true that the nature of phenomenal consciousness and modal reasoning combined make it natural to view the mind as a nonphysical substance, this will explain why something resembling substance dualism is ubiquitous across traditional cultures, religions, and philosophical theories. It would be no surprise if these traditions should then elaborate the core substance dualist picture for poetic, religious, or theoretical purposes.

Natural areas for elaboration include whether, under any circumstances, disembodied minds or souls become perceptible ghosts as in Plato's *Phaedo* (81c–d); whether there exist multiple nonphysical components of humans such as the Greek *psyche* and *pneuma*, the Egyptian *ba* and *akh*, or the Chinese *hun* and *po*; whether there exist immaterial minds or souls associated with animals, plants, rocks, and rivers, or floating free in the manner of angels and daemons; and whether various capacities such as respiration, perception, and cognition require just body, just soul, or both body and soul.

Scholars sometimes make out that because a given tradition has a distinctive perspective on the kind of issues listed here, it cannot be viewed as embracing a form of soul-body dualism comparable to that of paradigmatic dualists such as Plato or Descartes. But the divergences between views do not affect the fact that they share a common core. And it is plausible that that common core arises as a result of deep-seated factors in human nature, including the nature of our phenomenal concepts and modal reasoning.

I do not suggest that the insights of this enquiry are likely to exhaust the conceptual roots of common-sense dualism. I only highlight that some parts of the discussion might provide a useful complement to the psychological research. Research of both kinds suggests that nonphysical substances are likely to continue to play an important role in discussions of the mind-body problem in the future. It also confirms that the idea that 'the official doctrine … hails chiefly from Descartes' was a myth of Ryle's (1949, 1) own invention.

Appendix

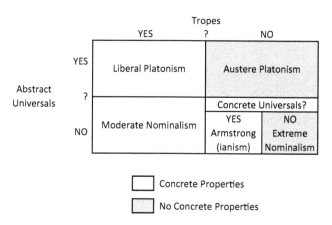

Figure A1.1 Five theories of properties.

Bibliography

Ackrill, J. L. (1963). 'Notes.' *Categories and De Interpretatione*. Trans. J. L. Ackrill. Oxford: Clarendon Press.

Alison, Henry. (1989). 'Kant's Refutation of Materialism.' *The Monist* 72.2, 190–208. https://doi.org/10.5840/monist19897227

Alter, Torin and Derk Pereboom. (2019). 'Russellian Monism.' *The Stanford Encyclopedia of Philosophy*. Ed. Edward N. Zalta (FALL 2019 EDITION) https://plato.stanford.edu/archives/fall2019/entries/russellian-monism/

Aristotle. (1949). *Aristotelis Categoriae Et Liber De Interpretatione*. Ed. L. Minio-Paluello. Oxford: Oxford University Press.

Armstrong, David. (1968). *A Materialist Theory of Mind*. London: Routledge.

Armstrong, David. (1978). *Universals and Scientific Realism*. Cambridge: Cambridge University Press.

Armstrong, David. (1997). *A World of States of Affairs*. Cambridge: Cambridge University Press.

Arnauld, Antoine and Pierre Nicole. (2012) [1662]. *Logic or the Art of Thinking*. Ed. Jill Vance Buroker. Cambridge: Cambridge University Press.

Augustine of Hippo. (1844–1864). *De Trinitate. Patrologiae Cursus Completus, Series Latina*. Vol. 42. Ed. Jacques Paul Migne. Paris: Apud Garnier Fratres.

Augustine of Hippo. (1948). *On the Immortality of the Soul. Basic Writings of Saint Augustine*. Vol. 1. Trans. Whitney Jennings Oates. New York: Random House.

Ayer, A. J. (1988). 'What I Saw When I Was Dead.' *The Sunday Telegraph*, 28th August 1988.

Azenabor, Godwin. (1999). 'African Theory of Mind-Body: An Essan Cultural Paradigm.' *African Quarterly* 39.4, 121–33

Bailey, A. M. (2012). 'No Bare Particulars.' *Philosophical Studies* 158, 31–41.

Bayne, Tim. (2010). *The Unity of Consciousness*. Oxford: Oxford University Press.

Bennett, Jonathan. (2001). *Learning from Six Philosophers: Descartes, Spinoza, Leibniz, Locke, Berkeley, Hume*. Oxford: Clarendon Press.

Bergman, Gustav. (1947). 'Russell On Particulars.' *The Philosophical Review* 56.1, 59–72.

Bergman, Gustav. (1967). *Realism: A Critique of Brentano and Meinong*. Madison, WI: University of Wisconsin Press.

160   Bibliography

Bering, Jesse. (2006). 'The Folk Psychology of Souls.' *The Behavioural and Brain Sciences* 29.5, 453–532. https://doi.org/10.1017/s0140525x06009101

Berkeley, George. (1948–1957). *The Works of George Berkeley, Bishop of Cloyne*. Vol. 9. Eds. A. A. Luce and T. E. Jessop. London: Thomas Nelson and Sons.

Berto, Francesco and Mark Jago. (2018). 'Impossible Worlds.' *The Stanford Encyclopedia of Philosophy*. Ed. Edward N. Zalta (Fall 2018 Edition). https://plato.stanford.edu/archives/fall2018/entries/impossible-worlds/

Bloom, Paul. (2007). 'Religion is Natural.' *Developmental Science* 10.1, 147–51. https://doi.org/10.1111/j.1467-7687.2007.00577.x

Boole, George. (1954) [1854].*The Laws of Thought*. London: Walton and Maberly.

Bourget, David and David Chalmers. (2014). 'What Do Philosophers Believe?' *Philosophical Studies* 170.3, 465–500.

Bourget, David and David Chalmers. (2022). 'Philosophers on Philosophy.' *Philosophers' Imprint* 22.

Bright, Liam Kofi. (2021). 'Why Do Scientists Lie?' *Royal Institute of Philosophy Supplement* 89, 117–129. https://doi.org/10.1017/S1358246121000102

Broackes, Justin. (2006). 'Substance.' *Proceedings of the Aristotelian Society* 106.1, 133–68. https://doi.org/10.1111/j.1467-9264.2006.00142.x

Broad, C. D. (1925).*The Mind and its Place in Nature*. London: Kegan Paul.

Brown, Warren S., Nancy Murphy and Newton H. Malony (eds.) (1998).*Whatever Happened to the Soul?* Minneapolis: Fortress Press.

Bryson, Cynthia. (1998). 'Mary Astell: Defender of the "Disembodied Mind".' *Hypatia* 13.4, 40–62. https://doi.org/10.1111/j.1527-2001.1998.tb01384.x

Burnet, John. (1920). *Early Greek Philosophy*. London: A. & C. Black.

Campbell, Keith. (1983). 'Abstract Particulars and the Philosophy of Mind.' *Australasian Journal of Philosophy* 61.2, 129–41. https://doi.org/10.1080/00048408312340931

Campbell, Keith. (1990). *Abstract Particulars*. Oxford: Blackwell.

Carnap, Rudolph. (1932). 'Psychologie in Physikalischer Sprache.' *Erkenntnis* 3, 107–42.

Carnap, Rudolph. (1959) [1931]. 'The Elimination of Metaphysics Through Logical Analysis of Language.' *Logical Positivism*. Ed. A. J. Ayer. New York: Simon and Schuster.

Carter, George. (2018). Biopsychism: A Novel Solution to the Subjective and Objective Problem as it Pertains to Consciousness, Personal Identity and Free Will. MA diss. University of Buckingham.

Chalmers, David. (1995). 'Facing Up to the Problem of Consciousness.' *Journal of Consciousness Studies* 2.3, 200–19.

Chalmers, David. (1996). *The Conscious Mind: In Search of a Fundamental Theory*. Oxford: Oxford University Press.

Chalmers, David. (2002). 'Does Conceivability Entail Possibility?' *Conceivability and Possibility*. Eds. Tamar Gendler and John Hawthorne. Oxford: Oxford University Press.

Chalmers, David. (2003). 'The Content and Epistemology of Phenomenal Belief.' *Consciousness: New Philosophical Perspectives*. Eds. Quentin Smith and Aleksandar Jokic. Oxford: Oxford University Press.

Chalmers, David. (2006). 'The Foundations of Two-Dimensional Semantics.' *Two-Dimensional Semantics*. Eds. Manuel García-Carpintero and Josep Macià. Oxford: Oxford University Press, 38–140.

Chalmers, David. (2010).*The Character of Consciousness*. Oxford: Oxford University Press.

Chalmers, David. (2016a). 'Panpsychism and Panprotopsychism.' *Panpsychism: Contemporary Perspectives*. Eds. Godehard Bruntrup and Ludwig Jaskolla. Oxford: Oxford University Press, 19–44.

Chalmers, David. (2016b). 'The Combination Problem for Panpsychism.' *Panpsychism: Contemporary Perspectives*. Eds. Godehard Bruntrup and Ludwig Jaskolla. Oxford: Oxford University Press, 179–211.

Chalmers, David. (2018). 'The Meta-Problem of Consciousness.' *Journal of Consciousness Studies* 25.9–10, 6–61.

Chalmers, David. (2021). 'Idealism and the Mind-Body Problem.' *The Routledge Handbook on Idealism and Immaterialism*. Eds. Joshua Farris and Benedikt Paul Göcke. London: Routledge, 591–613.

Chappell, Vere. (2008). 'Descartes on Substance.' *A Companion to Descartes*. Eds. Janet Broughton and John Carriero. Oxford: Blackwell.

Churchland, Paul. (1985). 'Reduction, Qualia, and the Direct Introspection of Brain States.' *The Journal of Philosophy* 82.1, 8–28. https://doi.org/10.2307/2026509

Clark, Desmond. (2003). *Descartes's Theory of Mind*. Oxford: Oxford University Press.

Cleeveley, Harry. (2022). 'The a Priori Truth of Modal Rationalism.' *The Philosophical Quarterly* 72.4, 816–36. https://doi.org/10.1093/pq/pqab061

Coleman, Sam. (2016). 'Panpsychism and Neutral Monism: How to Make Up One's Mind.' *Panpsychism*. Eds. Godehard Brüntrup and Ludwig Jaskolla. Oxford: Oxford University Press. https://doi.org/10.1093/acprof:oso/9780199359943.003.0011

Cooper, John. (2000). *Body, Soul and Life Everlasting*. Nottingham: Apollos.

Cooper, John. (2001). 'Biblical Anthropology and the Body-Soul Problem.' *Soul, Body and Survival: Essays on the Metaphysics of Human Persons*. Ed. Kevin Corcoran. Ithaca NY: Cornell University Press, pp. 153–76.

Cooper, John. (2007). 'The Bible and Dualism Once Again: A Reply to Joel B. Green and Nancey Murphy.' *Philosophia Christi* 9.2, 459–69. https://doi.org/10.5840/PC20079237

Cooper, John. (2009a). 'The Current Body-Soul Debate: A Case for Dualistic Holism.' *Southern Baptist Journal of Theology* 13.2, 32–50.

Cooper, John. (2009b). 'Exaggerated Rumors of Dualism's Demise: A Review Essay on Body, Soul, and Human Life.' *Philosophia Christi* 11.2, 453–64. https://doi.org/10.5840/pc200911240

Cooper, John. (2015). 'Scripture and Philosophy on the Unity of Body and Soul: An Integrative Method for Theological Anthropology.' *The Ashgate Research Companion to Theological Anthropology*. Eds. Joshua Farris and Charles Taliaferro. Farnham: Ashgate.

Cooper, John. (2018). 'Biblical Anthropology is Holistic and Dualistic.' *The Blackwell Companion to Substance Dualism*. Eds. Jonathan Loose, Angus Menuge, and J. P. Moreland. Oxford: Blackwell.

162 Bibliography

Cottingham, John. (1985). 'Cartesian Trialism.' *Mind* 94.374, 218–30. https://doi.org/10.1093/mind/XCIV.374.218

Cottingham, John. (1994). 'Introduction: Plus Una Vice Agendum: Cartesian Metaphysics Three and a Half Centuries On.' *Reason, Will and Sensation: Studies in Descartes' Metaphysics*. Ed. John Cottingham. Oxford: Clarendon Press.

Crane, Tim. (2001). *Elements of Mind: An Introduction to the Philosophy of Mind*. Oxford: Oxford University Press.

Cucu, Alin. (2022). Interacting Minds in the Physical World. Dissertation, University of Lausanne.

Cucu, Alin, and Brian Pitts. (2019). 'How Dualists Should (Not) Respond to the Objection from Energy Conservation.' *Mind & Matter* 17.1, 95–121.

Davidson, Donald. (1970). 'Mental Events.' *Experience and Theory*. Eds. L. Foster and J. W. Swanson. London: Duckworth. Reprinted in Donald Davidson. Essays on Actions and Events. Oxford: Oxford University Press, 1980.

Davies, Daniel. (2022). 'Theories of the Soul in Medieval Jewish Thought.' *Jewish/Non-Jewish Relations: Between Exclusion and Embrace. An Online Teaching Resource*. [Accessed 1 November, 2022] https://jnjr.div.ed.ac.uk/primary-sources/medieval/theories-of-soul-in-medieval-jewish-thought/

Demos, Raphael. (1948). 'Note on Plato's Theory of Ideas.' *Philosophy and Phenomenological Research* 8, 456–60.

Denkel, Arda. (1992). 'Substance Without Substratum.' *Philosophy and Phenomenological Research* 52.3, 705–11.

Dennett, Daniel. (1991). *Consciousness Explained*. Boston, MA: Little Brown & Co.

Di Gregorio, Mario. (2016). 'Ernst Haeckel and the Unity of Culture – Monism.' *Brewminate: A Bold Blend of News and Ideas*. 5 April 2016. [Accessed 14 July, 2022] https://brewminate.com/ernst-haeckel-and-the-unity-of-culture-monism/

Double, Richard. (1985). 'Phenomenal Properties.' *Philosophy and Phenomenological Research* 45.3, 383–92.

Farris, Joshua. (2015). 'Substance Dualism and Theological Anthropology.' *Philosophy and Theology* 27.1, 107–26. https://doi.org/10.5840/philtheol20155623

Farris, Joshua. (2020). *An Introduction to Theological Anthropology: Humans, Both Creaturely and Divine*. Ada, MI: Baker Academic.

Farris, Joshua. (2023). *The Creation of Self: A Case for the Soul*. Alresford: John Hunt.

Farris, Joshua and Benedikt Paul Göcke (eds.) (2021).*The Routledge Handbook for Idealism and Immaterialism*. London: Routledge.

Feldman, Fred. (1974). 'Kripke on the Identity Theory.' *Journal of Philosophy* 71, 665–76. https://doi.org/10.2307/2024805

Fine, Kit. (2001). 'The Question of Realism' Philosophers.' *Philosophers' Imprint* 1.1. https://quod.lib.umich.edu/p/phimp/3521354.0001.002/--question-of-realism?view=image

Fine, Kit. (2012). 'A Guide to Ground.' *Metaphysical Grounding*. Eds. Fabrice Correia and Benjamin Schneider. Cambridge: Cambridge University Press.

Francescotti, Robert. (2001). 'Property Dualism without Substance Dualism?' *Philosophical Papers* 30.2, 93–116.

García-Carpintero, Manuel and Josep Macià (eds.) (2006). *Two-Dimensional Semantics*. Oxford: Oxford University Press.

Gasman, Daniel. (1971). *The Scientific Origins of National Socialism: Social Darwinism in Ernst Haeckel and the German Monist League*. London: Macdonald.

Göcke, Benedikt Paul. (2012). *After Physicalism*. Notre Dame, IN: Notre Dame University Press.

Goff, Philip. (2009). 'Why Panpsychism Doesn't Help Explain Consciousness.' *Dialectica* 63.3, 289–311. https://doi.org/10.1111/j.1746-8361.2009.01196.x

Goff, Philip. (2010). 'Ghosts and Sparse Properties: Why Physicalists Have More to Fear from Ghosts than Zombies.' *Philosophy and Phenomenological Research* 81.1, 119–39. https://doi.org/10.1111/j.1933-1592.2010.00352.x

Goff, Philip. (2012). 'A Priori Physicalism, Lonely Ghosts and Cartesian Doubt.' *Consciousness and Cognition* 21, 742–46. https://doi.org/10.1016/j.concog.2011.02.007

Goff, Philip. (2014). 'The Cartesian Argument Against Physicalism.' *New Waves in Philosophy of Mind*. Eds. Mark Sprevak and Jesper Kallestrup. London: Palgrave Macmillan.

Goff, Philip. (2017). *Consciousness and Fundamental Reality*. Oxford: Oxford University Press.

Goff, Philip. (2021a). 'Essentialist Modal Rationalism.' *Synthese* 198, 2019–27. https://doi.org/10.1007/s11229-019-02109-9

Goff, Philip. (2021b). 'Replies to Critics.' *Journal of Consciousness Studies* 28.9–10, 289–328.

Goff, Philip. (Forthcoming) 'How Exactly Does Panpsychism Help Explain Consciousness?' *Journal of Consciousness Studies*.

Goldschmidt, Tyron and Kenneth Pearce (eds). (2017). *Idealism: New Essays in Metaphysics*. Oxford: Oxford University Press.

Gregory of Nyssa. (1993). *Homilies on Ecclesiastes: An English Version*. Ed. Stuart Hall. Berlin: De Gruyter.

Guyer, Paul and Rolf-Peter Horstmann. (2018). 'Idealism.' *The Stanford Encyclopedia of Philosophy*. Ed. Edward N. Zalta (Winter 2018 Edition). https://plato.stanford.edu/archives/win2018/entries/idealism/

Gyekye, Kwame. (1995). *An Essay on African Philosophical Thought: The Akan Conceptual Scheme*. Revised edition. Philadelphia: Temple University Press.

Harari, Yuval Noah. (2016). *Homo Deus*. Rochester: Vintage Digital.

Hasker, William. (1995). 'Concerning the Unity of Consciousness.' *Faith and Philosophy* 12.4, 532–47. https://doi.org/10.5840/faithphil199512429

Hasker, William. (1999).*The Emergent Self*. Ithaca, NY: Cornell University Press.

Haugeland, John. (1982). 'Weak Supervenience.' *American Philosophical Quarterly* 19.1, 93–103.

Hawkins, Mike. (1997). *Social Darwinism in European and American Thought*. Cambridge: Cambridge University Press.

Heil, John. (2003). *From an Ontological Point of View*. Oxford: Clarendon Press.

Heil, John. (2012). *Philosophy of Mind: A Contemporary Introduction*. London: Routledge.

Hempel, Carl. (1935). 'Analyse Logique de la Psychologie.' *Revue de Synthese* 10, 27–42.

Hendrischke, Barbara (trans.) (2006). *The Scripture of the Great Peace. The Taiping jing and the Beginnings of Daoism*. London: University of California Press.

164   Bibliography

Herodotus. (1954) [c. 430 BCE]. *Histories*. Trans. Aubrey de Selincourt. London: Penguin.

Hobbes, Thomas. (1651). *Leviathan or the Matter, Forme, & Power of a Commonwealth Ecclesiastical and Civil*. London: Andrew Crooke, at the Green Dragon in St. Paul's Churchyard.

Hoffman, Joshua and Gary Rosenkrantz. (1997). *Substance: Its Nature and Existence*. London: Routledge.

Horgan, Terence. 'Supervenience to Superdupervenience: Meeting the Demands of a Materialist World.' *Mind* 102.408 (1993) 555–86.

Hübinger, Gangolf. (2023). 'Monist League, German.' *Religion Past and Present*. Brill Reference Online. [Accessed 12 January, 2023] https://referenceworks.brillonline.com/entries/religion-past-and-present/monist-league-german-SIM_14399

Hughes, Samuel. (2021). 'German Idealism.' *The Routledge Handbook for Idealism and Immaterialism*. Eds. Joshua Farris and Benedikt Paul Göcke. London: Routledge.

Hume, David. (2007) [1739–40]. *A Treatise of Human Nature*. Eds. David Norton and Mary Norton. cOxford University Press.

Husserl, Edmund. (1982) [1913]. 'Ideas Pertaining to a Pure Phenomenology and to a Phenomenological Philosophy: First Book: General Introduction to a Pure Phenomenology.' Trans. F. Kersten. The Hague: Nijhoff.

Jackson, Frank. (1982). 'Epiphenomenal Qualia.' *Philosophical Quarterly* 32.127, 127–36. https://doi.org/10.2307/2960077

Jackson, Frank. (1986). 'What Mary Didn't Know.' *The Journal of Philosophy* 83.5, 291–95.

Jackson, Frank. (1998). *From Metaphysics to Ethics: A Defense of Conceptual Analysis*. Oxford: Clarendon Press.

Jackson, Frank. (2003). 'Mind and Illusion.' *Minds and Persons*. Ed. Anthony O'Hear. Cambridge: Cambridge University Press.

James, William. (1890). *The Principles of Psychology*. Vol. 1. New York: Henry Holt.

Kanada. (2022). *Vaiśeṣikasūtra: A Translation*. Trans. Moese, Ionut and Ganesh U. Thite. London: Routledge.

Kaphagawani, Nidier Njirayamanda. (2004). 'African Conceptions of a Person: A Critical Survey.' *A Companion to African Philosophy*. Ed. Kwasi Wiredu. Oxford: Blackwell.

Kim, Jaegwon. (2005). *Physicalism, or Something Near Enough*. Princeton, NJ: Princeton University Press.

Kim, Jaegwon. (2006). *Philosophy of mind* (2nd ed.). New York: Westview.

Knight, Nick. (1990). 'Introduction.' *Mao on Dialectical Materialism: Writings on Philosophy*, 1937. Ed. Nick Knight. London: M. E. Sharp.

Koons, Robert and George Bealer. (2010). *The Waning of Materialism*. Oxford: Oxford University Press.

Kripke, Saul. (1972). 'Naming and Necessity.' *Semantics of Natural Language*. Eds. Donald Davidson and Gilbert Harman. Dordrecht: Reidel.

Kripke, Saul. (1980). *Naming and Necessity*. Cambridge MA: Harvard University Press.

Levin, Michael. (1979). *Metaphysics and the Mind-Body Problem*. Oxford: Oxford University Press.

Bibliography 165

Levine, Joseph. (1983). 'Materialism and Qualia: The Explanatory Gap.' *Pacific Philosophical Quarterly* 64, 354–61. https://doi.org/10.1111/j.1468-0114.1983.tb00207.x

Lewis, David. (1966). 'An Argument for the Identity Theory.' *The Journal of Philosophy* 63.1, 17–2.

Lewis, David. (1983). 'New Work for a Theory of Universals.' *Australasian Journal of Philosophy* 61, 343–77. https://doi.org/10.1080/00048408312341131

Lewis, David. (1986). *On the Plurality of Worlds*. Oxford: Blackwell.

Liu, Michelle. (2021). 'Revelation and the Intuition of Dualism.' *Synthese* 199, 11491–515.

Locke, John. (1689). *An Essay Concerning Human Understanding*. Ed. R. Woolhouse. London: Penguin.

Lockwood, Michael, (1989). *Mind, Brain, and the Quantum*. Oxford: Blackwell.

Loeb, Louis. (1981). *From Descartes to Hume: Continental Metaphysics and the Development of Modern Philosophy*. St. Ithaca, NY: Cornell University Press.

Look, Brandon C. (2013). 'Simplicity of Substance in Leibniz, Wolff and Baumgarten.' *Studia Leibnitiana* 45.2, 191–208. https://doi.org/10.25162/stl-2013-0012

Loose, Jonathan, Angus Menuge, and J. P. Moreland (eds.) (2018). *The Blackwell Companion to Substance Dualism*. Oxford: Blackwell.

Lowe, E. J. (1998).*The Possibility of Metaphysics: Substance, Identity and Time*. Oxford: Clarendon Press.

Lycan, William. (2009). 'Giving Dualism its Due.' *Australasian Journal of Philosophy* 87.4, 551–63. https://doi.org/10.1080/00048400802340642

Lycan, William. (2013). 'Is Property Dualism Better off than Substance Dualism?' *Philosophical Studies* 164.2, 533–42. https://doi.org/10.1007/s11098-012-9867-x

Mackie, J. L. (1976). *Problems from Locke*. Oxford: Clarendon Press.

Maimonides, Moses. (1986–2007) [c.1176–c.1178]. *Mishneh, Torah, Repentance*. Trans. Eliyahy Touger. New York: Moznaim Publishing.

Majeed, Hassekei Mohammed. (2013). 'A Critique of the Concept of Quasi-Physicalism in Akan Philosophy.' *African Studies Quarterly* 14.1–2, 23–33.

Markie, Peter. (1994). 'Descartes' Concept of Substance.' *Reason, Will and Sensation: Studies in Descartes*. Ed. John Cottingham. Oxford: Clarendon Press.

Martin, C. B. (1980). 'Substance Substantiated.' *Australasian Journal of Philosophy* 58.1, 3–10.

Maxwell, Grover. (1979). 'Rigid Designators and Mind-Brain Identity.' *Minnesota Studies in the Philosophy of Science* 9, 365–403.

Mazis, Glen A. (2011). 'The Sky Starts at Our Feet: Anasazi Clues about Overcoming Mind/Body dualism Through the Unity of Earth/Sky.' *Environment, Space, Place* 3.2, 7–21. https://doi.org/10.7761/ESP.3.2.7

McEvilley, Thomas. (2002). *The Shape of Ancient Thought*. New York: Allworth Press.

McGinn, Colin. (1977). 'Anomalous Monism and Kripke's Cartesian Intuitions.' *Analysis* 37.2, 78–80. https://doi.org/10.1093/analys/37.2.78

McGinn, Colin. (1989). 'Can we Solve the Mind-Body Problem?' *Mind* 98, 349–66.

McPherson, Fiona. (2006). 'Property Dualism.' *Consciousness and its Place in Nature*. Ed. Anthony Freeman. Exeter: Imprint Academic.

166 Bibliography

Melnyk, Andrew. (2003). *A Physicalist Manifesto: Thoroughly Modern Material-ism* Cambridge: Cambridge University Press.

Mertz, D. W. (1996). *Realism and Its Logic.* New Haven, CT: Yale University Press.

Michel, Jean-Baptiste, Yuan Kui Shen, Aviva Presser Aiden, Adrian Veres, Matthew K Gray, Joseph P. Pickett, Dale Hoiberg, Dan Clancy, Peter Norvig, Jon Orwant, Steven Pinker, Martin A Nowak, and Erez Lieberman Aiden (2011). 'Quantitative Analysis of Culture Using Millions of Digitized Books.' *Science* 331.6014, 176–82. https://www.science.org/doi/10.1126/science.1199644

Mizrahi, Avshalom. (2011). 'The Soul and the Body in the Philosophy of the Rambam.' *Rambam Maimonides Medical Journal* 2.2. https://doi.org/10.5041/RMMJ.10040

Montero, Barbara. (2013). 'Must Physicalism Imply the Supervenience of the Mental on the Physical?' *The Journal of Philosophy* 110.2, 93–110. https://doi.org/10.5840/jphil2013110240

Montero, Barbara. (2015). 'Russellian Physicalism.' *Consciousness in the Physical World: Perspectives on Russellian Monism.* Eds. Alter and Nagasawa. Oxford: Oxford University Press.

Moore, G. E. (1903). 'The Refutation of Idealism.' *Mind* 12, 433–53.

Moran, Alex. (2018). 'The Paradox of Decrease and Dependent Parts.' *Ratio* 31.3, 273–84. https://doi.org/10.1111/rati.12185

Mørch, Hedda Hassel. (2014). 'Panpsychism and Causation: A New Argument and a Solution to the Combination Problem.' PhD diss. University of Oslo.

Moreland, J. P. (2014). *The Soul: How We Know It's Real and Why It Matters.* Chicago, IL: Moody.

Nagel, Ernest. (1961). *The Structure of Science: Problems in the Logic of Explanation.* New York: Harcourt Brace & World.

Nagel, Thomas. (1965). 'Physicalism.' *Philosophical Review* 74.3, 339–56.

Nagel, Thomas. (1974). 'What is it Like to be a Bat?' *Philosophical Review* 83.4, 435–50.

Newman, John Henry. (1849). 'On the Individuality of the Soul.' *Newman Reader.* [Accessed 17 October 2022] https://www.newmanreader.org/works/parochial/volume4/sermon6.html

Nida-Rümelin, Martine. (2006). 'Dualist Emergentism.' *Contemporary Debates in Philosophy of Mind.* Eds. Brian McLaughlin and Jonathan Cohen. Oxford: Blackwell.

Nida-Rümelin, Martine. (2007). 'Grasping Phenomenal Properties.' *Phenomenal Concepts and Phenomenal Knowledge.* Eds. Torin Alter and Sven Walter. Oxford: Oxford University Press.

Nida-Rümelin, Martine. (2010). 'An Argument from Transtemporal Identity for Subject Body Dualism.' *The Waning of Materialism.* Eds. George Bealer and Robert Koons. Oxford: Oxford University Press.

Nida-Rümelin, Martine. (2011). 'The Conceptual Origin of Subject Body Dualism.' *Self and Self-Knowledge.* Ed. Annalisa Colliva. Oxford: Oxford University Press.

Nida-Rümelin, Martine. (2012). 'The Non-descriptive Individual Nature of Conscious Beings.' *Personal Identity: Complex or Simple?* Eds. Georg Gasser and Matthias Stefan. Cambridge: Cambridge University Press.

O'Conaill, Donnchadh. (2022). *Substance.* Cambridge: Cambridge: Cambridge University Press.

Oliver, Alex. (1996). 'The Metaphysics of Properties.' *Mind* 105.417, 1–80. https://doi.org/10.1093/mind/105.417.1

Owen, G. E. L. (1965). 'Inherence.' *Phronesis* 10, 97–105.

Papineau, David. (2001). 'The Rise of Physicalism.' *Physicalism and its Discontents.* Eds. Carl Gillett and Barry Loewer. Cambridge: Cambridge University Press.

Papineau, David. (2002). *Thinking about Consciousness.* Oxford: Oxford University Press.

Papineau, David. (2009). 'The Causal Closure of the Physical and Naturalism.' *The Oxford Handbook of Philosophy of Mind.* Eds. Brian McLaughlin, Ansgar Beckermann, and Sven Walter. Oxford: Oxford University Press.

Pfeifer, Theresa H. (2009). 'Deconstructing Cartesian Dualisms of Western Racialized Systems: A Study in the Colors Black and White.' *Journal of Black Studies* 39.4, 528–47. https://doi.org/10.1177/0021934706298192

Pini, Giorgio. (2008). 'Reading Aristotle's Categories as an Introduction to Logic: Later Medieval Discussions about its Place in the Aristotelian Corpus.' *Medieval Commentaries on Aristotle's Categories.* Ed. Lloyd A. Newton. Leiden: Brill.

Pitts, J. Brian. (2020). 'Conservation Laws and the Philosophy of Mind: Opening the Black Box, Finding a Mirror.' *Philosophia* 48, 673–707. https://doi.org/10.1007/s11406-019-00102-7

Place, U. T. (1956). 'Is Consciousness a Brain Process?' *British Journal of Psychology* 47.1, 44–50. https://doi.org/10.1111/j.2044-8295.1956.tb00560.x

Plantinga, Alvin. (1970). 'World and Essence.' *The Philosophical Review* 79.4, 461–92.

Plato. (1977). *Plato: Complete Works.* Ed. John Cooper. Indianapolis, IN: Hackett.

Plumwood, Val. (1993). *Feminism and the Mastery of Nature.* London: Routledge.

Porter, Elizabeth. (2006). 'The Harm of Dualism.' *Peace Review* 17.2–3, 231–37.

Price, H. H. (1939). 'Presidential Address to the Society for Psychical Research.' *Proceedings of the Society for Psychical Research* 45.160, 307–23. Reprinted in F. B. Dilley (Ed.) *Philosophical Interactions with Parapsychology.* London: Palgrave Macmillan.

Priest, Stephen. (1991). *Theories of the Mind.* London: Penguin.

Priest, Stephen. (2000). *The Subject in Question: Sartre's Critique of Husserl in The Transcendence of the Ego.* London: Routledge.

Priest, Stephen. (2012). 'The Unconditioned Soul.' *After Physicalism.* Ed. Benedikt Paul Göcke. Notre Dame, IN: University of Notre Dame Press.

Putnam, Hilary. (1967). 'Psychological Predicates.' *Art, Mind, and Religion.* Eds. William H. Capitan and Daniel Davy Merrill. Pittsburgh PA: University of Pittsburgh Press.

Putnam, Hilary. (1973). 'Meaning and Reference.' *The Journal of Philosophy* 70.19, 699–711.

Quame, Safro. (2004). 'Quasi-Materialism: A Contemporary African Philosophy of Mind.' *A Companion to African Philosophy.* Ed. Kwasi Wiredu. Oxford: Blackwell. https://doi.org/10.1002/9780470997154.ch27

168 Bibliography

Quine, Willard Van Orman. 'Two Dogmas of Empiricism.' *Philosophical Review* 60 (1951) 20–43.

Quine, Willard Van Orman. (1995). *From Stimulus to Science*. Cambridge, MA: Harvard University Press.

Rickabaugh, Brandon. (2018a). 'Responding to N.T. Wright's Rejection of the Soul.' *The Heythrop Journal* 59.2, 201–20. https://doi.org/10.1111/heyj.12341

Rickabaugh, Brandon. (2018b). 'Dismantling Bodily Resurrection Arguments Against Mind-Body Dualism.' *Christian Physicalism?* Eds. Keith Loftin and Joshua Farris. Lanham, MD: Lexington Books.

Rickabaugh, Brandon. (2019). 'Alister McGrath's Anti-Mind-Body Dualism: Neuroscientific and Philosophical Quandaries for Christian Physicalism.' *Trinity Journal* 40, 215–40.

Rickabaugh, Brandon and J. P. Moreland. (2023). *The Substance of Consciousness: A Comprehensive Defense of Contemporary Substance Dualism*. Oxford: Wiley-Blackwell.

Robinson, Howard. (1982). *Matter and Sense*. Cambridge: Cambridge University Press.

Robinson, Howard. (2016). *From the Knowledge Argument to Mental Substance*. Cambridge: Cambridge University Press.

Rodriguez-Pereyra, Gonzalo. (2008). 'Descartes's Substance Dualism and His Independence Conception of Substance.' *Journal of the History of Philosophy* 46.1, 69–90. https://doi.org/10.1353/hph.2008.1827

Rosen, Gideon. (2018). 'Abstract Objects.' *The Stanford Encyclopedia of Philosophy*. Ed. Edward N. Zalta (Winter 2019 Edition). https://plato.stanford.edu/archives/win2018/entries/abstract-objects/

Ruhnau, Eva. (1995). 'Time Gestalt and the Observer: Reflections on the "Tertium Datur" of Consciousness.' *Conscious Experience*. Ed. Thomas Metzinger. Paderborn: Imprint Academic.

Russell, Bertrand. (1912). *The Problems of Philosophy*. London: Williams and Norgate.

Russell, Bertrand. (1927). *The Analysis of Matter*. London: Kegan Paul.

Russell, Bertrand. (1948). *Human Knowledge – Its Scope and Limits*. London: Allen and Unwin.

Ryle, Gilbert. (2009) [1949].*The Concept of Mind: 60th Anniversary Edition*. Ed. Julia Tanney. London: Routledge.

Sartre, Jean-Paul. (1957) [1936–7]. *The Transcendence of the Ego: An Existentialist Theory of Consciousness*. Trans. Forest Williams and Robert Kirkpatrick. New York: Noonday Press.

Sartwell, Crispin. (2019). 'Western Philosophy as White Supremacy.' *Los Angeles Review of Books*. 1 July 2019 [Accessed 31 December 2022] https://thephilosophicalsalon.com/western-philosophy-as-white-supremacism/

Schmaltz, Tad. (2007). *Descartes on Causation*. Oxford: Oxford University Press.

Schneider, Susan. (2012a). 'Why Property Dualists Must Reject Substance Physicalism.' *Philosophical Studies* 157, 61–76. https://doi.org/10.1007/s11098-010-9618-9

Schneider, Susan. (2012b). Non-Reductive Physicalism Cannot Appeal to Token Identity.' *Philosophy and Phenomenological Research* 85.3, 719–28.

Bibliography 169

Schwitzgebel, Eric. (2014). 'The Crazyist Metaphysics of Mind.' *Australasian Journal of Philosophy* 92.4, 665–82. https://doi.org/10.1080/00048402.2014.910675

Searle, John. (2002). 'Why I am Not a Property Dualist.' *Journal of Consciousness Studies* 9.12, 57–64.

Searle, John. (2004). *Mind: A Brief Introduction.* Oxford: Oxford University Press.

Shoemaker, Sidney. (1975). 'Functionalism and Qualia.' *Philosophical Studies* 27.5, 291–315. https://doi.org/10.1007/BF01225748

Sider, Ted. (2011). *Writing the Book of the World.* Oxford: Oxford University Press.

Slingerland, Edward. (2013). 'Body and Mind in Early China: An Integrated Humanities-Science Approach.' *Journal of the American Academy of Religion* 81.1, 6–55. https://doi.org/10.1093/jaarel/lfs094

Smart, J. J. C. (1959). 'Sensations and Brain processes.' *The Philosophical Review* 68.2, 141–56.

Societas Iesu. (1986) [1599]. *Ratio Atque Institutio Studiorem Societatis Iesu. Monumenta Paedagogica Societatis Iesu.* Ed. S. J. Ladislaus Lukács. Rome: Institutum Historicum Societatis Iesu, 355–453. English trans. by Allan P. Farrell (1970) at https://3eh4ot43gk9g3h1uu7edbbf1-wpengine.netdna-ssl.com/wp-content/uploads/documents/2019/09/ratio-studiorum-1599.pdf

Spackman, John. (2012). 'Contemporary Philosophy of Mind and Buddhist Thought.' *Philosophy Compass* 7.10, 741–51. https://doi.org/10.1111/j.1747-9991.2012.00506.x

Spade, Paul Vincent and Claude Panaccio. (2019). 'William of Ockham.' *The Stanford Encyclopedia of Philosophy.* Ed. Edward N. Zalta (Spring 2019 Edition). https://plato.stanford.edu/archives/spr2019/entries/ockham/

Stalin, Joseph. (1938). 'Dialectical and Historical Materialism.' *Joseph Stalin Internet Archive.* [Accessed 13 January 2023] https://www.marxists.org/reference/archive/stalin/works/1938/09.htm

Steadman, Lyle, Craig Palmer and Christopher Tiller. (1996). 'The Universality of Ancestor Worship.' *Ethnology* 35.1, 63–76. https://doi.org/10.2307/3774025

Strawson, Galen. (1994). *Mental Reality.* Cambridge, MA: MIT Press.

Strawson, Galen. (2003). 'Real Materialism.' *Chomsky and His Critics.* Eds. Louise Antony and Norbert Hornstein. Oxford: Blackwell. Reprinted in *Real Materialism and Other Essays.* Oxford: Oxford University Press, 2008.

Strawson, Galen. (2006). 'Realistic Monism: Why Physicalism Entails Panpsychism.' *Journal of Consciousness Studies* 13.10–11, 3–31.

Strawson, Galen. (2008). 'What Is the Relation Between an Experience, the Subject of Experience, and the Content of Experience?' *Real Materialism and Other Essays.* Oxford: Oxford University Press.

Strawson, Galen. (2011).*The Evident Connexion: Hume on Personal Identity.* Oxford: Oxford University Press.

Strawson, Galen. (2018). 'The Consciousness Deniers.' *The New York Review of Books,* 4 April, 2018. [Accessed 31 December, 2022] https://www.nybooks.com/online/2018/03/13/the-consciousness-deniers/

Stuart, Matthew. (2003). 'Descartes' Extended Substances.' *New Essays on the Rationalists.* Eds. Rocco J. Gennaro and Charles Huenemann. Oxford: Oxford University Press.

170 Bibliography

Stubenberg, Leopold. (2018). 'Neutral Monism.' *Stanford Encyclopedia of Philosophy*. Ed. Edward Zalter (Fall 2018 Edition). https://plato.stanford.edu/archives/fall2018/entries/neutral-monism/

Stump, Eleanor. (2012). 'Resurrection and the Separated Soul.' *The Oxford Handbook of Aquinas*. Ed. Brian Davies. Oxford: Oxford University Press.

Swinburne, Richard. (1986). *The Evolution of the Soul*. Oxford: Oxford University Press.

Swinburne, Richard. (2013). *Mind, Brain and Free Will*. Oxford: Oxford University Press.

Swinburne, Richard. (2018). 'Cartesian Substance Dualism.' *The Blackwell Companion to Substance Dualism*. Eds. Loose, Jonathan, Angus Menuge, and J. P. Moreland. Oxford: Blackwell.

Swinburne, Richard. (2019). *Are We Bodies or Souls?* Oxford: Oxford University Press.

Tanney, Julia. (2009). 'Rethinking Ryle: A Critical Discussion of the Philosophy of Mind.' *The Concept of Mind: 60th Anniversary Edition*. Ed. Julia Tanney. London: Routledge.

Tanney, Julia. (2015). 'Gilbert Ryle.' *The Stanford Encyclopedia of Philosophy*. Ed. Edward N. Zalta (Spring 2015 Edition). https://plato.stanford.edu/archives/spr2015/entries/ryle/

Toner, Patrick. (2011). 'Independence Accounts of Substance and Substantial Parts.' *Philosophical Studies* 155.1, 37–43. https://doi.org/10.1007/s11098-010-9521-4

Tononi, Giulio. (2008). 'Consciousness as Integrated Information: A Provisional Manifesto.' *Biological Bulletin* 215.3, 216–42. https://doi.org/10.2307/25470707

Ukwamedua, Nelson U. (2022). 'Immortality of the Soul in Classical Western Thought and in Igbo-African Ontology: A Discourse in Existential Metaphysics.' *Ethnicities* (online first). https://doi.org/10.1177/14687968221119622

Van Inwagen, Peter. (2014). *Existence: Essays in Ontology*. Cambridge: Cambridge University Press.

Ventriglio, Antonio and Dinesh Bhugra. (2015). 'Descartes' Dogma and Damage to Western Psychiatry.' *Epidemiology and Psychiatric Sciences* 24, 368–70. https://doi.org/10.1017/S2045796015000608

Walsh, Brian and Richard Middleton. (1984). *The Transforming Vision*. Downers Grove, IL: Inter Varsity Press.

Weir, Ralph Stefan. (2021a). 'Bring Back Substances!' *Review of Metaphysics* 75.2, 265–308. http://doi.org/10.1353/rvm.2021.0040

Weir, Ralph Stefan. (2021b). 'Can a Post-Galilean Science of Consciousness Avoid Substance Dualism?' *Journal of Consciousness Studies* 28.9–10, 212–28. Reprinted in Philip Goff and Alex Moran (eds.) *Is Consciousness Everywhere? Essays on Panpsychism*, Exeter: Imprint Academic, 2022.

Weir, Ralph Stefan. (2021c). 'Does Idealism Solve the Problem of Consciousness?' *The Routledge Handbook on Idealism and Immaterialism*. Eds. Joshua Farris and Benedikt Paul Göcke. London: Routledge.

Weir, Ralph Stefan. (2021d). 'Private Language and the Mind as Absolute Interiority.' *From Existentialism to Metaphysics: The Philosophy of Stephen Priest*. Eds. Benedikt Paul Göcke and Ralph Stefan Weir. Oxford: Peter Lang.

Bibliography 171

Weir, Ralph Stefan. (2022). 'Christian Physicalism and the Biblical Argument for Dualism.' *International Journal for Philosophy of Religion* 91, 115–38. https://doi.org/10.1007/s11153-021-09811-0

Weir, Ralph Stefan. (2023). 'Substance.' *Internet Encyclopedia of Philosophy*. Eds. James Fieser and Bradley Dowden.

Weir, Ralph Stefan. (Forthcoming). 'Science, Revelation and Biblical Dualism.' *Divine Revelation and the Sciences: Essays in the History and Philosophy of Revelation*. Ed. Balázs Mezei.

Whitehead, Alfred North. (1969). *Process and Reality*. Toronto: Collier-Macmillan.

Williams, D. C. (1953a) 'On the Elements of Being I.' *The Review of Metaphysics* 7.1, 3–18.

Williams, D. C. (1953b). 'On the Elements of Being II.' *The Review of Metaphysics* 7.2, 171–92.

Williamson, Timothy. (2013). *Modal Logic as Metaphysics*. Oxford: Oxford University Press.

Wilson, Jessica. (2006). 'On Characterising the Physical.' *Philosophical Studies* 131, 61–99. https://doi.org/10.1007/s11098-006-5984-8

Wilson, Natalie. (2009). 'Mind/Body Dualism and the Un-Just Gendered Logistics of Militarization.' *(Re)Interpretations: The Shapes of Justice in Women's Experience*. Eds. Lisa Dresdner and Laurel S. Peterson. Cambridge: Cambridge Scholars Press.

Wiredu, Kwasi. (1983). 'The Akan Concept of Mind.' *Ibadan Journal of Humanistic Studies* 3, 113–34.

Wittgenstein, Ludwig. (1953). *Philosophical Investigations*. Trans. G. E. M. Anscombe. Oxford: Blackwell.

Wolff, Christian. (1751). *Vernünfftige Gedancken von Gott, der Welt und der Seele des Menschen, auch allen Dingen überhaupt, den Liebhabern der Wahrheit mitgetheilet. Neue Auflage hin und wieder vermehret*. Halle: Renger.

Wood, Ledger. (1944). 'Abstract.' *Dictionary of Philosophy*. Ed. Dagobert Runes. London: Routledge.

Wright, N. T. (2016). 'Mind, Spirit, Soul and Body: All for One and One for All.' *N. T. Wright Online*. [Accessed 31 December 2022] https://ntwrightpage.com/2016/07/12/mind-spirit-soul-and-body/

Yang, Eric. (2015). 'The Compatibility of Property Dualism and Substance Materialism.' *Philosophical Studies* 172, 3211–19. https://doi.org/10.1007/S11098-015-0465-6

Žabkar, Louis. (1963). 'Herodotus and the Egyptian Idea of Immortality.' *Journal of Near Eastern Studies* 22.1, 60–2. https://doi.org/10.1086/371711

Zimmerman, Dean. (2006). 'Dualism in the Philosophy of Mind.' *Encyclopedia of Philosophy* (2nd edition). Ed. Donald M. Borchert. Farmington Hills, MI: Macmillan, 113–22.

Zimmerman, Dean. (2010). 'From Property Dualism to Substance Dualism.' *Aristotelian Society Supplementary* 84.1, 119–50. https://doi.org/10.1111/j.1467-8349.2010.00189.x

Index

abstraction 52
Abstract Particulars (Campbell) 46, 52, 56–57, 136
abstract universals 45–46, 49, 51; *see also* concrete universals
African views of soul-body dualism 14–15
afterlife beliefs 21
Akan 14
Alison, Henry 148
Alter, Torin 74, 87, 89–91
Anaxagoras 15
anti-physicalist Russellian monism 87, 89–92, 116, 120, 139
Aquinas, Thomas 1, 14, 31, 74, 84–86, 138, 140, 154
Archimedes 26
Aristotle 8, 31, 38–41, 46, 60, 75, 82, 84–86, 143, 153, 154
Armstrong, David 46, 48, 50, 71
Arnauld, Antoine 40
Astell, Mary 20
attribute dualism 35, 136
Augustine of Hippo 1, 31, 32, 43, 84–86, 154
austere platonism 46, 47, 50, 54–56
Avicenna 15
Azenabor, Godwin 14

ba (Egyptian concept) *see* Egyptian views of soul-body dualism
Bayne, Tim 148
Bennett, Jonathan 58, 65
Bergman, Gustav 41, 144
Berto, Francesco 74
Bible 8–11, 154; *see also* New Testament

bodily death 9, 10
Boole, George 67
Bourget, David 33, 110, 113, 150
bridge laws 48
Broackes, Justin 143
Broad, C. D. 31–32

Campbell, Keith 46, 52, 56–57, 136
Carnap, Rudolph 32, 119
Categories (Aristotle) 38–41, 43, 44, 153
causal-closure argument 28–29, 32, 34, 35, 152
Chalmers, David 2, 3, 32, 33, 35–37, 44, 50, 87, 88, 92, 95, 105, 107
Chinese views of soul-body dualism 14
Christian views of soul-body dualism 8
Churchland, Paul 35
Clark, Desmond 42
Coleman, Sam 92
compresence argument 101–105, 109, 135, 140
conceivability argument 3, 34, 95–97, 100, 105, 109–133, 149–153; ghosts 111–113, 119–121; influence 150–151; modal rationalism 113–121; transparent concepts 116–119; two-dimensional semantics 113–116; zombies 110–111, 113–119; *see also* phenomenal disembodiment argument
The Concept of Mind (Ryle) 21
concrete properties 45, 51–56; concrete universals 46, 49, 50, 71; defined 45; liberal platonism 45–46, 50;

Index 173

metaphysically incomplete
see metaphysical incompleteness;
moderate nominalism 46; property
dualism with and without 51–56;
proponents *vs.* opponents 45;
theories 45–47; token-identity and
51; as tropes 52
concrete universals 46, 49, 50, 71; *see
also* abstract universals
consciousness 22–27, 91; arguments
against materialism about 23–27;
functional 23; meta-problem 156;
phenomenal *see* phenomenal
consciousness; conceivability
argument
contingentism 73; *see also* necessitism
Cooper, John 10
Cottingham, John 42, 154
Cucu, Alin 29

Davidson, Donald 48, 51
Davies, Daniel 11
Denkel, Arda 144
Dennett, Daniel 2, 135
Descartes, Rene 1, 7, 8, 16, 21, 27, 53,
57, 136–138, 140, 154; bundle
view 42–43; *Categories* definition
and 43, 44; Clark on 42;
conceivability argument 108;
Cottingham on 42, 154; on created
substances 40, 59; developmental
psychologists and 155;
disembodiment argument 105,
107–108, 122–131; *Fifth
Objections and Replies* 42;
independence definition of
substance *see* independence
definition; *Meditations* 15, 39, 113,
141; method of doubt 141; as
paradigm substance dualist 41–44,
84, 86–87, 136, 157; *Principles of
Philosophy* 39, 40; property-
dependence objection 64–71; on
space and time 73; on substance 39,
40, 41, 74; theory of mind 18, 41,
147, 154
developmental psychologists 155
Di Gregorio, Mario 17
Double, Richard 3, 5, 31, 33
dualism 9–10, 50; arguments for
dualism 95–97, 106–108; definition

of 31; evils 16–17; Haeckel's
hostility to 17; holistic 9, 13, 14;
hostility to 8–21, 26–30; opposition
to 7; paradigmatic substance
dualists 15–16, 84–87, 154–155;
property versus substance dualism
31–38, 82–84; Russellian monist
property dualism 88–92; *see also*
monism; properties/property
dualism; substance/substance
dualism

ecofeminism 17–19, 20
ectoplasm 35, 37
Egyptian views of soul-body dualism
12–13
Elizabeth of Bohemia 27–28
*Essay Concerning Human
Understanding* (Locke) 40–41
evolutionary psychology 156–157
explanatory gap argument 96,
150, 151
extreme nominalism 46, 54–56

'Famous Trick Donkeys' (Loyd) 24–26
Farris, Joshua 10
Feminism and the Mastery of Nature
(Plumwood) 17–20
Francescotti, Robert 33
functional consciousness 23, 110–111

Gassendi, Pierre 27–28
German Metaphysics (Wolff) 1, 91
German Monist League 17, 20
ghosts 111–113; conceivability argument
and 109, 111–113, 119–121; modal
rationalism and 119–121
Goff, Philip 29, 91, 92, 108, 111–113,
116–118, 120, 123–124, 126, 127,
131, 138–141, 143, 147, 150, 151
Gregory of Nyssa 20
grounding physicalism 48–50, 54–56,
69–71, 78–81, 87–88
Gyekye, Kwame 14

haecceity 128, 132
Haeckel, Ernst 17
Harari, Noah 27
Haugeland, John 78
Heil, John 33
Hempel, Carl 32, 163

174 *Index*

Heraclitus 155
Herodotus 12
Hobbes, Thomas 1, 8, 9, 11, 26, 77
Hoffman, Joshua 58, 63–64, 68, 70,
   72–73
holism 9, 13
Homo Deus (Harari) 27
Hume, David 41, 57, 86, 147
Husserl, Edmund 3, 146

idealism 1–3, 5, 7, 35, 77, 79–84, 88,
   91, 93, 96, 111, 135, 138–141, 155
identity 69–70, 78, 80, 122, 128–133,
   152; independence 64; intuitions
   about 125; token-identity theory
   48–51, 55, 122; type-identity theory
   48–49
immaterial soul 4, 7, 9, 13, 15, 21–22,
   27–30
independence definition of substance 4,
   38, 85, 137, 143, 153; *Categories*
   definition 39–41, 43, 44; causal
   reading 58–61; created substances
   and 40; defence 58–76; four
   theories of mind and 82–84; further
   objections and refinements 72–76;
   metaphysical reading 58–63;
   properties 44, 51–53; property-
   dependence objection 57, 58, 60,
   63–71; substance dualism 41–44;
   threat of necessitism 73–74
interaction problem for soul-body
   dualism 27–29; *see also causal-*
   closure argument
intrinsic properties 87

Jackson, Frank 2, 32, 35, 44, 96, 105,
   111, 134, 150, 151
Jago, Mark 74
James, William 22, 148
Jewish views of soul-body dualism 11

Kant, Immanuel 1, 145, 146, 148
Kim, Jaegwon 2, 31–32, 34–36, 37,
   42, 44, 105, 150
knowledge argument 34, 95–97, 105,
   148–151
Kong Yingda 15
Kripke, Saul 72, 113, 115–118,
   122–129, 131, 137, 151
Krishna, Isvara 15

L'Art de Penser (Arnauld and Nicole)
   40, 97, 99
Leibniz, Gottfried Wilhelm 1, 2, 36,
   37, 79–80, 87, 89, 140
Levine, Joseph 32
Lewis, David 32, 34, 45, 46, 48, 67
Liu, Michelle 117
Lloyd, Sam: 'Famous Trick Donkeys'
   24–26
Locke, John 38, 40–42, 72, 74,
   135, 143
Lockwood, Michael 87
Loeb, Louis 58
Loose, Jonathan 33
Lowe, E. J. 58, 61, 63, 64, 68, 70,
   73, 102

Mackie, J. L. 143
Maimonides 11
Majeed, Hassekei Mohammed 14
Mao 20
Maqala fi'l-nafs (Avicenna) 15
Markie, Peter 58, 59–60, 64–65,
   66, 70
Martin, C. B. 144
materialism 1, 77–79; Christian 8–11;
   rejection or arguments against
   21–30; *see also* conceivability
   argument; knowledge argument;
   physicalism
Matthew 10:28 (Gospel of Matthew)
   8, 10
Mazis, Glen 14–15
Mcevilly, Thomas 12
McGinn, Colin 32
Meditations (Descartes) 15, 39, 67,
   113, 141
Meno (Plato) 18
metaphysical complements/
   incompleteness 53–54, 56–57, 62,
   74–75, 82–86, 99–101, 106, 130,
   142–144
meta-problem of consciousness 156
metempsychosis 12
Michel, Jean-Baptiste 32
microphysical truths 110
mind stuff 2, 38
Mizrahi, Avshalom 11
modal rationalism: ghosts 119–121;
   phenomenal disembodiment
   119–121; transparent concepts

Index 175

116–119; two-dimensional semantics 113–116; zombies 113–119
moderate nominalism 46, 50
monism 9; holistic 9, 13; *see also* dualism; Russellian monism
Montero, Barbara 88, 93
Moore, G. E. 79
Moran, Alex 57
Mørch, Hedda Hassel 90
Moreland, J. P. 10

Nagel, Ernest 48, 49
Nagel, Thomas 32, 48, 51, 68, 95
Nazism 20
necessitism 73–74
neutral monism 93–94; *see also* Russellian monism
Newman, John Henry 29
New Testament 8, 9–11
Nicole, Pierre 40
Nida-Rümelin, Martine 44, 86, 113, 116, 123, 124, 147, 149
nominalism: extreme 46, 54–56; moderate 46, 50
noninteractionist property dualism 36
nonphysical properties 2–4, 27, 30, 35, 36, 49, 83, 95, 103, 105, 106, 139, 149, 154
nonphysical substances 2–4; individual soul and 137–139; phenomenal disembodiment argument 121–133; *see also* conceivability argument; properties/property dualism
nonreductive physicalism 47–51; grounding physicalism 48–50, 54–56, 69–71, 78–81, 87–88; nonphysical properties and 49; supervenience physicalism 48, 49, 51, 55, 69, 78; token-identity theory 48, 49–51, 55, 122

Organon (Aristotle) 39, 40
Orphism 18

Palmer, Craig 15
panpsychism 89–90; *see also* Russellian monism
Papineau, David 34
paranormal research 22–23

parity argument 105–108, 121–122, 131–133; nonphysical substances and 137–139; reasons why this being overlooked 134–137; Russellian monism and 139–141; threat to 142; *see also* conceivability argument; phenomenal disembodiment argument
particulars 45, 46
Paul the Apostle 8–10
Pereboom, Derk 74, 87, 89–91
Phaedo (Plato) 15, 157
Phaedrus (Plato) 18
phenomenal concepts 111, 113, 116–120, 128, 148–149, 151–152, 156
phenomenal consciousness 23, 95; conceivability arguments and *see* conceivability argument; knowledge argument and 95–97; modal reasoning and 157
phenomenal disembodiment argument 106–108; conceivability argument and 109–113; Descartes's disembodiment argument and 122–127; ghosts and *see* ghosts; Kripke's disembodiment argument and 122–127; modality, duplication and 129–131; modal rationalism and 119–121; nonphysical substances and 121–133; objections to 123–125, 126; zombies and *see* zombies
phenomenal properties 32, 97–101, 103–104, 106, 112, 128, 140, 144, 146, 148
physicalism 1–3, 69, 77–79, 93; grounding 48–50, 54–56, 69, 70–71, 78–81, 87–88; history of 47–48; nonreductive 47–51; reductive 48, 50; referential 90–91; supervenience 48, 49, 51, 55, 69, 78; token-identity theory 48–51, 55, 122; type-identity theory 48–49
physical properties 6, 7, 49, 55, 78, 83, 98, 100, 103, 104, 106, 132, 138, 140, 145
Pitts, Brian 29
Place, U. T. 48, 69, 78
Plantinga, Alvin 32, 43, 135

176 *Index*

Plato 1, 14–16, 18–19, 31, 32, 43, 46, 67, 84–86, 136, 138, 140, 154, 155, 157
platonism: austere 46, 47, 50, 54–56; liberal 45–46, 50
Plumwood, Val 17–19, 20
Port Royal Logic *see L'Art de Penser* (Arnauld and Nicole)
Price, H. H. 22
Priest, Stephen 146, 147
properties: concrete *see* concrete properties; mental 3, 6–7, 91, 102; necessary 65–66; nonphysical 2–4, 27, 30, 35, 36, 49, 83, 95, 103, 105, 106, 139, 149, 154; phenomenal 32, 97–101, 103–104, 106, 112, 128, 140, 144, 146, 148; physical 6, 7, 49, 55, 78, 83, 98, 100, 103, 104, 106, 132, 138, 140, 145; relational 72, 87, 100, 101; role of 56–57; second-order properties 39; spatial 87, 89, 91, 139; spiritual 6–7; structural 87–88; substances *vs.* 38–41, 60, 68; theories 44–47; third-person properties 23; unified 92; *see also* property dualism
property dualism 2–3, 6–7; concrete properties *see* concrete properties; defences 44; intuitive problem 97–99; metaphysical incompleteness *see* metaphysical incompleteness; noninteractionist 36; *vs.* nonreductive physicalism 47–51; preference for 33–38, 57; role of properties 56–57; sensible constraint on simplicity 75; strong necessity 118, 132, 151–153; substance dualism *vs.* 31–38, 82–84; theories 44–47; transcendental egos 3, 145–149; *see also* compresence argument; conceivability argument; parity argument; Russellian monism; symmetry argument; properties
psychephobia 7
Putnam, Hilary 48–49, 113
Pythagoras 15

Quame, Safro 14
quasi-physicalism 14

quiddities 87, 88–90, 93
Quine, Willard Van Orman 7, 46, 47

Rambam *see* Maimonides
reductive physicalism 48, 50
referential physicalism 90–91
religion 8, 13
Revelation 117
Rickabaugh, Brandon 10
Rodriguez-Pereyra, Gonzalo 58, 60, 61, 63, 65–66
Rosenkrantz, Gary 58, 63–64, 68, 70, 72–73
Ruhnau, Eva 33
Russell, Bertrand 31–32, 41, 87, 94, 135–136, 143
Russellian monism 24–25, 35, 77, 87–94; anti-physicalist 87–92, 116, 120, 139; combination problem 149; defining 87–88; dualist 89; neutral monism 93–94; as a panacea 141; panpsychist 89–90; parity argument and 139–141; property dualist 89, 91–92; referential physicalism and 90–91; substance dualist 89
Ryle, Gilbert 2, 4, 21, 31–32, 34, 43, 84, 87, 135, 154, 157

Samkhyakarika (Krishna) 15
Sartre, Jean-Paul 3, 146, 147
Schneider, Susan 32, 33, 83, 98, 102
Searle, John 1–2, 33, 87, 97–99, 101, 102, 106
The Shape of Ancient Thought (Mcevilly) 12
Sheldrake, Rupert 22
Sidgwick, Henry 22
Slingerland, Edward 13
Smart, J. J. C. 48, 69, 78
Society for Psychical Research 22
Socrates 18
solipsism 18
soul-body dualism 6–30; African views 14–15; Chinese views 14; Christian views 8–11; as cognitive default 155; consciousness and 23–27; Egyptian views 12–13; historical exceptions 15–16; indigenous/ traditional cultures 15; interaction problem for 27–29; Jewish views

Index 177

11; paranormal research and 22–23; putative societal evils/ills of 16–21; *see also* substance dualism

spatial properties 87, 89, 91, 139

spirits 13, 15, 37, 43

Stalin 20

Steadman, Lyle 15

Strawson, Galen 32, 79, 87, 88, 90–92, 116, 139, 140, 147, 150, 151

strong necessity 118, 132, 151–153

structural properties 87–88

Stuart, Matthew 58, 65

Stubenberg, Leopold 93

substance 2, 4, 27; characterisations 38–41; nonphysical *see* nonphysical substances; properties *vs.* 38–41, 60, 68; unclarity about 36–38; *see also* independence definition; substance dualism

substance dualism 1, 2; *Categories* definition 38–41, 43, 44; characterisations 38–41; decline/fall of 31–33, 34; distinctive feature 36; four theories of mind 82–84; independence definition *see* independence definition; paradigmatic dualists 84–87; sensible constraint on simplicity 75; unclarity 36–38; *see also* property dualism; substratum

substratum 38, 41–43, 72, 74–75, 92, 135–136, 142–145

as bare particulars 41, 144

supervenience physicalism 48, 49, 51, 55, 69, 78

Swanson, Guy 15

Swinburne, Richard 32, 43, 66, 124, 135, 147

symmetry argument 99–101, 106, 107, 109, 139, 140, 141; compresence argument *vs.* 103–104; relational properties and 100–101; significance 105; zombies and 99–101

Taiping jing 15

Tattvarthasutra (Umaswati) 15

Tiller, Christopher 15

token-identity theory 48–51, 55, 122

transcendental egos 3, 145–149

transparency argument 150

transparent concepts 116–119, 124, 128, 132, 145–147

trope dualism 136

Turing, Alan 22

two-dimensional semantics 113–116, 118, 123

type-identity theory 48–49

Ukwamedua, Nelson 14

universals 45; abstract 45–46, 49, 51; concrete 46, 49, 50, 71

Vaisheshikasutra (Kanada) 15

Van Inwagen, Peter 46, 47, 54, 55

Weir, Ralph Stefan 10, 29, 34, 38, 39, 79, 143

Wiles, Andrew 26

Williams, D. C. 45–46, 52–54, 56–57, 101, 103

Williamson, Timothy 74

Wiredu, Kwasi 14

Wittgenstein, Ludwig 32, 34, 135, 154

Wolff, Christian 1–5, 91, 139

Wright, N. T. 9–10

Wujing Zhengyi (Kong Yingda) 15

Yang, Eric 33

Žabkar, Louis 12

Zimmerman, Dean 32, 33, 36, 37, 136, 149

zombies 9/–100; conceivability argument and 110–111, 113–119; metaphysical possibility of 151; modal rationalism and 113–119; symmetry principle and 99–100

Milton Keynes UK
Ingram Content Group UK Ltd.
UKHW020751231124
451456UK00007B/46